THE ORIGINS OF
PROHIBITION

THE ORIGINS OF PROHIBITION

BY

JOHN ALLEN KROUT

New York

RUSSELL & RUSSELL

TO MY FATHER AND MOTHER

FOREWORD

On January 29, 1919, the Secretary of State announced that the required number of states had ratified the Eighteenth Amendment to the Constitution. The subsequent passage of the Volstead Act by Congress, defining and enforcing the provisions of the Amendment, gave the Anti-Saloon League and its allies a victory in their fight for a "saloonless nation." To many Americans prohibition came with something of a shock. Though they were aware of the political power possessed by the enemies of the liquor traffic, they had not realized that the reformers were so near the goal. The immediate reaction of some was to cry fraud, since it seemed impossible that the people of a great nation could be fairly persuaded to write into their fundamental law so radical a change in social customs. To others, the restrictions on personal liberty were plainly contrary to that individualism which had always been the genius of American institutions. To a great many, it was all a mystery. Accordingly, publicists set forth elaborate theories to explain to the country how and why prohibition had emerged from remote possibility into startling reality.

These theories dealt chiefly with the forces and events which seemed to be immediately responsible for the ratification of the Eighteenth Amendment. The present study, while offering no complete solution of the riddle of prohibition, attempts to present some of the factors which prepared the way for the destruction of the saloon. It seeks the origin of the prohibitory movement in early evidences of social concern over the intemperate use of intoxicants.

FOREWORD

How the temperance crusade became a national campaign for restrictive legislation against the liquor traffic is to be the theme of the following pages. From the seventeenth and eighteenth century protests against drunkenness the slowly growing hostility to the use of intoxicants is traced, through many devious turnings, to the Maine Liquor Law of 1851. The latter time limit is imposed because the enactment of the Maine Law marked the end of an epoch in temperance reform. Henceforth, the battle was to be waged not by precept and example, but by political action. How this transition occurred is a story which the author hopes may throw a ray of light here and there on the liquor problem of today.

To Professor Dixon Ryan Fox of Columbia University, who suggested the possibilities of this subject, the author is deeply indebted for constant encouragement and inspiration, and for that constructive criticism which only a friend can offer. At the sacrifice of many hours, Professor Fox has reviewed the entire manuscript. Dean Herbert E. Hawkes of Columbia College kindly loaned the manuscript of Reverend Ebenezer Sparhawk's temperance sermon, preached at Templeton, Massachusetts, in 1776. The author wishes also to acknowledge the assistance of Mr. Victor Hugo Paltsits of the New York Public Library, of Mr. Clarence S. Brigham, Librarian of the American Antiquarian Society, and of the staff of the American history room in the New York Public Library. He is under many incidental obligations to his associates in the department of history at Columbia for valuable suggestions and willing co-operation. Also, he is indebted to his wife, Marion Dorothy Krout, for corrections in the proof. For the imperfections which remain, whether in form or content, the author alone is responsible.

John Allen Krout.

Columbia University, May, 1925.

CONTENTS

CHAPTER I

THE BASIS OF REGULATION

A RECENT publication from the press of the Anti-Saloon
League is responsible for the dictum that the "American
liquor problem is as old as the white man's knowledge of
the American continent." [1] If this be true, the problem
long existed in the midst of a people who little comprehended
its real significance. Though the establishment of the first
English settlements was marked by the transit of European
drinking customs to the New World, the seventeenth century
colonists did not regard that fact as a cause for unusual
anxiety. For two centuries after the founding of Jamestown
there was no organized attempt to restrict the normal use
of intoxicants or to define their influence on the interests of
the group. Save in the case of Georgia, where Oglethorpe's
futile efforts directed attention to the destructive nature of
distilled spirits, there was no widespread condemnation of
spirituous liquors. Puritan clergymen, Dutch merchants
and Virginia planters agreed that the use of alcoholic beverages was not only beneficial, but also necessary. They
were quick, however, to rebuke individual excesses; for all
such indiscretions signified an abuse of nature's wholesome
gifts, and were, therefore, violations of the Divine will in
regard to man's use of natural blessings. The liquor problem, they felt, embraced little beyond the occasional lapse
of individuals from judicious self-control. The line of

[1] Ernest H. Cherrington, *The Evolution of Prohibition in the United
States*, p. 9.

1

moderation was drawn variously in different communities, making some localities more sober, or at least less indulgent, than others; but all were solicitous that there be an adequate and cheap supply of good liquor available. Restraint was necessary only for those incorrigibles who insisted on flaunting the evidence of their over-indulgence in the faces of their more abstemious fellows.

The regulative measures of the colonial period, inspired in part by the desire to outlaw drunkenness, were not designed to reform social customs. In them was continued that thread of public control traceable in such employments as common carriage and inn-keeping from the manorial and municipal regulations of fourteenth century England. They reflected the familiar outlines of a system which had been taking form for over two hundred years. By their provisions the freeholder of the new Ipswich in Massachusetts Bay, conferring on his town the boon of a public tavern, was subject to restrictions closely resembling those which burdened the busy inn-keeper in old Ipswich across the sea.[2] This similarity signified neither a conscious imitation of English methods, nor a general translation of liquor laws from England to America. Rather did it indicate the fact that men do not suddenly abandon a system of action under which they have long lived even if they move into a strange environment. They cannot altogether escape the ideas and institutions of their former experience. Since the English migration to the New World began in the opening decades of the seventeenth century, just as a reasonably effective control over the liquor traffic had been achieved through the device of licensing, it was natural for the colonists to meet a novel situation with variations of an old and well-known plan. In a few instances they re-enacted statutes of the mother country, but such legislation was merely a temporary

[2] *Cf.* Joseph B. Felt, *Ipswich, Essex and Hamilton,* p. 112; Nathaniell Bacon, *Annalls of Ipswiche,* pp. 199, 204.

expedient till more satisfactory measures could be formulated.[3]

A wide variety of motives, usually unrelated to any abstract theory of social control, persuaded the governing authorities in the several colonies to interfere with the natural development of the trade in intoxicants. The chief impulse probably was furnished by the desire to prevent personal excesses and public disorders, but this was complicated by a whole host of minor considerations. The discovery, confirmed by harrowing experiences, that the American Indian under the influence of the "good creature" was a menace to life and property,[4] the necessity of providing adequate accommodations for travellers, the importance of the brewing and distilling industries and the fact that sorely needed revenues could be most easily secured from an assessment against the liquor traffic, all played their part in determining the character and course of regulation. Each was a force responsible for specific statutes in every one of the thirteen colonies.

The suppression of drunkenness was early advanced as a reason for restrictive measures. In 1622 Sir Francis Wyatt, governor of Virginia, was advised by the council of the London Company to effect a "speedie redress" of the enormous excess of drinking, the "cry whereof cannot but have gone to Heaven, since the infamy hath spread itself to all that have heard the name of Virginia." [5] The General Court of Massachusetts Bay in 1637 discovered that "much drunkenness, waste of the good creature of God, mispence

---

[3] For an excellent brief account of the licensing system in England see Sidney and Beatrice Webb, *The History of Liquor Licensing in England*, pp. 1–14. *Cf.* J. F. Grimke, editor, *The Public Laws of South Carolina* (1790), 1, 15; François Martin, *A Collection of the Statutes of England now in force in the State of North Carolina* (1792).

[4] This term was commonly used in the English colonies during the seventeenth century to designate distilled spirits.

[5] Letter of August 1, 1622, Edward D. Neill, *History of the Virginia Company of London*, p. 322.

of precious time, and other disorders" in the inns of the colony required special attention.[6] Connecticut's code of laws, approved in 1650, recognized the "necessary use" of ordinaries and houses of common entertainment where liquor was sold, but established strict rules governing the conduct of proprietor and patron.[7] So in every colony, the person who lacked both self-control and a sense of social responsibility furnished the pretext for governmental interference.[8]

In the matter of observing the accepted canons of moderate drinking the American Indian was an inveterate transgressor. Finding the ecstasies of intoxication the most attractive feature of the white man's "fire-water," he failed to appreciate the advantages of self-restraint. To the colonists, the degradation of scores of peaceful natives, and the transformation of hundreds of others into marauding savages strikingly signified the need for definite regulation of the Indian trade.[9] Virginia's unfortunate experience with an uncontrolled trade was so well known that Governor Endicott was warned by the Massachusetts Bay Company in 1629 to take precautions lest the savages "be induced to the excessive use or rather abuse of strong waters." [10] The early laws universally forbade the sale or gift to Indians

[6] *Records of the Governor and Company of Massachusetts Bay*, I, 213. (To be cited *Mass. Col. Doc.*)

[7] *Public Records of the Colony of Connecticut*, 1, 533. (To be cited *Conn. Pub. Rec.*)

[8] One searches in vain in the colonial records to find a clear distinction between the various types of public houses. "Inn," "ordinary" and "tavern" are used indiscriminately to indicate a house which lodged travellers and usually sold liquor as part of its entertainment. "Retailers" sold in small quantities to all comers, but provided no accommodations. They were not allowed to entertain customers in their establishments. The term "ale-house," so common in England, was rarely used in America.

[9] John Winthrop, *The History of New England*, I, 406–407.

[10] For typical regulations of this nature, see *Mass. Col. Doc.*, I, 106; *Conn. Pub. Rec.*, 1, 256; *Records of the Colony of Rhode Island and Providence Plantations*, I, 279 (to be cited R. I. Col. Rec.); *Colonial Laws of New York*, I, 41; *Archives of Maryland*, XXXVIII, 15.

of wine or distilled spirits, but beer and malt liquors usually escaped the ban.[11] In spite of the tremendous difficulties of enforcement, an earnest effort was made in certain sections to apprehend violators of the law, and heavy penalties were frequently imposed. Connecticut, for example, administered corporal punishment to any servant found guilty of furnishing Indians with liquor, while New Netherland sent some of its substantial citizens back to Holland for the same offence.[12] Total prohibition of the traffic, however, was undesirable from the standpoint of those interested in the development of colonial commerce. In the hands of shrewd traders ardent spirits were an open sesame to the riches of the fur-trade, and many an ambitious landholder found them efficacious in suppressing Indian claims to choice tracts which he desired. Thus, economic considerations, more powerful than any fear of drunken savages, wrought a gradual withdrawal of governmental restrictions. Rhode Island, which originally trusted only Roger Williams to dole out wine and "strong water" for Indian consumption, in 1655 permitted two ordinary-keepers in each town to sell limited quantities.[13] Massachusetts, likewise, selected in each town dealers who might sell on condition that they did not supply any Indian with more than a pint at a time. In Pennsylvania the assembly authorized the governor to suspend the prohibitory legislation, if the tribal chiefs consented to have their drunken subjects punished in accordance with the provincial laws. Everywhere the profits of commercial intercourse tended to break down the safeguards which the legislators threw about the traffic.[14]

---

[11] Cf. *Records and Files of the Quarterly Courts of Essex County, Mass.*, VIII, 435-6; *Early Records of the Town of Providence*, II, 83.

[12] *Conn. Pub. Rec.*, III, 228; *Documents Relative to the Colonial History of the State of New York*, XII, 69; XIII, 67-8. (To be cited *N. Y. Col. Doc.*)

[13] *R. I. Col. Rec.*, I, 308.

[14] *Mass. Col. Doc.*, III, 369. The difficulties encountered by the au-

But restriction was not the sole objective of colonial legislatures which framed bills regulating the liquor trade. Many statutes were plainly intended to encourage inn-keeping, brewing and distilling. Since spirituous as well as malt liquors were considered an integral part of the daily diet, their sale was intimately associated with the furnishing of entertainment for travellers. Each colony desired that the public-houses within its borders should be adequate to meet the steadily increasing demands made upon them by expanding commercial activity, and whenever the number of inns seemed insufficient, it was expected that the legislature would provide relief. With his great faith in the efficacy of written law, the American colonist believed that the proper statute could produce accommodations for travellers where private initiative had failed. Maryland presented a conspicuous example of a regulation which was designed to encourage. Until 1662 the province was without regular public-houses, though well supplied with tippling-houses of a low order.[15] This situation the assembly endeavoured to remedy by an act for the encouragement of ordinary-keepers. The preamble explained, with customary completeness, the motives which the legislators thought had influenced them. The absence of proper accommodations for travellers exposed persons attending the county courts or transacting business in remote parts of the province to great inconvenience and even danger. Besides, it often placed an unpleasant burden on private families to supply food and lodging for some belated and importunate wayfarer. In order to encourage prospective inn-keepers, a special licence was to be granted by the Proprietor or his representative, conferring on the licensee a monopoly of the sale of liquors in his dis-

thorities in Pennsylvania are clearly set forth in Shepherd, *History of Proprietary Government in Pennsylvania*, pp. 107–110.

[15] George Alsop, *A Character of Maryland*, N. D. Mereness, editor, p. 50.

trict.[16] That this special permission assumed the aspect of coercion, when trade was dull and debts hard to collect, is evidenced by the petition of William Smith, an inn-keeper at St. Mary's, who begged to be relieved of his licence because he had been compelled to keep a public-house and give credit throughout the province much to his financial detriment.[17]

Maryland was not peculiar in the attempt to foster the location of inns and taverns at strategic places. In 1637 the General Court of Massachusetts had ordered each town to present a man to be allowed to sell wine and "strong water," lest the public suffer from the lack of proper accommodations.[18] Connecticut placed upon each town the duty to choose from the freemen a suitable person to keep an ordinary where beer and ale were sold.[19] As an inducement to Rhode Islanders to provide accommodations for the travelling public, two dealers in each town were granted a monopoly of the liquor trade.[20] In all parts of the colonies operators of important ferries and toll-bridges were compelled to furnish all the conveniences of a tavern under the terms of a special licence.[21] From these acts it is evident that the spirit controlling the regulation of the liquor traffic manifested no tendency toward prohibition. The legislators appreciated the vast social importance of the trade and desired to utilize its manifold possibilities for the best interests of the community.

In the machinery of regulation the device of licensing was of primary importance. Ancient in origin, and tested for over a century in England, it possessed advantages that could not be disregarded. Although the English experience had not been uniformly successful, a decided improvement in

[16] *Archives of Maryland*, I, 447. (To be cited *Md. Arch.*)
[17] *Ibid.*, II, 50.
[18] *Mass. Col. Doc.*, I, 221.
[19] *Conn. Pub. Rec.*, I, 103.
[20] *R. I. Col. Rec.* I, 280.
[21] *Colonial Records of North Carolina*, XXIII, 728.

the operation of the system occurred during the seventeenth century. From a plan thus ready to hand, the colonists picked the features which satisfied the conditions peculiar to their new environment. With the exception of New Netherland and Georgia the colonial establishments developed the licensing function along similar, if not identical, lines. The authority to license was early assumed by the legislatures, which delegated the power as they saw fit,[22] usually vesting the right of selection in one of three agents; the governor or proprietor, the county court, or the town board of selectmen. These agents were virtually free to make whatever choice they pleased, though the law assumed that they would license only persons of good standing in the community. They were expected to locate the public-houses at places frequented by the justices holding county court, along main-travelled roads, and near important bridges and ferries, lest any traveller should fail to secure accommodations while meeting the demands of justice or trade.[23] As population increased and it became correspondingly difficult for the governor, or the proprietor's representative, to select intelligently the persons to be favoured with licences, the selective power was generally placed in the hands of the county court. By the mid-eighteenth century in all of the colonies, save Pennsylvania, Delaware and Rhode Island, this transition had taken place.[24] Pennsylvania and Delaware still recognized the governor as the licensing agent, though the licensee had to be recommended by the justices in the county courts.[25] With its usual emphasis upon local government,

[22] In Massachusetts the General Court selected the keepers of public-houses until 1644. See *Mass. Col. Doc.*, II, 188.

[23] Consult: *Mass. Col. Doc.*, I, 140; *R. I. Col. Rec.*, I, 185–6; *Md. Arch.*, I, 447; W. W. Hening, editor, *Statutes at Large . . . of Virginia*, I, 287.

[24] Hening, VI, 71–6; *Md. Arch.*, VII, 65–8; *Conn. Pub. Rec.*, II, 76; *Colonial Records of North Carolina*, XXIII, 182–5.

[25] *Laws of the State of Delaware (1797)*, I, 192–6. For the contest

Rhode Island confirmed to the town selectmen the choice of tavern-keepers [26]

The designation of the county court as licensing agent paralleled the English system at its best, for justices of the peace in special sessions, acting under Parliamentary authorization, controlled the granting of liquor licences throughout England.[27] Unlike their English prototype, however, the colonial justices in the eighteenth century no longer possessed full discretionary powers in making selections. They were subject to statutory mandates which reduced them to the level of mere registrars of licences. In Massachusetts, for instance, their choice was conditioned by the opinion of the town selectmen on the fitness of applicants.[28] Likewise, the endorsement of the town meeting was a necessary qualification for any successful petitioner to the county court in Connecticut.[29] Under the Duke's Laws the justices in New York could issue a licence only upon receipt of a certificate of good behaviour from the constable and two overseers of the parish.[30] The assembly of Maryland forbade the courts to license anyone who held public office within the province.[31] Thus, while the justices could create valuable business monopolies, they could not award them to their personal or political friends, unless the specific requirements of the law were satisfied.

The idea of selling the liquor monopoly for a definite district at a high price, either to raise revenue or to limit the number of licensees, was not evident in the early legislation. A small clerical fee usually constituted the

over authority of the governor in Pennsylvania see W. R. Shepherd, *History of Proprietary Government in Pennsylvania*, pp. 80–81.

[26] *R. I. Col. Rec.*, IV, 418.
[27] Webb, *op. cit.*, pp. 5–14.
[28] Joseph B. Felt, *The Annals of Salem*, I, 419.
[29] *Conn. Pub. Rec.*, IV, 145.
[30] *Duke of Yorke's Book of Laws*, p. 30.
[31] *Md. Arch.*, XXXIX, 290.

only charge made for a licence. But, as the trade became more profitable and the establishments more numerous, statute followed statute imposing constantly increasing fees. The charges in New England, graduated according to the profits of the dealers, were generally higher than in the colonies to the south. The Boston taverner paid £15 for his licence, while the keeper of a public-house in Philadelphia was charged £3. Rhode Island placed a maximum limit of £10 and instructed the towns to regulate the fee according to the needs of the community. Throughout the colonies the sale of malt liquors was favoured by the imposition of merely a nominal fee for a permit to conduct a house retailing only beer and ale.

The disposition of the revenue from licences was the cause of much friction between local and provincial authorities and between governors and the popularly elected assemblies. While the fees were ordinarily a perquisite of the governor in the royal colonies and of the proprietor in the proprietary provinces, Connecticut and Rhode Island granted them to the respective towns.[32]   In Maryland the struggle over the proprietor's prerogative in the matter of licence fees constituted an interesting episode in the general conflict waged during the eighteenth century between the colonial governors and the popular assemblies. From the outset the Calverts had regarded the fees as a part of their income, and the assembly had entered no protest until 1739, when an attempt was made to appropriate the money for an extension of the military establishment.[33]   Lord Baltimore was obstinate and vetoed the bill as often as the assembly passed it, with the result that for sixteen years the governor was embarrassed by the tactics of a legislative body which refused to vote important funds at critical periods. After Braddock's

[32] Cf. *Colonial Laws of New York*, IV, 729–730; *Colonial Records of North Carolina*, XXIII, 182–185; *Laws of Delaware*, I, 192–196; *Md. Arch.*, XV, 78–79; Hening, VI, 71–76.

[33] Letter of Governor Sharpe, *Md. Arch.*, VI, 235.

disastrous defeat in 1755, the proprietor withdrew from his position and allowed the licence fees to be expended in meeting the existing military emergency.[34] As soon as the danger had passed, however, the struggle was renewed, throwing the whole licensing system into such confusion that Governor Sharpe reported in 1764 that anyone who pleased kept a tavern.[35] Sharpe sought relief under the terms of the Stamp Act, which empowered colonial governors to issue licences in case no other regulation existed, but his faith in that ill-fated measure was sadly misplaced.[36] Finally, the governor's council handed down a decision, denying the proprietor's claims and affirming the assembly's power to suppress undesirable public-houses under the English common law.[37] This opinion served as a *modus vivendi* until the outbreak of the Revolution removed all effective opposition to the assembly's control.

The case of Maryland was an exception to the normal administration of the licence system. Ordinarily, the chief source of friction was the selection of successful applicants. The question of renewals was also important, since the authorities could suppress any public-house by refusing to renew the licence at the expiration of a year's time.[38] Such refusals might be based on the misconduct of the licensee, the decision of the court that the quota of taverns had been exceeded, or on some personal preference of the justices. Colonial assemblies urged the courts to suppress disorderly houses, and the law-breaking publican was liable to have his sign torn down by the constable.[39] To what extent the

[34] *Md. Arch.*, XXXI, 495.

[35] *Ibid.*, XIV, 172.

[36] *Ibid.*, XIV, 201.

[37] *Ibid.*, XXXII, 145-6.

[38] *Cf.* Hening, VI, 71–76; *Pa. Statutes at Large*, III, 291–295; *Colonial Records of North Carolina*, XXIII, 182–185.

[39] Following the English custom, removal of the sign-board signified the withdrawal of the licence. See Webb, *op. cit.*, p. 10 n.

justices revoked licences for reasons of public policy or personal pique could be determined only by a careful analysis of the county court records, few of which have been preserved in available form. The scant evidence consulted, however, seems to indicate that there were few complaints of arbitrary action on the part of the justices.[40] The tendency was rather toward a too generous awarding of licences in most localities. In New England local favourites were chosen tavern-keepers year after year with as much regularity as marked the re-election of the town magistrates.[41] Where no numerical limit was fixed by statute, the justices were prone to increase the public-houses on the slightest pretext, thus creating unnecessary and sometimes objectionable businesses. This situation in Massachusetts called forth a vigorous protest to the Court of Quarter Sessions against the excessive number of inns and taverns in Haverhill and Salisbury. Similarly, a Philadelphia grand jury, of which Benjamin Franklin was foreman, presented a report in 1744 decrying the existence of over one hundred public-houses in the city and recommending that the court exercise more freely its power of suppression.[42]

With regard to the conditions imposed upon the innkeeper, the colonial statutes were so definite and complete that the discretionary power of the justices was reduced to a minimum. In harmony with a strongly paternalistic philosophy the legislatures devised a multitude of restrictions so comprehensive that it was a wise host who, after giving bond to obey the laws, knew all the limitations of his occupa-

[40] For forfeiture of licence, see *Mass. Col. Doc.*, V, 305; *Records and Files of the Quarterly Courts of Essex County, Mass.*, I, 154, 159; *Oyster Bay Town Records*, I, 268; Lyman Chalkley, *Chronicles of Scotch-Irish Settlement in Virginia*, I, 29; Alfred S. Hudson, *History of Sudbury, Mass.*, pp. 605–606.

[41] *Cf.* Spencer P. Mead, *Ye Historie of Ye Towne of Greenwich*, p. 50; Lucius R. Page, *History of Cambridge*, pp. 223–224.

[42] G. W. Chase, *History of Haverhill*, pp. 283–284; *Pa. Historical Society, Collections*, I, 267–268.

tion.[43] Legislative enactments determined the amount of liquor he might sell at one time, the character of the amusements he might offer in his house, and the prices he might charge for his entertainment. In the New England of the seventeenth century the patron of the tavern could spend only a limited time "tippling" unless he chanced to be a traveller, in which case he was warned not to accompany his thirst-quenching with dancing, loud singing or other unseemly noise.[44] The host was enjoined to see that his guest did not drink after nine o'clock in the evening or violate the cardinal principle of self-restraint by becoming "bereaved or disabled in the use of his understanding." [45] Neither townsman nor traveller could while away his idle moments by playing games of chance.[46] Throughout New England the laws either forbade the sale of liquor on the Sabbath, or closed the bar of the public-house during the hours of divine worship.

Such restrictions, for which there was abundant precedent in the regulations governing English ale-houses, were not peculiar to New England; nor can they be explained, as some writers have supposed, by a mere reference to Puritan asceticism. Their counterpart is met beyond the confines of the Puritan colonies. The dictatorial Stuyvesant in New Netherland, strengthening certain ordinances of his predecessor, William Kieft, antedated Massachusetts and Connecticut in refusing the hospitality of the tavern to

43 In North Carolina, for instance, the Act of 1715 bound the licensee to keep "this law and all other laws and statutes governing the retail of liquors within the Kingdom of Great Britain." *Colonial Records of North Carolina*, XXIII, 79–80. South Carolina, Georgia, Virginia and Rhode Island empowered justices of the peace to put in force the laws of England. *Cf. The Public Laws of South Carolina*, I, 15; *The Colonial Records of the State of Georgia*, XVIII, 218–224.

44 *Mass. Col. Doc.*, II, 100–101; IV, pt. i, 40; *Records of the Colony of New Plymouth*, XI, 222.

45 *Conn. Pub. Rec.*, I, 533.

46 *R. I. Col. Rec.*, I, 185–186.

idlers and tipplers. He forced the worthy Dutch burghers to put out their pipes and go home, when the curfew sounded the hour of nine. Although these restrictions were not retained by the English, their general tenor was preserved in the Duke of York's code of laws for his new province.[47] Likewise, in the colonies south of New York, the conditions imposed upon the liquor dealer, not unlike those of Massachusetts Bay, included the prohibition of gaming, dancing and excessive drinking. The statutes were clearly designed to provide a legal sanction for the dominant theory that the individual should not be permitted to misuse a commodity or institution intended for his good. As the Puritan was under an especially compelling concern to safeguard the welfare of his fellow-citizens, he removed with great care numerous temptations to over-indulgence, but in so doing he was merely carrying one step farther a policy which was generally recognized throughout the colonies.

Of special significance was the definition of the true function of a tavern as set forth in the colonial legislation. A statute of New Jersey, based on English precedents, declared that taverns, inns and ordinaries should be places for the accommodation of strangers and travellers, the transaction of public business and the "refreshment of mankind in a reasonable manner."[48] In the attempt to secure conformity to such a definition no error was made on the side of inadequate legislation. The records during the seventeenth and eighteenth centuries are liberally sprinkled with acts relating to the character of accommodations, as well as the quality and price of liquors. The Maryland taverner, whose establishment was located near the court house, was obliged to provide "six good and substantial beds" and "sufficient warm covering for the same," that the dispensers

[47] *The Records of New Amsterdam*, B. Fernow, ed., I, 4; *Duke of Yorke's Book of Laws*, pp. 30–31.

[48] *Acts of the General Assembly of the Province of New Jersey*, Samuel Allinson, editor, p. 102.

of justice might not be inconvenienced during the sessions.[49]
No licence could be issued in New Jersey to any save those
who possessed two spare beds and sufficient accommodations
for the stabling and pasturing of horses. In Rhode Island
the retailing of liquors was limited to such houses as maintained at least one bed for the convenience of travellers.
With more or less particularity each colony recorded the
kind of accommodations to be provided by one serving the
public as a tavern-keeper.[50]

Not content with careful attention to the physical welfare
of the traveller the legislators indulged in a series of interesting, but frequently ludicrous, experiments to safeguard
his financial interests. From the first, the scarcity of liquor
in the New World, and the operation of the licensing system,
tended to place in the hands of a few dealers in each colony
a virtual monopoly. To prevent the exorbitant prices
which might result from such a situation, the assemblies
undertook the difficult task of regulating them. As early
as September 3, 1634, an ordinance in Massachusetts, following an act of the reign of James I, fixed the price of
beer at one penny a quart.[51] Virginia attacked the high
prices in 1644 by listing the value of all liquors in terms of
the accepted currency, tobacco.[52] Fluctuations in the
tobacco crop from year to year necessitated an annual read-
justment of the published prices, which perplexed the legislators and irritated the liquor dealers. Charges of unfair
discrimination became common and the retailers sought
redress by petitioning the legislature to abandon the practice.[53] When no relief was forthcoming, the more un-

[49] Md. Arch., XXVI, 306.

[50] R. I. Col. Rec., I, 441; Conn. Pub. Rec., II, 244; Mass. Col. Doc.,
II, 286, Colonial Records of North Carolina, XXIII, 182; N. Y. Col.
Laws, V, 583–584; Hening, VI, 71–72.

[51] Mass. Col. Doc., I, 126.

[52] Hening, I, 287.

[53] Ibid., I, 521–522.

scrupulous, fearing to sell above the legal rate, resorted to the profitable device of fraudulent measures and adulterated drinks. As a result the assembly was forced to supplement the annual price-lists with clauses against "fraudulent corrupting and mixing of wines and strong waters," much after the fashion of modern pure food legislation.[54]

The possibility of encouraging domestic production of liquors by a policy of price-fixing appealed to the legislators of both Virginia and Maryland, but the methods adopted were singularly well conceived to thwart the avowed purpose. Based on a strange conception of the psychology of the consumer, the law provided that drinks of domestic production should sell at higher rates than those of foreign origin. The Virginia act of 1667, for instance, explains that Virginia "drams" and "syder" have greater rates in order to encourage anything that is produced in the province.[55] Though such reasoning may have been welcomed by the retailer, it contributed little to the popularity of domestic drinks. These experiments in price regulation, however, are typical of the attempts made by other colonies. Taken as a whole, they comprise a curious record of enactments, repeals and re-enactments based on the success or failure of the moment, with scant regard for comprehensive policy or fixed principles. The objective appears to change with each successive statute, varying from the desire to curb excessive prices to an eager encouragement of liquor production. If there is any basic element present, it is a confused idea, perhaps a by-product of the existing mercan-

[54] Hening, II, 112–113.
[55] Ibid., II, 263. Similarly, Maryland in 1671 placed the price of foreign cider, perry and quince at one shilling a gallon, while the domestic product was listed at one shilling six-pence. Md. Arch., II, 295–297.

tile theory, that some sort of regulation is better than none.[56]

Of all the conditions imposed upon the liquor traffic none was more important from the social standpoint than the prohibition of the sale of intoxicants to Negroes, servants and apprentices. There was nothing novel about excluding certain classes from the pleasant conviviality of the tavern, but the colonial restrictions went far beyond the English practice. At the opening of the eighteenth century, Massachusetts and Connecticut forbade the licensed dealer to entertain apprentices and servants, lest the time belonging to the master should be spent in dissolute idleness.[57] Virginia sought to keep the menial class within bounds by limiting the credit which the taverner might grant to his patrons. This was designed to control the indentured servant, who often incurred such heavy debts during his period of servitude that on the expiration of his indenture he dared not face his creditors. As stated in the act, the inability of these debtors to meet their obligations caused "many newly free to run away to the neighbouring plantations to the great disadvantage of the country."[58] New York, likewise, protected the master's interests by prohibiting the sale of strong liquor to any servant, while Georgia and the Carolinas placed a ban on the sale of intoxicants to slaves unless the consent of the owner was obtained.[59] These restrictions, inspired in part by the fear of slave insurrections and designed to promote labour efficiency, were undoubtedly advantageous to master and em-

[56] For miscellaneous price regulations, see *Pa. Statutes at Large,* II, 222; *Conn. Pub. Rec.,* IV, 286–287; *Duke of Yorke's Book of Laws,* p. 31; *Colonial Records of North Carolina,* XXIII, 182–185.

[57] *Conn. Pub. Rec.,* IV, 7.

[58] Hening, III, 44–45; Jennings C. Wise, *Eastern Shore of Virginia,* p. 196.

[59] *N. Y. Col. Doc.,* VI, 17; *Colonial Records of Georgia,* XVIII, 126.

ployer, but they contributed to the rapid increase in the number of illegal tippling-houses. The conscientious tavern-keeper, jealous of the good name of his house and eager to entertain respectable patrons, preferred not to extend his hospitality to persons against whom the law discriminated. Apprentices, indentured servants and Negroes, therefore, sought out places where they could obtain credit illegally, and where they could loiter, gaming and drinking, reasonably safe from detection. Many an unlicensed dealer throve in secluded corners of the towns, harbouring all sorts of questionable characters from runaway slaves to deserters from the British navy. Complaints against these undesirable establishments were numerous during the eighteenth century, and an enormous amount of legislation was enacted in the hope of remedying an intolerable situation. But, in spite of laws and threatening proclamations, the law-breakers were able to maintain their merry haunts without much fear of constable or sheriff.[60]

The colonial officials were not primarily interested in an efficient administration of the licence system, or in the enforcement of incidental regulatory measures. Their chief concern was to raise a revenue from the liquor traffic. The importations of wines and distilled spirits were sufficiently large to make import duties attractive, and the domestic production of liquor was capable of enduring the burden of excise taxes during the eighteenth century. While the British colonial policy was still in its formative period, Massachusetts began to defray a part of its governmental expenses by levying an *ad valorem* duty on wines and spirits.[61] With apparent disregard of the interests of other portions of the Empire, the duty was imposed on all

[60] For example, *Conn. Pub. Rec.*, IV, 7; *R. I. Col. Rec.*, VI, 461; *Documents and Records Relating to the Province of New Hampshire*, IV, 76; *Colonial Records of Georgia*, XVIII, 218–224.

[61] *Mass. Col. Doc.*, I, 186.

commodities, but a revision of the act in 1648 exempted goods of the production of England.[62] Not satisfied with the returns from the customs, the General Court in 1644 placed an excise tax on all wine sold at retail by licensed vintners.[63] Later the excise was extended to distilled liquors as well, and was usually collected from the retailer on the basis of his sales. The elementary priciples contained in these early acts were applied with slight modifications in all the colonies during the next century.[64] The revenues thus secured were used to finance a wide range of local and provincial activities, though the largest appropriations were made for defence of the frontier and maintenance of the military establishment.[65] Maryland chose to vote the money for "repairing court-houses and prisons, increasing the salaries of justices and reimbursing an agent to represent the province in England."[66] Education in Connecticut received a considerable forward impetus from the sums accruing to the treasury in the form of customs duties and excise taxes. In 1721 a rector's house was built for Yale College, and six years later the assembly voted that the rum revenue should be appropriated for one year to the "use, benefit and better support of the said college, its rector and tutors." An act of 1766 awarded the excise money to the towns to be used for the benefit of the local schools.[67] More common, however, was the practice of Pennsylvania, which set aside this particular revenue as an emergency fund to meet extraordinary expenses, thus insur-

[62] *Mass. Col. Doc.*, II, 106, 246.

[63] *Ibid.*, II, 246.

[64] *Conn. Pub. Rec.*, I 146; *N. Y. Col. Doc.*, III, 217; *Colonial Records of North Carolina*, VI, 1113; *Ga. Col. Rec.*, III, 68–69; *N. H. Prov. Papers*, III, 819; *Md. Arch.*, XXVI, 281–283.

[65] *N. H. Prov. Papers*, VI, 473; *Colonial Records of North Carolina*, XXV, 352.

[66] Act of 1692, *Md. Arch.*, XIII, 466.

[67] *Conn. Pub. Rec.*, VI, 282; VII, 133; XII, 463.

ing the government against too frequent financial embarrassment.[68]

Although revenue production was the primary purpose of tariffs and excise taxes, the regulation of commerce was by no means negligible. If the colonial legislatures were anxious to have their acts approved by the Privy Council, they were careful to conform to the regulations of the British colonial system. Preferential treatment was accorded to liquors produced in Great Britain, and any deviation from the rule was ultimately brought to the attention of the offending colony. For example, in 1718 Robert Hunter, the liberal and public-spirited governor of New York, was busy explaining to the Lords of Trade that the provincial duty on wine did not extend to importations from Great Britain. He admitted that no specific exemption was contained in the act, but promised that a special declaratory measure would correct the omission.[69]   Maryland's famous act of 1704, imposing a duty upon rum, wine, brandy and Negroes, expressly exempted all English ships.[70] While the various colonies usually recognized the peculiar rights of the mother country, they did not hesitate to erect customs barriers against each other. The assembly of Maryland discovered in 1694 that a great part of the money of the province was being carried into Pennsylvania to purchase beer, rum and other liquors, much to the detriment of local enterprises. In order to discourage the practice a tariff wall was erected against the neighbouring province, and ten years later the importation of beer and malt from Pennsylvania was totally prohibited, that domestic malting

[68] *Pa. Statutes at Large*, III, 415. For suggestions that Parliament should create a colonial revenue from taxes on alcoholic liquors to defray the cost of a permanent civil and military establishment in America, see George L. Beer, *British Colonial Policy, 1754–1765*, pp. 37–42.

[69] *N. Y. Col. Doc.*, V, 509.

[70] *Md. Arch.*, XXVI, 349. Also *Colonial Records of North Carolina*, XXIII, 372.

and brewing might be encouraged in Maryland.[71] Massachusetts and New Hampshire waged a tariff war during 1721 caused by the northern province's resentment over the profits realized by Boston merchants from the rum and wines shipped into its towns.[72] Further proof that each colony desired to be economically independent of its neighbours was contained in the North Carolina act of 1751, which levied prohibitory duties on liquor from South Carolina on the ground that the inhabitants of the colony were able to produce sufficient quantities for their own use.[73]

The failure of many laws of this character to mention malt liquors has led some writers to conclude that there was a general tendency to favour mild beverages and encourage their use in place of ardent spirits.[74] Such a conclusion, however, does not seem to be warranted by the facts. In the first place malt beverages were an insignificant commodity in the commerce of the seventeenth and eighteenth centuries in comparison with wines and distilled spirits. No legislative body, therefore, would consider them an ideal object of taxation from the standpoint of revenue production. Furthermore, the industries of malting and brewing did not receive any more attention from colonial lawmakers than did distilling and wine-making, for laws purporting to encourage the production of the milder beverages can be matched by acts designed to foster the manufacture of spirituous liquors.[75] As has been pointed out, the excise was not a piece of restrictive legislation, and its application cannot be regarded as an attempt to regulate the drinking customs of the people. Indeed, it was applied to beer and ale as well as to ardent spirits, for the tapsters'

[71] *Md. Arch.*, XXXVIII, 63; XXVI, 314–316.
[72] *N. H. Prov. Papers*, III, 819, 827–828.
[73] *Colonial Records of North Carolina*, XXIII, 363–364.
[74] *Cf.* G. Thomann, *Colonial Liquor Laws*, pp. 42–43.
[75] For examples, see *Mass. Col. Doc.*, I, 258; *Pa. Statutes at Large*, III, 415.

tax, first used in New Netherland, subsequently became popular in the English colonies and malt liquors bore a part of the tax burden.[76]

As the taxing power bore with increasing severity upon the liquor traffic, the problems of the revenue collector grew apace. Smuggling was easy when customs officers were few and not overly sensitive in regard to their duties, a fact which was reflected in the slowly mounting revenues from a rapidly expanding commerce.[77] Inasmuch as honest importers and the public treasury suffered from such a system, efforts were made to detect those who evaded the law. Special officers were appointed in some colonies to supervise the customs service, and the justices issued writs to the constables, authorizing search of all premises suspected of harbouring illegal importations. Confiscation of such shipments not infrequently increased the colony's current funds.[78] Difficult as it was to enforce the tariff laws, the collection of the excise presented an even more troublesome problem. The fact that this form of tax had been used in England long before the seventeenth century made it no more acceptable to the seventeenth century colonist in America. He regarded it as a pernicious form of direct taxation, and bore it unwillingly, even when imposed by his own representatives in the colonial assembly. To the retailer it signified the unpleasant interference of government in private business, as well as the highly objectionable activity of spies and informers.[79] The consumer saw the tax as a peculiarly heavy burden, because it tended to in-

[76] N. Y. Col. Doc., I, 424–425; Pa. Statutes at Large, II, 105; Mass. Col. Doc., IV, pt. ii, 365–366.

[77] H. A. Scomp, King Alcohol in the Realm of King Cotton, pp. 140–144. Some interesting figures on the loss of revenue in the Carolinas are cited.

[78] Conn. Pub. Rec., VI, 224, 282, 350; Colonial Records of North Carolina, XXIII, 363, 364.

[79] Conn. Pub. Rec., IV, 249–250; S. G. Arnold, History of the State of Rhode Island, I, 368–369.

crease the price of an indispensable commodity. This unpopularity of the excise was manifest in numerous unsuccessful attempts during the eighteenth century to find a device which would yield a maximum of revenue with a minimum of friction.[80]

One can best understand the intimate relation between regulation and revenue production, and the increasing importance of the latter, by noticing the succession of statutes in a single colony. New York, for example, where the English developed a licensing system from the Dutch beginnings, tried one plan after another for almost a century. Control by municipal authorities and county justices gave way to the ancient practice of farming out the excise to the highest bidder. At first this auction was under the supervision of the mayor and council in New York City and Albany, and of the justices in the various counties, but in 1714 special commissioners were named by the legislature to administer the system in certain designated districts.[81] Both arrangements proving futile from the standpoint of financial returns, a law of 1753 sought to resolve the difficulty by establishing the minimum amount to be realized in each district, and by empowering the commissioners to license all retailers, apportioning the excise among them in proportion to the gross sales of each.[82] Though the collection of an adequate revenue was thus assured, the licensing system was deprived of that slight semblance of restriction which it had formerly possessed. Since more retailers with greater sales would lighten the burden of each dealer and facilitate the task of collection for the commissioners, the test for granting a licence came to be not the need of the

[80] So widespread was the opposition to the excise in Connecticut that an act was passed in 1756 fining a town £200 if it failed to appoint collectors for the excise. *Conn. Pub. Rec.*, X, 451.

[81] *Colonial Laws of New York*, I, 785–786, 838.

[82] *Ibid.*, III, 951–957.

community, but the exigencies of the excise situation. Differing from the New York system in particular details, the other colonies revealed the same general tendency, which may be characterized as a growing insistence upon the ability of the liquor traffic to contribute to the financial support of the government. The expenses of the French and Indian War, placing an added burden on the colonial treasuries, confirmed this tendency, and American finances during the Revolution would have been in worse plight than they were, had it not been for the revenues from liquor taxes.

The transition from colony to state, which marked the period of the American Revolution, did not alter the fundamentals of colonial legislation. In so far as they were applicable, the liquor laws were re-enacted by the new state governments, and with minor variations remained in force until the early part of the nineteenth century.[83] While there was still a noticeable lack of uniformity, certain features were common to all the state laws. Nowhere could intoxicants be sold legally except by dealers licensed under the minute and all-inclusive provisions of the statutes. The sale of liquors was universally associated with the business of keeping a tavern, but other dealers might be licensed. The retailer, who did not provide entertainment for travellers, was seldom permitted by the terms of his licence to sell small quantities to be drunk on the premises. His place of business contained no bar, and his patrons were persons, unable to buy large quantities from importers or manufacturers, who desired to secure a gallon or less for home consumption. The laws usually limited the sale of drinks by draught to the keeper of the tavern. The manufacturer and importer did not come within the provisions of the licence system, but at times special permits were required from those who sold wholesale.

Although laws are usually the reflection of current so-

[83] Scomp, *op. cit.*, pp. 180–192.

cial standards, no adequate portrayal of the manners and morals of a people is found between the covers of statute books. The legislator, influenced by a host of conflicting considerations, seldom is able to reproduce faithfully the popular attitude toward particular institutions and customs. Personal prejudice, economic interest and political expediency combine to render him incapable of accurately judging the wishes of his fellows and uncertain in regard to his own motives for supporting specific bills. His attempts to set forth in lengthy preambles the purposes of the laws he frames serve to confuse rather than to clarify. And he cannot be certain, after his work is finished, that those who follow him will interpret the statutes as he intended. So, if the student of colonial liquor customs were guided solely by the legislation on the subject, he might reach a conclusion far removed from the realities of the situation. His survey might conceivably convince him that the English colonist in America early formulated and consistently supported a policy of hedging the liquor trade about with such minute restrictions that it had no opportunity to expand. A multitude of statutes, containing hostile preambles and heavy penalties, might confirm the idea that in the New World the use of intoxicants was condemned to a sure destruction. Such was the apparent import of numerous laws, but not the real purpose of the law-makers. They agreed with their fellows that liquor was generally beneficial, that its use was constantly increasing, and that, if certain evils could be remedied, the increase should be encouraged for the welfare of the community. They sought to confirm the respectability of the trade by regulating it for the benefit of the group. The dealer accepted this public interest in his business with little protest. Specific restrictions he frequently evaded, but with the principles underlying them he did not quarrel. Apparently, he failed to see that at some future date regulation might lead to the destruction of his business.

CHAPTER II

GLIMPSES OF AN OLD ORDER

FROM the day in 1642 that William Bradford confided to his journal his astonishment at the growth of drunkenness, the use and abuse of alcoholic beverages has been an important factor in determining the characteristics of American life.[1] John Winthrop might persuade himself by means of a faultless syllogism that laws suppressing immoderate drinking were wholesome, but his fellow-countrymen were not ready to abandon customs which had afforded them much pleasure under English skies.[2] Rather, they seemed bent on indulging themselves more freely in the New World than in the Old, achieving in the process a reputation for unusual devotion to the flowing bowl. Their habits have been ascribed by their descendants to various circumstances; the hereditary influence of a hard-drinking Anglo-Saxon ancestry, the hardships and exposure of frontier life, the universal contemporary belief in the medicinal properties of alcohol and the ascetic character of Puritanism, which forced the individual to seek recreation and relief in the joys of the cup.[3] Each explanation affords an opportunity for interesting speculation; but all are significant because they rest upon the hypothesis that excessive drinking was

[1] William Bradford, *History of Plymouth Plantation* (Original Narratives of Early American History), pp. 363–364.

[2] John Winthrop, *History of New England* (Savage edition), I, 44n.

[3] Charles F. Adams, *Three Episodes of Massachusetts History*, II, 785–786; P. A. Bruce, *Economic History of Virginia*, II, 231; Arethusa Hall, *Life and Character of Sylvester Judd*, pp. 315–316.

the rule rather than the exception during the colonial period. Whether the hypothesis be true or not, the Puritan fathers seem to have convicted their own generation. In their opinion their fellows needed watching. Intemperance, resulting from flagrant abuse of nature's gifts, conflicted with Calvinistic ideas of frugality and respectability, which had it that liquor was given to man for the benefit of the group and not for the wasteful gratification of individual appetites. Therefore, by moral precept and statutory pro-vision, the ban was placed upon drunkenness. He, who stepped over the shadowy line of moderation, was an outcast from the community. His pathway was in side streets and back alleys, lest his presence offend his more sober fellows. Summary punishment was his lot if he dared to parade his offence on the public highway. So insistent were the mag-istrates in their early attempts to suppress over-indulgence, that they succeeded in preserving for future generations an exaggerated idea, perhaps, of the extent of intemperance.

Even the way of the prospective transgressor was hard in New England. Though possessed of the means and the inclination to drink to excess, he found it difficult to ac-complish his purpose. If he repaired to the public-house for his liquor, he was apt to be watched carefully by some pub-lic officer, lest he violate the rules and regulations of the place. Unless his previous conduct had been good, he might learn to his sorrow that his name was on the list of those denied the right to purchase liquor.[4] If he secured intoxi-cants and drank unwisely and too long, he was likely to fall into the clutches of the constable. His first offence war-ranted a fine, usually five shillings, or, in default of payment, a sojourn of from one to six hours in the stocks.[5] In case

---

[4] *Mass. Col. Doc.*, IV, pt. ii, 463; *Conn. Pub. Rec.*, II, 282. Josselyn tells of the annoying vigilance of town officers in the taverns of Boston. John Josselyn, *Two Voyages to New England*, pp. 132–133.

[5] *R. I. Col. Rec.*, I, 186; *Conn. Pub. Rec.*, V, 5; *Mass. Col. Doc.*, III, 139; *Laws of New Hampshire*, I, 21.

his tippling became habitual, he could be whipped or forced
to wear some mark of his shame.[6] At the discretion of
the magistrates his kind were frequently put to work on the
fortifications or assigned to some task that would save money
for the town. Thus the treasury was reimbursed for the
expense of justice, and the town received service in lieu of
money from a fine.[7]

In the middle Atlantic and southern colonies the law-
makers frowned as fiercely upon intemperance as did the
New Englander. That it might be less difficult for the
justices to detect offenders, Maryland in 1639 defined drunkenness as "drinking with excess to the notable perturbation
of any organ of sense or motion." [8] From everyone discovered in such a state the Lord Proprietor was to receive
the usual fine of five shillings. If the guilty party chanced
to be a servant, corporal punishment or confinement in the
stocks for twenty-four hours was the penalty.[9] The experience of a few years demonstrated that servants were
not the only incorrigibles, and in 1658 the suffrage was
taken from all free-holders who were convicted for the third
time.[10] None of the neighbouring colonies were quite so
severe in the penalties inflicted, but all provided a fine or the
stocks for the first offence, and hard labour or whippings in
the case of any who indulged in repetitions.[11] During the
eighteenth century, however, the tendency was toward a
mitigation of the punishment, though the drunkard still remained under the ban of social disapproval.

[6] *Mass. Col. Doc.*, I, 112. A scarlet D was sometimes worn by the
habitual drunkard.

[7] *Ibid.*, I, 108.

[8] *Md. Arch.*, I, 53.

[9] *Md. Arch.*, I, 159.

[10] *Ibid.*, I, 375.

[11] *Pa. Statutes at Large*, II, 99; Allinson, *Acts* . . . *of New Jersey*, p.
3; Hening, I, 126, 167; *Colonial Records of North Carolina*, XXIII,
173–174.

It is doubtful whether these laws were as strictly enforced in the plantation provinces as in the Puritan colonies. In the easy social intercourse of the "cavalier" South there was not that compelling concern for the behaviour of the other fellow that so generally permeated New England thought and action. The authorities were more apt to be lenient in their application of the law than the stern magistrates to the north of them. Besides, had the officials of Maryland, Virginia, and the Carolinas been ever so vigilant, they would not have been able to equal the ease with which officers in the northern towns detected offenders. Take North Carolina as an example. According to the law of that colony, a person could be convicted of drunkenness only if seen by a justice of the peace or on the oath of one or more witnesses to the fact, and the information was worthless unless presented within ten days of the offence. In view of the sparsely settled character of the colony, the great distances and the difficulties of communication in the early part of the eighteenth century, it is probable that many escaped even the most conscientious servants of the law. In the more populous colony of Virginia conditions seem to have been different. Proof that drunkenness was severely dealt with during the seventeenth century has been set down by the most distinguished student of the social life of the colony.[12] His numerous citations from the records of the county courts closely resemble the entries in the early records of the Massachusetts General Court, when almost every session witnessed several presentments for intemperance.[13] Although these entries do not reveal the true state of enforcement, they are sufficient to indicate that the law against drunkenness was not a dead letter.

In the aggregate the evidence of prosecutions for intem-

[12] P. A. Bruce, *Institutional History of Virginia*, I, 39–40.
[13] *Mass. Col. Doc.*, I, 98–100 *et seq; Records and Files of the Quarter Courts of Essex County, Mass.*, I, 134–136, 150–152, 154–157.

perance seems to constitute an impressive indictment against
the sobriety of the American colonist. There are witnesses,
however, to answer the accusation. Governor Berkeley did
not hesitate to inform the Commissioners for Foreign Plantations that he considered the Virginia planters generally
more temperate than the English gentlemen.[14] John
Winthrop recorded with evident satisfaction the circumstances of a great training at Boston in 1641, when 1200
men drilled for two days without one case of drunkenness
being observed, although the supply of wine, small beer and
other liquors was abundant.[15] An observer of Massachusetts
life during the middle years of the same century found little
evidence of intemperance even in the busier towns of the
seaboard.[16] As late as 1686 Judge Samuel Sewall, who was
extremely sensitive to every public disturbance, could write
of a few townsmen who had become boisterous over their
drinks that such high-handed wickedness had hardly been
heard of before in Boston.[17] Doubtless there were similar
convivial parties of which the worthy judge was not
cognizant, but they did not make Boston a disorderly town.
Indeed, against the dark background of conditions in England during the early decades of the eighteenth century, town
life in America stood out as a model of orderliness and
sobriety. It was the time when residents of England's
greatest city feared to venture abroad after dark unless
protected by armed retainers, for gangs of drunken ruffians
roamed the dark streets at night, setting upon all they
met, not even excepting the officers of the watch. Young
men of the nobility, as well as servants and apprentices,
committed wanton outrages upon sober citizens with entire
impunity. Drunkenness was characteristic of the lawless

[14] P. A. Bruce, *Social Life of Virginia*, p. 178.
[15] Winthrop, *op. cit.*, II, 49–50.
[16] Thomas Lechford, *Plain Dealing*, p. 69.
[17] *Diary of Samuel Sewall*, *M. H. S. Collections*, Fifth series, V, 151.

element, and was manifest to the most disgusting degree.[18] The colonies were sober and decorous by comparison. No bands of the irresponsible or vicious made the streets of Charleston or Williamsburg or New Haven a terror for the late straggler. True, there was little activity after candle-light, but no one who chanced to be abroad at night was in much danger of molestation. The immediate descendants of Judge Sewall would have been as surprised as he at any unseemly disturbance in Boston.

But the eighteenth century was not many years old, when a change came over colonial drinking customs. It was caused largely by the increasing popularity of distilled spirits in general, and rum in particular. The earliest settlers had brought to the New World a decided preference for wines and malt liquors, a preference which they sought to gratify by domestic production of their favourite drinks, thus supplementing or replacing importations from Europe.[19] Skill was required in the making of palatable ale or beer, and good brewers and maltsters were greatly in demand in all the settlements.[20] Malt houses were early established in New England, but in spite of the fact that the towns encouraged them, successful maltsters were few. The consequent scarcity of high quality malt was a constant handicap to the brewing industry.[21] That substitutes were frequently used with some success is indicated by an optimistic stanza of the period:

> If barley be wanting to make into malt,
> We must be content and think it no fault,

[18] W. E. H. Lecky, *A History of England in the Eighteenth Century,* I, 478–483.

[19] See the chapter "Old Colonial Drinks and Drinkers" in Alice M. Earle, *Customs and Fashions in Old New England.*

[20] See, for instance, the request for brewers from the Virginia plantations in 1609 and 1610. Alexander Brown, *The Genesis of the United States,* I, 353, 356.

[21] For example, Joseph B. Felt, *Ipswich, Essex and Hamilton,* p. 97.

For we can make liquor to sweeten our lips,
Of pumpkins, and parsnips, and walnut-tree chips.[22]

Although Virginia, Maryland and New England supplemented domestic production by importations of barley and beer from the Dutch settlements on the Hudson and the Delaware, the supply of malt liquors was not adequate to meet the growing demand.[23]

Many of the colonists were confident that in time the New World would surpass the Old in the production of choice wines. French vine-growers were sent to Virginia in 1621 by the London Company to instruct the people in the cultivation of grapes.[24] Their efforts seem to have been futile, for forty years later Thomas Woodward, surveyor of Albemarle County in Carolina, estimated that, if the Virginians had been able to produce their own wines, they would have possessed a greater per capita wealth than that of the most opulent country in Europe. Woodward, accordingly, encouraged the Carolina proprietors in their purpose to make the colony a wine-producing country.[25] Wild grapes grew in such abundance in Georgia that the trustees endeavoured to establish viticulture. Cuttings of malmsey from Madeira and tubs of vines from Burgundy were sent to ambitious land-holders in the colony.[26] Although a few succeeded in cultivating the vines and making a sweet wine, many found the experiment decidedly unprofitable after the expiration of a few years.[27] Faith in the ultimate success of such projects still persisted, however, for in 1700 the Earl of Bellomont assured the Lords of Trade that it was possible to

[22] Scomp, *op. cit.,* p. 42.

[23] *N. Y. Col. Doc.,* I, 436, II, 211; *N. C. Col. Rec.,* I, 714.

[24] Lyon G. Tyler, *The Cradle of the Republic,* p. 159; Bruce, *Economic History of Virginia,* I, 243–245.

[25] *Shaftesbury Papers, N. C. Col. Rec.,* I, 101.

[26] *Ga. Col. Rec.,* I, 96, 234.

[27] *Ga. Col. Rec.,* V, 347, 500.

produce enough wine in the continental colonies to supply all the dominions of the Crown. He cited as evidence the wild grapes which grew in great profusion along the Hudson River and were palatable in spite of their wildness. The successful French vineyards in the neighbourhood of Montreal convinced him that New York was not too far north. Besides, he had tasted wine produced in the Narragansett country in Rhode Island, where the climate was not unlike that of the upper Hudson valley.[28]   But Bellomont's enthusiasm was not vindicated by actual results. Although groups of Palatine refugees, expert vine-dressers, were settled in Virginia, the Carolinas and along the Hudson during the eighteenth century, natural handicaps of climate and soil were too much for their skill, and native wines seldom replaced the imported on the colonial gentleman's table.

One drink of domestic production that achieved a well-merited popularity was apple-cider. Foreign travellers found that, if properly served, it ranked with the best drinks to which they were accustomed. Wherever they journeyed from Boston to Savannah, it was served by their hosts and at the public inns. In 1663 Josselyn enjoyed it spiced and sweetened with sugar at the tap-houses in Boston.[29]   Hugh Jones declared that the Virginia beverage was not much inferior to Herefordshire, if kept until the proper age, but no one seemed able to keep it, for the planters were too good companions and hosts while the cider lasted.[30]   The Labadist missionaries, Dankaerts and Sluyter, considered the New York cider the best they encountered during their travels in 1679 and 1680.[31]   During the seventeenth century the New England colonies produced the greatest quantities

[28] *N. Y. Col. Doc.*, IV, 787–788.

[29] Josselyn, *op. cit.*, p. 145.

[30] Hugh Jones, *The Present State of Virginia*, p. 41. Originally published in London in 1724.

[31] *Journal of Jasper Dankaerts* (Original Narratives), p. 66.

of the beverage. Henry Wolcott of Windsor, Connecticut,
had an extensive orchard from which he annually secured
nearly five hundred small hogsheads of cider.[32] In 1648,
when he began to sell, the price was 2s. 8d. a gallon, but
thirty years later production had so increased that he was
forced to sell at 10s. a barrel. The constant addition of
new orchards with the attendant increase in production sent
the price down still further, till in 1700 anything above 6s.
a barrel was considered a fair return.[33]

Although the use of cider became universal, imported wines
were quite as much in demand among those who could afford
them. Madeira was the favourite, while next in popular
esteem came port, canary, claret, burgundy and other French
wines.[34] Brandy, malaga and sherry, the Spanish sack
which Shakespeare praised and drank at the Mermaid in
Cheapside, enjoyed a limited vogue in the colonies. In fact
almost every wine of merit was to be found on the tables of
the wealthier classes and in the bars of the more pretentious
taverns.[35] Though individual tastes differed, people of
fortune in New England were generally partial to canary in
preference to the harsher madeira, which was so favourably
received in the middle Atlantic and southern colonies.[36] It
was a bottle of canary upon which Judge Sewall relied to win
the favour of his lady love, and he was pleased when his
preference, canary or burgundy, was served to the guests

[32] Josselyn, op. cit., p. 145.

[33] Judd, History of Hadley, p. 66.

[34] Peter Kalm, Travels in North America, I, 257; Israel Acrelius,
Description of the Present Condition of the Swedish Churches, p. 160;
"Journal of Lord Adam Gordon," Travels in the American Colonies,
N. D. Mereness, ed., p. 406.

[35] W. B. Weeden, Economic and Social History of New England,
II, 586; Bruce, Economic History of Virginia, II, 215–216.

[36] C. M. Andrews, Colonial Folkways (The Chronicles of America),
pp. 107–108; Hugh Jones, op. cit., p. 52; James Birket, "Some Cursory
Remarks," Travels in the American Colonies, p. 10.

at the weddings he attended.[37]   But the New Englander's taste was not infallible.   So Josiah Quincy discovered when he visited Virginia and the Carolinas in 1773.   At Charleston he found the richest wines he had ever tasted and thought them better than the varieties commonly served in Massachusetts.[38]   Peter Kalm, the Swedish naturalist, and Adam Gordon, the Scotch peer, were equally generous in their praise of the superior vintages possessed by the hospitable merchants and planters southwest of the Hudson.[39]   Kalm was particluarly interested in the native wines, which were still in the experimental stage as late as the middle of the eighteenth century.   In Pennsylvania and Maryland he drank excellent beverages made from blackberries, cherries and wild grapes, but he considered peach-brandy, used extensively in all the colonies, "not good for people who have a more refined taste, but only for the common kind of people, such as workmen and the like." [40]   Burnaby thought that the imitation burgundy of Maryland production, which he drank at the table of Governor Hamilton of Pennsylvania, was not bad "for the first tryal." [41]

An excellent idea of the customary drinks of colonial days can be gained from a list carefully compiled by Israel Acrelius, provost of the Swedish churches in America, while making a survey of the congregations under his control. Since he had an excellent opportunity to observe the everyday habits of the communities he visited, his record, dated 1759, is unusually complete.   Over thirty drinks, well-known at the time, are listed and described.   Besides the wines

[37] *Diary*, III, 301, 364.

[38] "Journal of Josiah Quincy, Jr.," *M. H. S. Proceedings*, XLIX, 443, 448, 464.

[39] *Travels in the American Colonies*, p. 400; Kalm, *op. cit.*, I, 87.

[40] Kalm, *op. cit.*, I, 87, 95.

[41] Andrew Burnaby, *Travels through the middle settlements in North America, 1759–1760*, pp. 70–71.

already noticed, a number of mixed drinks are mentioned; punch, flip, sling, mead and sillibub. The latter, made by adding milk and sugar to wine, was long a favourite as a cooling beverage in the summer-time. Punch usually consisted of lemon or lime juice, spices, and Jamaica spirits, diluted with sweetened water. It was the popular drink for all social gatherings at which the thirst of a large number had to be satisfied. Flip and sling were variations of a single ingredient, Jamaica or New England rum. The former, containing small beer, rum and brown sugar, was served after a hot poker had been thrust in to give it a bitter flavour, while the latter was a simple concoction, half rum and half water, sweetened to the taste. Mead, of ancient fame in England, was prepared by allowing honey and water to ferment. For milder beverages the colonists had a strong beer of American brew, porter and bottled beer from England, and a fermentation of honey and yeast, known as metheglin.[42]

More significant than any enumeration of choice drinks is the revelation contained in Acrelius' list that rum had become the chief stimulant for many Americans. When the New England trade with Barbados commenced, shortly after 1650, the product of the colonists' small stills or "limbecs" was supplanted by a more satisfying distillation from the West Indies.[43] Molasses, brought by adventurous traders from England's island possessions to the energetic merchants of Connecticut and Massachusetts, supplied the ingredient necessary for a large-scale production of rum. Although the New England liquor never equalled that of the West Indies, it was produced more cheaply and soon became popular in all the colonies. Men, engaged in the hard labour of forest and field, and fisher-folk, constantly following the

[42] Acrelius, *op. cit.*, pp. 160–163.
[43] Judd, *op. cit.*, p. 66; *Conn. Pub. Rec.*, I, 322.

sea, demanded a strong stimulant to lighten the burden of
their exacting toil.   The effect of a diet consisting chiefly
of salt meat did not tend to discourage the consumption of
distilled spirits.   As the demand for rum increased, more
merchants ventured to risk their surplus in the business of
distilling, till almost every important town possessed a still-
house of its own.   Some manufactured solely for local consumption, but larger establishments were not lacking in the
important trade centres of Rhode Island, Connecticut and
Massachusetts.   Newport, during the eighteenth century,
grew rich from its distilleries, and the product of the Medford firms was far-famed for its quality.   While the industry
was largely concentrated in the New England colonies, New
York, Pennsylvania and the Carolinas boasted establishments able to compete with the northern distillers.[44]   Philadelphia rum was pronounced as good as the New England
product and commanded an equal price in the American
market.   New York City combined distillation with sugar
refining, which had grown to be the most important element in its industrial life.[45]   Indeed, the multiplication of
distilleries was responsible for the change which came over
colonial industry during the first half of the eighteenth
century, a change marked by notable social and economic
consequences.

Whether spirituous liquor was of domestic or foreign
origin, it penetrated deeply into the social life of Americans.
Rum seemed to be ubiquitous.   It was found in the finest
tavern and the vilest road-house.   The traveller seldom
journeyed far enough to escape it, even in the mountains of
the frontier.   People of fortune kept a stock of good quality

[44] Weeden, *op. cit.*, II, 501; J. M. Usher, *History of the Town of
Medford*, p. 431; *N. C. Col. Rec.*, VIII, 496.

[45] J. F. Watson, *Annals of Philadelphia*, I, 238–239; Burnaby, *op. cit.*,
p. 110; *N. Y. Col. Doc.*, VI, 511.

in their homes, while the servant and common labourer regarded it as indispensable.[46]   Parents gave it to children for many of the minor ills of childhood, and its wholesomeness for those in health, it appeared, was only surpassed by its healing properties in case of disease.[47]   No other element seemed capable of satisfying so many human needs. It contributed to the success of any festive occasion and inspirited those in sorrow and distress.   It gave courage to the soldier, endurance to the traveller, foresight to the statesman, and inspiration to the preacher.   It sustained the sailor and the plowman, the trader and the trapper. By it were lighted the fires of revelry and of devotion.   Few doubted that it was a great boon to mankind.

Along with milder liquors, rum served as a pleasing beverage for special occasions.   No child was properly christened unless all present drank to the health and future prosperity of the infant.   At weddings the tankards passed from hand to hand, and mugs or tumblers were frequently filled with punch, liberally seasoned with Jamaica spirits. The gentlemen enjoyed the customary race for a choice bottle of wine, which the winner was privileged to present to the bride.[48]   The time-honoured practice of serving drinks to the mourners at a funeral was almost universally observed, though occasionally some sterner soul, fearful lest unseemly levity mar the last sad rites, left instructions in his will that no intoxicants should be provided.[49]   Church, as well as home festivities, were made the merrier by reason of

[46] Birket, *op. cit.*, p. 11; *Records of the Court of New Castle, Pa.*, p. 351.

[47] "William Logan's Journal" (1745), *Pa. Mag.*, XXXVI, 3–5.

[48] Helen E. Smith, *Colonial Days and Ways*, pp. 171–172; *Diary of Samuel Sewall*, II, 18; W. S. Bartlett, *A Memorial of Reverend Jacob Bailey*, p. 10.

[49] H. M. Jenkins, *Historical Collections of Gwynedd*, p. 389; H. S. Nourse, *The Early Records of Lancaster, Mass.*, p. 154; Bruce, *Economic History of Virginia*, II, 217; *Md. Arch.*, IV, 108; Felt, *Ipswich, Essex and Hamilton*, pp. 198–199.

the "good creature." The building of a new edifice, the
installation of new pews, and especially the ordination of a
new minister were occasions when slight restraint was placed
upon the appetite.[50]   In Boston John Vyall was requested
to keep a house near the Second Church that thirsty sinners,
going to hear John Mayo or Increase Mather preach, might
be satisfied.[51]   The vestries of certain Episcopalian churches
met at the tavern, where the chief business transacted was
the consumption of good rum at the expense of the congregation.[52]   To the tavern also resorted the town selectmen
and the county justices that the business of government
might have the benefit of the clarifying influence of ardent
spirits.[53]   There over a bowl of toddy or a mug of flip
matters of local and colonial concern were decided, and civil
and criminal cases were heard.

In its intimate relation to the interests and activities of
the community, the tavern was the most significant factor
in the colonial liquor traffic.   Though there was a vast
difference in architectural form between the stately "King's
Arms" in Boston and the rude, wooden shack, which served
as a public-house in the back country of North Carolina,
both were symbols of an influence widely felt in eighteenth
century America.   They represented not only the performance of a public service for private profit, but also the
strengthening of bonds of unity within and between communities.   As centrally located as either the town-hall or
the meeting-house, the tavern in New England served as a

[50] Alice M. Earle, *The Sabbath in Puritan New England*, pp. 269–
270; "Letters of Jonathan Boucher," *Md. Hist. Mag.*, VII, 14; C. C.
Coffin, *History of Boscawen and Webster*, pp. 30–31.

[51] W. R. Bliss, *Side Glimpses from the Colonial Meeting House*,
pp. 13–14.

[52] Letter of John Urmston, *N. C. Col. Rec.*, I, 765–770.

[53] *R. I. Col. Rec.*, V, 267; Babson, *History of Gloucester*, pp. 316–
317; *History of Carroll County, N. Y.*, Georgia D. Merrill, editor,
p. 60.

sort of community centre, housing in cases of emergency the worshipping congregation or the voters assembled for town-meeting. To it came the traveller from distant parts, bringing his welcome news of unusual occurrences and interesting experiences of the journey, and receiving in return an account of local happenings with which to regale his audience at the next stop. Town idlers loved to gather on Saturday afternoons in the great room near the bar and listen to the discussions of politics, religion and current events. Often the conversation was of more than passing interest, for the politically prominent used these informal gatherings to formulate policies, select candidates for office and consider matters of moment in the colony. Such was the nature of the meetings at the "Raleigh" in Williamsburg, which have forever associated that tavern with the cause of American independence.[54]

Training days, county court sessions, town-meetings and convocations were seasons of extraordinary business and profit for the owner of the public-house. Those who attended a muster, appetite whetted by the liquor doled out at the officers' expense, were generous in their patronage at the bar after the day's drilling was finished. Officers and men mingled in good comradeship, while the treats were going round, and toasts were drunk to everyone in authority from the governor to the company captain. Newly appointed officers were expected to "wet" their commissions by liberal purchases of liquor for the benefit of the men. So the preparation for military service became a day of social jollification and for some a time of gross over-indulgence.[55] Boisterousness, rowdyism and rough-and-tumble fighting were likewise characteristic of the crowds that assembled for

[54] Edward Field, *The Colonial Tavern, passim;* W. R. Bliss, *Colonial Times on Buzzard's Bay,* pp. 123–126; James M. Usher, *op. cit.,* p. 389; Mary M. Stanard, *Colonial Virginia,* p. 151.

[55] *Alexander Hamilton's Itinerarium,* A. B. Hart, editor, pp. 81–82.

the sessions of the county court, and occasionally the temptation of the tavern's good cheer was too much for the presiding justices. The colonist journeyed to the county seat on such occasions with no idea of devoting his time entirely to weighty matters of law and business. Usually he had travelled a considerable distance over roads that made the trip anything but pleasant, and he was bent upon making merry for several days as compensation for the hardships of the journey. In the South horse-racing, cock-fighting, and wrestling matches, mingled with much gambling and hard drinking, were favourite diversions after the demands of justice had been satisfied. The convocations of the clergy, north as well as south, called for the best liquors that the local hostelry could supply, for the clergyman was as discriminating as the layman in the use of intoxicants. The New England tavern was frequently located near the meeting-house that visiting ministers might find comfortable lodging and a well-ordered bar conveniently situated.[56]

It was from the tavern, as a rule, that the colonial householder secured his supply of liquor. A few fortunate individuals, like Colonel William Byrd of Virginia, could indulge their love of conspicuous consumption by importing the best wines and brandies directly from Europe, but for the majority this was an impossibility.[57] Often traders, calling themselves wholesalers, purchased hogsheads of rum and spirits from the merchant-importers in the larger towns and travelled up and down the countryside selling their commodity in five and ten gallon lots. Such a dealer was Joshua Hempstead during the first quarter of the eighteenth century. He has left in his diary a detailed statement of

[56] Hening, II, 384; S. G. Fisher, *Men, Women and Manners in Colonial Times*, I, 71; Watson, *Men and Times of the Revolution*, pp. 261–262; Chastellux, *Travels in North America*, 292–293.

[57] *Writings of Colonel William Byrd*, J. S. Bassett, editor, pp. xxxi-xxxii.

the manner in which he supplied his Connecticut neighbours
with their year's supply of rum, until larger business interests took his entire attention.[58]   Most families, however,
influenced either by loyalty to the local taverner or by the
necessity of buying in small quantities, made their purchases
at the public-house, whenever they did not make sufficient
liquor for their own use.[59]   In some communities the profits
of the tavern-keeper constituted a reasonably accurate indication of the prosperity of the group.

Many writers, looking back upon the colonial period
through a romantic haze, have idealized the tavern.   They
have described its cheerful, spacious great-room, its commo-
dious bar, well-stocked with choice and popular beverages,
and its huge, open fire-place, where the crackling of the
logs invited one to while away the long winter evenings.
Here, they would have us believe, gathered the wit and talent
of the town, as well as the interesting travellers who chanced
to share the hospitality of the genial host.   Such public-
houses there were in favoured spots, but they were few and
the way was long between them.   John Dunton tells us that
jovial George Monck made the "Blue Anchor" at Boston a
delight to the most fastidious.   His place was famed far
and wide for the beauty of its special rooms and the ex-
cellence of its fare.[60]   Alexander Hamilton, the Maryland
physician, closely observing manners and customs as he
visited the northern colonies in 1744, found much to praise
in the New York taverns, though the people frequenting
them were extremely annoying.[61]   More often, however, the
record left by the critical traveller is a severe denunciation
of both taverns and tavern-keepers.   Birket considered the

[58] "Diary of Joshua Hempstead," *New London County Historical
Society, Collections,* I, *passim.*

[59] J. S. Barry, *Historical Sketch of the Town of Hanover, Mass.,*
pp. 171–172.

[60] John Dunton, *Letters from New England* (1686), pp. 85–86.

[61] *Alexander Hamilton's Itinerarium,* pp. 50, 106–107.

New England houses either "very indifferent'" or "intolerably dirty," and his experiences with the proprietors caused him to seek refuge in a private home wherever possible.[62] His unfavourable opinion is paralleled by that of William Logan with regard to the region south of Pennsylvania. Called to South Carolina by business interests, Logan rode down the coast from New Jersey to Charleston, noting in his journal as he progressed the sort of entertainment he encountered from day to day. With the exception of a few good houses in Virginia, the farther south he journeyed the worse he fared. "Poor liquor," "dirty food" and "nasty rooms" are frequent entries in his detailed account of the trip.[63] Although the accommodations were so often unsatisfactory, the places offering to care for travellers were numerous. A group of Moravian brethren, making their way through the back-country from Bethlehem, Pennsylvania, to Wachovia in North Carolina, experienced little difficulty in 1753 in finding an inn of some sort during the course of the day's journey.[64] In the sparsely settled sections these inns were usually nothing more than a private house, where the head of the family had secured a licence that he might exact legal rates from his guests. One petitioner in western Virginia urged his case on the ground that he was "very much infested with travellers" and needed a licence to save himself from their impositions.[65] Establishments of such a character seldom pretended to satisfy the needs of the guest in a business-like fashion. He shared what the family ordinarily enjoyed in the way of food and lodging and considered himself fortunate, if he was not discriminated against. His host

---

[62] Birket, *op. cit.*, pp. 10, 25–26, 31.

[63] "William Logan's Journal," *Pa. Mag.*, XXXVI, 2, 3–5, 13, 16.

[64] "Diary of a Journey of Moravians," *Travels in the American Colonies*, pp. 331–334.

[65] J. N. Harmon, Sr., *Annals of Tazewell County, Va.*, p. 19.

probably provided cider, if he was ambitious enough to cultivate an orchard, and a cheap grade of rum, pronounced by foreigners to be "execrable stuff," but which the average American drank with considerable satisfaction.[66]   After experiencing the accommodations of the western country, the traveller was quite willing to give the taverns of the seaboard towns a more favourable report.

In the eastern communities, particularly in New England, the host of the public-house enjoyed considerable prestige. The towns from the beginning presented men of good reputation to be licensed by the justices, and the tradition continued well into the eighteenth century.   Cambridge was long served at the tavern by the most prominent deacon in the church, and upon his retirement his son succeeded him. The tendency to license the same person year after year vested the calling with a sort of dignity which it otherwise would have lacked.   The high esteem in which the occupation was held is evident from the pages of the early Harvard records, on which the names of students were listed not alphabetically, but according to the relative social position of families.   In the class of 1653 Joshua Long, son of an English inn-keeper, precedes Samuel Whiting, whose father was a clergyman.   John Harriman, son of a prominent taverner at New Haven, led the class of 1667, including among his social inferiors the son of Rev. Peter Hobart.   Certainly no more emphatic testimony could be given in regard to the social position of the tavern-keeper in the community.[67] It was not unusual for the town clerk, the deputy to the General Court and the justice of the peace in Massachusetts to round off a public career by securing a licence to run a

[66] "A New Voyage to Georgia" (1737), *Ga. Hist. Soc., Collections,* II, 44; "Narrative of George Fisher" (1755), *William and Mary College Quarterly,* XVII, 173–174.

[67] F. B. Dexter, "On Some Social Distinctions at Harvard and Yale," *American Antiquarian Society, Proceedings,* October, 1893, p. 50.

public-house.[68] During the eighteenth century, however, the occupation lost caste rapidly. Sons of tavern-keepers failed to retain their high rank on the college rolls at Harvard. The courts began to award licences with a greater liberality, which meant a rapid decline in the type of men licensed. The position became less a man's job, as many widows were granted permission to keep public-houses that they might not become dependent upon the community. In some localities persons of influence obtained licences and then employed someone to conduct the business, in order that they might escape responsibility for any unpleasantness or scandal connected with the trade. This practice became common in the middle and southern colonies, where the respectable host, considerate of his good name, was being replaced by a horde of unscrupulous keepers of rude huts, bent upon making a maximum of profit.[69] No reproach, however, attached to the proprietor of a reputable house. At the close of the Revolution a considerable number of officers sought to recoup their fortunes, financially and politically, by entering a business that was profitable and kept them constantly before the public. In the closing decade of the century an English visitor was impressed by the number of lawyers, ex-judges and former members of the legislature who kept tavern in New York state. His observations convinced him that the lawyer and the taverner had found the open sesame to riches and honour in the newer communities of the country.[70] Nevertheless, neither the reflected glory of a military reputation, nor the prestige of a judicial career could restore the occupation to its former high place.

[68] For example see the lists in H. S. Nourse, *The Early Records of Lancaster, Mass.*, pp. 334–338; C. W. Baird, *History of Rye, N. Y.*, p. 150.

[69] "Narrative of George Fisher," pp. 167, 170–171.

[70] John Harriott, *Struggles Through Life*, II, 110, 114, 117.

During the eighteenth century intoxicants became a vital element in determining the course of colonial commerce. The English settlers had early realized the power of ardent spirits to control the valuable Indian trade. Though legal restrictions were imposed in all the colonies to prevent wholesale debauching of the natives, desire for profits broke through legal barriers and enterprising traders paid scant heed to the morality or legality of their methods. By bringing the Iroquois under their domination, the English in New York cleverly schemed to divert the fur-trade of the northern lakes from Montreal to Albany. Indispensable to their plans was rum, less tasty than French brandy, but possessing the merit of cheapness, which enabled the Indian to secure a greater quantity in exchange for his priceless bundles of beaver and mink. Craftily, the English traders, using their brand of "fire-water" to lure the northern tribes, despoiled their rivals and increased their own treasure of furs. Wherever the Indian had pelts for sale, there the independent trader or the merchant's agent might be found, usually provided with a stock of liquor as his medium of exchange.[71] He preceded the settler into the regions beyond the frontier, gathering invaluable information along with his supply of furs. So devastating, however, was the influence of ardent spirits upon the tribes with which he came in contact, that the colonial records are filled with denunciations of unscrupulous traders little better than "abandoned wretches."

Cotton Mather blamed the traffic for the tragedy of King Philip's War, and charged his fellow citizens with deliberately debauching the red men.[72] A decade after the war Dankaerts and Sluyter encountered numerous evidences of

[71] *Travels in the American Colonies,* pp. 524–525.
[72] Mather, *History of the War with the Indians in New England,* S. G. Drake, editor, pp. 91, 99, 175–176; *Diary of Cotton Mather,* [*M. H. S. Collections,* Series vii, vol. vii–viii], I, 342.

the disastrous results which followed in the wake of the Indian trade.[73] Conditions became so intolerable in some sections that the Indians themselves were aroused to denounce the practice. In 1738 the Alleghenies adopted a plan of spilling all rum brought among them, and seven years later George Thomas, lieutenant-governor of Pennsylvania, issued a proclamation giving all tribes in the province the right to destroy liquor offered to them for sale.[74] There was published in London during 1754 a pamphlet entitled *Speech of a Creek Indian Against Immoderate Use of Spirituous Liquors.* In eloquent phrase this spokesman for his nation pictured the artful manner in which the English had introduced ardent spirits among the Indians, supplying it plentifully as soon as its trade possibilities were understood. He passionately attacked a system which based commercial profit upon the degradation of a people, declaring that if the practice were continued many decades longer the Creek nation would perish from the ravages of intemperance.[75] His accusations against the English were substantiated a generation later by the testimony of David Tait after he had travelled extensively among the tribes of the southeast. Desperate as Tait found the situation, he realized that conditions would have to become much worse before the desire for profits would yield to higher considerations of justice. Too many still believed with the seventy-two Albany merchants that any restriction on the use of rum in the fur-trade would end the prosperity of those engaged in an important branch of colonial commerce.[76]

But the rôle of rum in the Indian trade was less important,

[73] *Journal of Jasper Dankaerts,* pp. 179–180.

[74] *Pa. Archives,* First series, I, 549–550; Third series, VIII, 542–544.

[75] *Speech of a Creek Indian,* pp. 12–14.

[76] *N. Y. Col. Doc.,* VII, 613–615. A group of Albany merchants in 1764 petitioned the Lords Commissioners for Trade and Plantations against any prohibition of the use of rum in the trade with the Indians.

from the standpoint of the economic interests of a majority
of the colonists, than its moving power in other forms of
commercial activity. Its importance in determining the
course of trade and the development of industry has been
clearly pointed out by Weeden in his *Economic History of
New England*.[77] Beginning with the importation of the
first considerable quantities of molasses in 1684, Rhode
Island began to build upon a foundation of rum distillation
and exportation. In 1723 some enterprising merchants introduced the liquor as a substitute for French brandy, long
an element indispensable to the African slave-trade, and before the middle of the century Newport and Providence had
become the chief bases for this trade in North America.[78]
Distilleries at Medford, Boston, Newport, and the large
establishments of James Brown at Providence supplied merchants with a commodity readily exchangeable for gold,
ivory and slaves along the African coast.[79] Governor
Cranston reported that between 1698 and 1708 over one
hundred vessels were built in Rhode Island to engage in the
Guinea trade. After 1730 the colony annually exported
1800 hogsheads of rum to be exchanged for slaves.[80] The
correspondence of the larger firms with their captains and
agents throws a flood of light upon the character of the
traffic. Captain John Cahoone, Jr., was off the Guinea
coast in 1736, attempting to realize a good profit from a
cargo of rum which he had taken out of Newport for Daniel
Ayrault. Competition for slaves was so keen, he wrote to
his employer, that he had been able to secure only twenty-
seven in a month. There were nineteen rum ships, both
French and English, in the road at one time, and the

77 II, 641, 649.

78 *R. I. Col. Rec.*, VI, 380.

79 Samuel Hopkins, *Works*, II, 615; Gertrude Kimball, *Providence in
Colonial Times*, pp. 251-252.

80 *R. I. Col. Rec.*, IV, 191-193, 225, VI, 380.

regular stations for slaves were unable to supply the demand. He was taking any slaves that he could get by sending the small boat ashore under supervision of the mate, who was to bargain for Negroes wherever he had an opportunity. Sixteen years later David Lindsay, sailing for Ayrault, reported the same conditions in regard to the rum trade. He spent several months securing 61 slaves and a few ounces of gold, but was forced to start a return voyage before he had disposed of all his rum. In 1755 Wilkinson and Ayrault of Newport sent Lindsay with a cargo of 38 hogsheads of rum to the African coast under orders to secure gold and slaves, the latter to be sold in Barbados, St. Christopher or Jamaica at not less than £27 a head. He was to invest the proceeds in molasses for the New England distilleries. Newport was credited in 1763 with twenty vessels which carried 9000 hogsheads of rum to the African coast. The ventures were becoming less profitable, however, for the price of slaves had risen to 250 gallons of rum for each prime man,[81] while no proportionate increase in the value of slaves was evident in the West Indies. The agents of Aaron Lopez, wealthy Rhode Island merchant, could secure only £33 for prime Negroes in the British and French islands in 1770. During the next few years decreasing profits, re-enforced by the restrictions of the "Association" and the difficulties of war-time, tended to wean the New England shippers from the African trade.[82]

Not all of the product of New England distilleries was destined for the famous triangle of molasses, rum and slaves. As early as 1710 Salem merchants were supplying the continental colonies with sugar, molasses and rum. Philip English, William Pickering and George Curwen, heavily in-

---

[81] New England rum was worth approximately 2s. per gallon.

[82] For interesting material in regard to the rum trade, see *Commerce of Rhode Island, M. H. S. Collections,* Seventh series, IX, 46-47, 59-60, 64, 96, 339, 517, X, 14; Kimball, *op. cit.,* pp. 247-248.

terested in the trade to Virginia and the Carolinas, were amassing considerable fortunes in the early years of the century.[83] Thomas Amory in Boston was testing with favourable results the possibilities of commercial intercourse between Massachusetts, the West Indies and Carolina. His ships carried fish, lumber and foodstuffs to the sugar planters of Jamaica and Barbados, whence sugar and spirits were taken to satisfy the increasing demand of the continental colonies. It was the day when Peter Faneuil, James Brown, and the Derbys, of Salem, were building solid fortunes from the trade with the West Indies.[84] A little later Stephen Hopkins of Providence, disgruntled with the scant profit in the slave-trade, turned his attention more particularly to the English and French islands.[85] Boston merchants, though Birket thought their trade was declining in 1750, were still supplying their customers with fish and rum, receiving in return drygoods from England, flour and provisions from the middle colonies, pitch and turpentine from North Carolina and tobacco from Virginia.[86]

On the eve of the Revolution, then, spirituous liquor was one of the greatest factors in moving colonial commerce. In whatever branch of trade the merchant invested his capital he relied upon rum or some other form of ardent spirits to earn profits for him. Since the traffic in intoxicants was consistently profitable for all who engaged in it, the public accorded it that approbation which attaches to most things indispensable to the world of business. Nothing short of a revolution in public opinion could remove it from its important place in American life.

[83] G. F. Cheever, "Some Remarks on the Commerce of Salem," *Essex Institute Collections*, I, 85, 172.

[84] R. E. Peabody, "The Derbys of Salem," *Essex Institute Collections*, XLIV, 207.

[85] Kimball, *op. cit.*, 257–258, 275–277.

[86] Birket, *op. cit.*, p. 23.

CHAPTER III

VOICES IN THE WILDERNESS

THE half-century following the achievement of American independence was marked by a gradual change in the popular attitude toward the use, manufacture and sale of intoxicants. There is a temptation to find the genesis of this movement for social reform in the isolated protests of the seventeenth century, but no continuing element seems to run through the early denunciation of intemperance. Condemnation of excessive drinking came from various sources, and the underlying motives were as different as the individuals and groups who voiced the warning. An exception might well be made, however, in the case of the Puritan clergy, for the sombre background of Calvinism gave unity and continuity to numerous attempts to restrain individual excesses. Puritanism had not been established fifty years upon American soil, when its high priests took alarm at the serious inroads made by the prevalence of intemperance. A gradual lowering of religious and moral standards among the people caused John Higginson to take action against an evil, which John Winthrop had noticed a generation earlier. In 1670, while pastor of the church at Salem, Higginson addressed a note of admonition to the magistrates, advising them to exercise greater care in their regulation of the sale of liquor.[1] Several years later he followed up this warning with a statement of his reasons for cautioning the authorities. Inasmuch as he had been set in his place by God and men to guard his people from sin, he had been vigilant in searching out the influences which combat religious and moral princi-

[1] *Essex County Court Files, Essex Institute Collections*, XLIV, 192.

ples.   His observations had convinced him that drunkenness
was such an influence, that it was constantly increasing in
Massachusetts and that the magistrates were responsible,
since they had licensed too many ordinaries and public
drinking-houses.[2]

Higginson belonged to a group of conservative clergy, who
were defending the bulwarks of orthodox Puritanism against
the increasing attacks of anti-Calvinistic liberalism.   In
this defence none were more conspicious than the Mathers,
father and son.   Increase Mather, sensing that the manners
of the younger generation might be partially responsible for
its unwillingness to recognize authority in high places, published a pamphlet in 1673, calling upon the colony to discourage tippling and to banish the habitual drunkard.   In
realistic terms he delineated the evils which befall a society,
tolerant of intemperance in its midst.[3]   So earnest was he in
the matter, that he saw a causal relation between the first
case of smallpox in Boston in 1675 and the fact that the
victim was the daughter of an ordinary-keeper.   It was a
testimonial of God's displeasure against the sin of drunkenness.[4]   Although Mather's sermons were sufficiently personal
to earn him a mild rebuke from Governor Bradstreet, he
continued to preach against the increase of ordinaries,
confiding to his diary that the Governor himself was responsible.[5]   In 1686 he had the opportunity in a dramatic
setting to state his cause before a great multitude.   With his
colleague, John Moody, he was invited to preach a public
sermon to James Morgan, a prisoner condemned to death
for a murder committed while under the influence of liquor.
Both clergymen denounced the ravages made upon the youth
of the colony by a new drink recently come into the country.

[2] *Essex Institute Collections*, XLIII, 180.
[3] Increase Mather, *Woe to Drunkards* (1673).
[4] Elizabeth D. Hanscom, *The Heart of the Puritan*, p. 177.
[5] *Diary by Increase Mather*, S. A. Green, editor, pp. 23, 24.

They attributed to this rum or "killdevil" the increase in drunkenness, which was weakening the moral fibre of the younger generation. Dunton recorded the solemnity of the discourses and the profound impression made on the curious crowd assembled to witness the execution.[6]

The mantle of Increase Mather fell upon the shoulders of his son, Cotton. Both in the defence of true religion and in the attack upon intemperance the son was more active than the father. Ever alert to detect heresy, he thought that he observed a close connection between loose-living and free-thinking. How could one explain the reckless running after false gods of a perverse generation except as a result of profligate and degenerate manners? In his own mind the solution was clearly outlined. The commanding voice of the clergy must be raised to enforce the sober conduct and conversation, which had distinguished the colony in its early days. Accordingly, Mather joined with the other ministers of Boston in 1694 to petition the General Court for effective regulation of ordinaries. The deplorable state of religion in the colony, reasoned the petitioners, was due to excessive tippling, and the civil authorities were obligated to assist their ecclesiastical brethren in suppressing the evil.[7] Independent of any action by the law-makers, Mather began his campaign against the enemy. In his diary he recorded the opinion that "the flood of excessive drinking" had begun to "drown Christianity." [8] With this in mind he devoted his Fast Day discourse in 1698 to a consideration of the forces of good and evil in Boston. Although he lamented the enormous number of drinking houses and feared their influence, he admitted that the keepers of the houses were engaged in an honest and legal employment. He challenged the proprietors, however, to suppress drunkenness, revelling

[6] Dunton, *op. cit.*, pp. 125–132.

[7] Waters, *Ipswich in the Massachusetts Bay Colony*, II, 75–76.

[8] *Diary of Cotton Mather*, II, 215.

and wasting of time in their establishments that they might fulfil their proper mission in the community.[9] In order to reach a wider audience he published a pamphlet entitled *Sober Considerations on a Growing Flood of Iniquity*, which supplemented an earlier tract denouncing the sale of rum to Indians.[10] For his own congregation at Second Church he had frequent examples of the ruinous effects of intemperance upon the colony.[11] Nor did he confine his attention to Massachusetts. Reports from Connecticut in 1711 so moved him that he considered writing a strong letter of protest to the principal ministers in that section, calling their attention to the "fearful circumstances into which love of rum had brought some of their number." [12] This concern for the moral welfare of the community, Mather never considered less worthy of his time and attention than his religious and scholarly activities. As late as 1726, only two years before his earthly labours were over, he published in collaboration with others *Seasonable Advice Concerning the Tavern*, which proved that he appreciated the true rôle of the public-house, but hated the excessive use of ardent spirits.

The Mathers were not the only protestants against intemperance. Judge Samuel Sewall heard Benjamin Wadsworth preach earnestly against the foolish custom of health drinking and the wickedness it encouraged.[13] No doubt he also read Wadsworth's pamphlet on the same subject, or that of Samuel Danforth, pastor at Bristol, on the *Woful Effects of Drunkenness*. The *New England Courant* printed and profitably sold in 1724 an interesting satire known as *The Tryal of Sir Richard Rum*. At a court held at Punch Hall

9 Cotton Mather, *The Bostonian Ebenezer*, Old South Leaflets, 67, p. 14.
10 Charles Evans, *American Bibliography*, I, 142, 196.
11 *Diary*, I, 21.
12 *Ibid.*, I, 51.
13 *Diary of Samuel Sewall*, III, 68.

*in the colony of Bacchus. The Indictment and Tryal of
Sir Richard Rum, a person of noble birth and extraction,
well known to both rich and poor throughout all America.*[14]
Of the popularity of the defendant there could be no doubt,
but more serious indictments than the one returned at Punch
Hall were being presented for popular judgment. To the
Society of Friends must be attributed the most effective
and consistent opposition to the increasing use of intoxicants. Although the Quaker ideal everywhere was moderation, the attitude of the various communities was not
uniform. The Welsh societies in Pennsylvania disciplined
members for excessive drinking, but placed no ban upon
members engaging in the liquor traffic until the closing years
of the eighteenth century.[15] The Philadelphia Friends in
1721 supported a movement to prevent the sale of ardent
spirits in the province and to encourage the brewing of
beer as a substitute.[16] The custom of serving liquor at
public vendues was denounced at a meeting of the Bucks
County societies in 1724, and two years later the Yearly
Meeting took similar action.[17] After 1736 the Yearly
Meeting issued periodic warnings to all Quakers against the
too frequent use of spirits, but the sect was not committed
to any hard and fast rules of abstinence.

Thomas Chalkley was typical of the most earnest temperance workers among the Friends during the eighteenth
century. Zealously striving to improve moral conditions in
Pennsylvania and the neighbouring provinces, he was often
moved by the Spirit to extol the virtues of moderation.
According to his inward light, he was certain that no drunkard could hope to enter the kingdom of heaven. By sermons

[14] Felt, *Annals of Salem*, II, 453. This pamphlet was republished in
Boston in 1750. Evans, *Bibliography*, II, 414.

[15] Jenkins, *op. cit.*, pp. 388–389.

[16] *History of Bucks County, Pa.*, W. H. Davis, editor, p. 385;
Watson, *Annals of Philadelphia*, III, 344.

[17] Watson, *Annals of Philadelphia*, I, 97.

filled with sorrowful instances of the terrible effect of intemperance, he sought to frighten the young from temptation and bring the old to repentance. In 1727 he devoted his time particularly to Philadelphia, where the great sins committed by the inhabitants in the public-houses had aroused the "anger of the Lord." [18] As his ministry grew in years, he became more pessimistic about the manners and morals of his generation, crying out in despair against flippant, gambling, tippling youngsters, who spent their time in frivolous pursuits, which they learned while idling around the taverns.[19] That Chalkley was not alone in his concern for his generation is evident from a report submitted in 1744 by a Philadelphia grand jury of which Benjamin Franklin was foreman. Never an intemperate drinker, Franklin could well voice the consternation with which he and his associates viewed the rapid increase in public-houses selling ardent spirits. The report to the justices recommended that the number of licences be restricted, since it appeared that the tippling-houses were responsible for the increased number of poor, the common use of profane language in the streets, and the growing indifference to God and religion.[20]

Puritan priest and Quaker missionary were joined in their temperance efforts by English philanthropists, for the founders of Georgia sought to insure sobriety by sumptuary legislation. No sooner had the first settlement been made than the trustees began their propaganda against ardent spirits. In 1734 they sent to the colony 100 copies of Dr. Hale's *Friendly Admonition to the Drinkers of Brandy*, an English pamphlet advocating the use of malt liquors. To each settler the trustees granted 44 gallons of strong beer and 64 gallons of molasses for brewing, with the hope that

---

18 *Journal of Thomas Chalkley*, pp. 254, 258, 291.
19 *Ibid.*, pp. 288–289.
20 *Pa. Hist. Soc., Collections*, I, 267–268.

beer would become the popular beverage.[21] In 1735 they
enforced an act, approved by the King in Council the previous year, prohibiting the importation or sale of ardent
spirits within the confines of the province.[22] From the
records of the futile attempts to make this prohibition
effective one could write tales of adventure and romance,
comparable to the modern short stories which have cast a
glamour over violations of the Volstead Act. Eighteenth
century rum-runners, with greater ease and less fear of
detection than is experienced by twentieth century boot-
leggers, landed their valuable cargoes in secluded Georgia
coves, or packed their heavy loads along the wilderness
trails from a neighbouring province. When General Oglethorpe visited his colony in 1736, he found the northern
section supplied with rum which came in by way of South
Carolina.[23]

At Savannah the rum-runners demanded and received jury
trial, with the result that the decision of their peers was
usually acquittal, no matter how incriminating the evidence.[24] William Stephens, secretary to the trustees, reported that at the trial of one dealer the presiding justice
instructed the jury to bring in a verdict of guilty, but the
jury refused to follow instructions.[25] Oglethorpe, although
a strong supporter of the law, was convinced that no twelve
men in the colony could be trusted to punish a person who
sold ardent spirits. The majority of people in Georgia
simply refused to regard the sale and use of rum as a
criminal offence. Obedience to the law seems to have been
limited to the German Salzburgers, who were satisfied with

[21] *Ga. Col. Rec.*, I, 121; Scomp, *op. cit.*, p. 63; *An Account Showing
the Progress of the Colony of Georgia in America*, p. 39.

[22] *Ga. Col. Rec.*, I, 44–48.

[23] *Ga. Hist. Soc., Collections*, III, 45.

[24] *Ibid.*, III, 73.

[25] *Ga. Col. Rec.*, IV, 78, 90.

the malt beverages permitted under the regulations.[26]
Stephens wrote to his employers vivid accounts of the
scandalous practice of selling rum in private houses, which
soon became "nurseries of all villainy," where servants were
debauched, and idleness and profaneness encouraged. He
suspected that some of the officials were making a profit out
of the business, since tippling-houses were becoming as
numerous as gin-houses in London.[27]   In 1739 a riot, inspired by hoodlums under the influence of liquor, frightened
the Savannah magistrates into a decision to enforce the law,
but the situation had gotten beyond control. Suppression
of illegal sales was too large a task for the officials.[28]   Convinced that the liquor law could not be enforced, and persuaded by British merchants that the rum trade was highly
profitable, the trustees abandoned their experiment in prohibitory legislation. After 1742 no attempt was made to
restrict the sale of spirits, except by the regulatory provisions of a licensing system.[29]   Several years later Stephens
testified that the change had been a wise one, for trade was
prospering under the impulse of rum, and there was less
drunkenness in the colony than before the law's repeal.[30]   So
Oglethorpe and his friends, sincere though they were, had
failed to foster temperance by legislative enactment in the
face of a hostile public opinion.

The popularity of distilled spirits with all classes increased
constantly during the latter half of the eighteenth century.
Students of the period have attributed the apparent lowering
of moral standards to the demoralizing influence of the
colonial wars, which wrought havoc with the simple life of the

26 P. A. Strobel, *The Salzburgers and Their Descendants,* p. 102.

27 *Ga. Col. Rec.,* XXII, pt. i, 164, 195; IV, 62, 121–122; XXII, pt. ii,
84.

28 *Ibid.,* IV, 388–389; V, 330, 342, 500.

29 *Ga. Col. Rec.,* I, 398, 403, 407.

30 *Ibid.,* XXV, 137–138.

colonists.[31]   Though this generalization may be a trifle too sweeping, it is certain that the experiences of camp and battlefield did not encourage temperance and sobriety.   Horatio Sharpe, governor of Maryland, wrote to Lord Baltimore shortly before the French and Indian War that the consumption of rum had become the disgrace of the colony.   A few years later he condemned the morals of the clergy in no uncertain terms, naming several whom he knew to be habitual drunkards and expressing contempt for a community which tolerated such leadership.[32]   Dr. Archibald Alexander, practising physician in the western part of Virginia, observed a great increase in drunkenness as an accompaniment of the French and Indian War.[33]   During the war Pennsylvania was forced to place unusual restrictions upon the liquor traffic in order to prevent disorderly conduct among the colonial troops.   Rhode Island blamed the vendors of strong drink for the numerous desertions from His Majesty's service.[34]   John Adams was so disturbed by the situation in Massachusetts that he presented a resolution to the selectmen of Braintree, providing for the limitation of licensed dealers in the town.   His action was prompted by "the present prevailing depravity of manners through the land in general and this town in particular and the shameful neglect of religious and civil duties, so highly offensive in the sight of God, and injurious to the peace and welfare of society." [35]

The fears, which Adams expressed in 1761, though overshadowed by the eventful decade preceding the Revolution, were not proved groundless by subsequent developments.

[31] C. F. Adams, *op. cit.*, p. 786; S. G. Fisher, *op. cit.*, I, 287; A. D. Mellick, *Story of an Old Farm*, pp. 614–615; H. Hollister, *History of the Lackawanna Valley*, pp. 141–142; George Duffield, *Samson Shorn*, p. 14; *American Quarterly Temperance Magazine*, February, 1833.
[32] *Md. Arch.*, VI, 164; XIV, 507.
[33] O. F. Morton, *History of Rockbridge County, Virginia*, pp. 181–182.
[34] *Pa. Arch.*, First series, III, 132; *R. I. Col. Rec.*, VI, 186–187.
[35] S. A. Bates, *Records of the Town of Braintree*, pp. 378–379.

The popularity of New England rum and Jamaica spirits was challenged during this period by a product of the west—whisky. Originally distilled from grain by the western farmer for home consumption, it soon became a favourite beverage with a high commercial value. Bulky grain was marketed with difficulty over roads little better than Indian trails or hunters' traces, but whisky, representing concentrated value, was readily salable. It even passed in some districts as an acceptable substitute for currency. Its popularity was enhanced during the Revolutionary War because of the difficulty experienced in securing good rum. The military records are eloquent testimonials of the important rôle it played in the economy of those who fought and those who sold supplies. Each colony sought to provide its militia with the best liquor obtainable, but complaints were numerous that poor whisky was the chief drink furnished.[36] The Continental troops were allowed either a gill or a half-pint of whisky per day, according to the state of the stores.[37] Frequently, however, even a gill was not forthcoming. The Supreme Executive Council of Pennsylvania, having ordered rum or whisky to be distributed to the militia daily, feared that difficulty might arise when the troops joined the Continental forces, since General Washington might see "inconvenience in distributing strong liquors, of which the people are fond, to one part of his army while another is neglected." Accordingly, the spirit ration was commuted to a pay equivalent.[38] So keen was the desire of the men for liquor, however, that the Quartermaster-General was authorized to allow one sutler to each brigade of the Continental line, who might sell whisky, rum, gin, brandy and cordials.[39] A visitor to the army during the terrible

[36] *Md. Arch.*, XII, 139; *Pa. Arch.*, First series, VIII, 640–641.
[37] "Bicker's Orderly Book of the Second Pennsylvania Continental Line," *Pa. Mag.*, XXXVI, 30–31; *N. C. State Records*, XIV, 133.
[38] *Pa. Arch.*, First series, V, 561–562.
[39] *Pa. Mag.*, XXXVI, 31.

winter at Valley Forge heard the complaint of the soldiers constantly voiced in the refrain: "No pay, no clothes, no provisions, no rum." [40] Between two and three hundred gallons of whisky a week were consumed by the workmen at Trenton, engaged in building a fleet for Pennsylvania. William Crispin, the commissary agent, wrote to the Council of Safety that he had seized several hogsheads of liquor in the neighbourhood, but the labourers were clamouring for more, and he feared that his safety depended upon an adequate supply of rum or whisky.[41] In 1780 Congress sought to meet the general demand by apportioning the responsibility for providing liquor among the various states. Connecticut's share was over 68,000 gallons, and the state Council of Safety began purchasing molasses for distillation at Middletown and Norwich.[42] Massachusetts circulated broadsides calling upon all patriotic citizens to sell their supplies to the public authorities.[43] General Gates, president of the Board of War, threatened to seize all stocks of ardent spirits which were being held out of the army stores by speculators.[44]

These strenuous efforts to provide sufficient quantities of liquor are but an indication of the widespread use of the product of the still. That the war served to increase this use is evident from contemporary records. Chastellux, during his extensive travels in America in 1780 and 1781, lamented the scarcity of good wines, but was gratified by the regularity with which he encountered the punch bowl. Whether he was drinking toasts at General Washington's table, or reading Ossian with Jefferson till far into the night, or penetrating the hills and valleys of western Virginia, he

[40] James Thacher, *A Military Journal*, p. 154n.
[41] *Pa. Arch.*, First series, VI, 203.
[42] *State Records of Connecticut*, II, 521; III, 248, 448.
[43] *Broadsides, Ballads . . . in Massachusetts, 1639–1800*, M. H. S., *Collections*, LXXV, 287.
[44] *Pa. Arch.*, First series, VI, 205.

was constantly cheered by some form of distilled spirits.[45] He considered the American practice of drinking healths at meals absurd and barbarous, for each person indulged in a ridiculous comedy of drinking successively the health of every other person present, till excessive politeness resulted in boisterous uproar. Unlike the German toasts, however, the custom seldom caused any unseemly over-indulgence, in spite of the fact that it was practised by the servant class as well as in higher social circles.[46] In his visits to the homes of prominent Americans, Claude Blanchard, commissary to the French army in America, discovered that the restrictions of war-time had not deprived his hosts of cider and ardent spirits. In the western sections he encountered little else in the way of beverages, but European wines were not uncommon on the tables of the wealthier class.[47] Brissot de Warville, writing of conditions in New England during 1788, expressed surprise at the abundance and variety of the wines and brandies and noticed that most people preferred ardent spirits to milder liquors.[48]

Distillations from grain were becoming more popular in all parts of the country. Domestic production was augmented in 1790 by the importation of 3,678,000 gallons of spirits, and two years later 4,869,000 gallons were brought into the country.[49] Soon afterward the Whisky Rebellion against the federal excise on spirituous liquors dramatically revealed the importance of domestic distilling in the western counties of Pennsylvania, where almost every family manufactured its own supply. In rural communities throughout the country little work was done without the stimulus of in-

[45] Chastellux, *op. cit.*, pp. 23, 67–68, 226, 229.

[46] *Ibid.*, pp. 92–93; *Journal of Claude Blanchard*, pp. 65–66, 116–117, 119.

[47] Blanchard, pp. 78–79, Chastellux, p. 234.

[48] J. P. Brissot de Warville, *New Travels in the United States of America*, pp. 103–104.

[49] Tench Coxe, *A View of the United States of America*, pp. 421, 492.

toxicants, while occasions such as haying, corn-husking, barn-raising and fence-building were times of special indulgence for the entire neighbourhood.[50] Wages were quoted in terms that included the customary daily allowance of rum, and few labourers cared to accept more money in lieu of the liquor.[51] Merchants carried larger stocks of "wet goods" than dry goods, selling in large or small quantities without regard to the terms of their licences. No grocer seemed to prosper unless he kept a barrel on tap and treated his customers whenever they settled their accounts. For trainings, musters and other public ceremonies the town was supposed to furnish the refreshments, while at ordinations, installations and district councils the church supplied the inevitable wines and spirits.[52]

Meanwhile, the abundance and cheapness of intoxicants, permitting their constant use by all classes, caused intemperance to grow apace, with the result that efforts to suppress the vice increased.[53] Once again the warning was sounded by the Puritan and the Quaker. Jonathan Edwards made his conduct more than his speech a plea for the "strictest temperance in drinking." Before he reached the age of twenty he solemnly decided that he would follow a rule of abstinence except in cases of necessity. Although his resolution was not often paraded in his sermons and writings, he frequently recorded in his journal the benefits of the course

[50] J. E. Pilcher, *Life and Labors of E. H. Pilcher*, pp. 16–17.

[51] Letter of Jeremiah Libbey to Jeremy Belknap, December 17, 1789. *Belknap Papers,* [*M. H. S., Collections,* Fifth Series, ii–iii, Sixth Series, iv] III, 456.

[52] Ida G. Adams, "The Passing of Intemperance in a Country Town," *Granite Monthly,* XXXII, 300; A. S. Hudson, *History of Sudbury, Mass.,* p. 606; J. W. Headland, *History of Loudoun County, Va.,* p. 118; F. P. Wells, *History of Newbury, Vt.,* pp. 255–256; Louise W. Murray, *Old Tioga Point and Early Athens, Pa.,* pp. 52–54; A. D. Mellick, *op. cit.,* 617–619.

[53] At the close of the 18th century whisky generally retailed for 40 or 50 cents a gallon.

he was pursuing. Experiences of the passing years confirmed his opinion that temperance kept a man "sprightly and healthy in mind and body." [54]   Edwards' mild testimony against spirituous liquors was not unlike the attack of that lovable preacher of the gospel of humility, John Woolman. Almost apologetically Woolman advised the Friends to whom he ministered to consider carefully the consequences of intemperate drinking. He understood full well that those who toiled long hours in the heat of summer found a welcome stimulant in strong drink, but in this very practice, he believed, lurked the danger. With that direct simplicity so characteristic of all his writings he recorded in 1769 his reasons for preaching temperance.

I have found [he wrote] that too much Labour in the summer heats the Blood, that taking Strong Drink to support the Body under such Labour, increaseth that Heat, and though a Person may be so far temperate as not to manifest the least Disorder, yet the Mind, in such a circumstance, doth not retain that calmness and serenity which we should endeavor to live in. Thus toiling in the Heat, and drinking Strong Liquor, makes men more resolute and less considerate, and tends very much to disqualify them from successfully following Him who is meek and low of Heart.[55]

More vigorous in his protests, and hence more representative of the determined reformers, was Anthony Benezet. A Quaker of Huguenot descent, he had settled in Philadelphia in 1731 after his family had felt the heavy hand of persecution in France. Having dedicated his life to ceaseless war against "whatever has a tendency to abridge the comforts, increase the sorrows, or endanger the safety of men," Bene-

[54] *Memoirs of the Rev. Jonathan Edwards by Samuel Hopkins,* John Hawksley, ed., pp. 12, 20, 31.

[55] *The Journal and Essays of John Woolman,* Amelia M. Gummere, ed., pp. 183–184, 281, 293, 388–389.

zet soon became a force in the life of his adopted city. After teaching for thirteen years in the William Penn school he established a school for girls, based upon his own educational theories, where an attempt was made to devise a curriculum which would meet the needs of each pupil. Ever a pioneer in educational matters, he conducted an evening school for free Negroes and from his contacts with the scholars was persuaded that the cause of the black race required his full time and attention. Through correspondence with Patrick Henry and Henry Laurens, he endeavoured to interest leaders of thought in the southern colonies in a plan for gradual emancipation. Along with his labours to improve the condition of the Negro, he manifested a benevolent interest in the welfare of the American Indian, which brought him for the first time into close contact with the problem of intemperance in an aggravated form.[56] Discerning the ensnaring influence which intoxicants exercised over the red man, Benezet began to study seriously their effect upon the people amongst whom he lived. As a result of his observations he published in 1774 his first attack against the habitual use of ardent spirits.[57] It was a small pamphlet setting forth an analogy between the ravages of strong drink and the havoc wrought by a prolonged war. The poverty, disease and death, following in the wake of intemperance, convinced Benezet that liquor was as grim a reaper as war itself. To his own satisfaction he proved that a community could better afford to endure the inevitable horrors of armed conflict than the desolation secretly effected by the product of the still. Four years later he circulated at his own expense an analysis of the opinions of distinguished physicians in regard to the effect of intoxicants upon the human body.[58] His edition of the Pennsylvania Spelling Book in 1779 con-

[56] Roberts Vaux, *Memoir of the Life of Anthony Benezet.*
[57] *The Mighty Destroyer Displayed* (1774).
[58] *Remarks on the Nature and Bad Effects of Spirituous Liquors* (1778).

tained a list of one hundred questions, comprising a temperance catechism for the instruction of the young. Questions and answers sought to impress the lesson that ardent spirits were harmful as a beverage and that popular approval of their use was based on a false conception of their true relation to the health of the drinker.[59] More significant than Benezet's publications, however, was his activity in bringing the Society of Friends to the point of defining its position in regard to the use, manufacture and sale of intoxicants. Although no action was taken during his lifetime, his work bore fruit three years after his death, when the Yearly Meeting of 1787 adopted a resolution recommending to the membership that all refrain from dealing in spirituous liquors.[60]

Meanwhile, another religious sect was using its influence in the interests of temperance. The American Methodist societies were governed by the same discipline as those in England, and the general rules formulated by the Wesleys were theoretically in force. According to the original rule of 1753, all Methodists in good standing were subject to disciplinary measures for "drunkenness, buying or selling spirituous liquors, or using them, unless in cases of extreme necessity." [61]   Actually this regulation received scant attention from the followers of John Wesley in America, but in 1780 the General Conference of preachers placed itself on record. Two questions were propounded and answered in the affirmative: "Shall we disapprove of the practice of distilling grain into liquor? Shall we disown our friends who will not renounce the practice?" Three years later a similar conference decided to admonish the membership to abandon the manufacture, sale and use of spirituous liquors,

---

[59] *The Pennsylvania Spelling Book* (A. Benezet, compiler).

[60] Letter of Benjamin Rush to Jeremy Belknap, *Belknap Papers*, III, 419–420.

[61] Henry Wheeler, *Methodism and the Temperance Reformation*, pp. 45–46.

but the admonition did not purge the Methodist societies of all who refused to give up the trade in intoxicants. When Thomas Coke visited the United States in 1784, for the purpose of investing Francis Asbury with the episcopal dignity, he found great need in the newly organized church for his exhortations against intemperance.[62] Bishop Asbury, likewise, had occasion to enforce the lessons of temperance, as he carried a sense of unity to the widely scattered societies of the South and West. Everywhere he voiced in plain speech his condemnation of communities which allowed intemperance to hinder the work of the Christian church.[63] New England clergymen were paying their compliments to "Demon Rum" with increasing frequency, basing their protests on considerations of public welfare. A sermon preached at Templeton, Massachusetts, in 1776 by Rev. Ebenezer Sparhawk was typical of the pulpit pronouncements of the period. The minister realized that his congregation might be surprised at his choice of a subject, but he justified himself by quoting from the Scriptures to prove that intemperate drinking was a sin in the sight of the Lord. His denunciation was directed chiefly against the waste of money involved, the misuse of valuable time, and the ruinous effect upon the health of a community. In an unscientific, but none the less vivid fashion, he outlined the influence of spirituous liquor on the body. It "puts the blood and juices into a most terrible ferment, and disturbs the whole animal economy. It vitiates the humor, relaxes the solids, spoils the constitution, fills the body with diseases, brings on meager looks, a ghastly countenance, and very bad tremblings: yea, when the abuse

[62] *Minutes of the Methodist Conference Annually Held in America,* I, 26, 41; *Extracts from the Journals of the late Reverend Thomas Coke,* pp. 43, 60.

[63] *Journal of Francis Asbury,* II, 219, 248. In 1796 the General Conference voted that any member using or selling ardent spirits might be censured or suspended at the discretion of the local preacher. *Journals of the General Conference of the Methodist Episcopal Church,* I, 28.

of it is persisted in, it quite ruins the health, destroys the strength, introduces decay of nature, and hastens death faster than hard labour." But higher concerns than those relating to the physical being demanded consideration. Intemperance was equally harmful to the things of the spirit. It deprived its victim of all sense of religious duties, removed him from the sanctifying influence of the Holy Spirit, and made it impossible for him to share in the heavenly inheritance. Therefore, the servants of Christ were under compulsion to bear witness, even in the face of popular displeasure, against so grievous a destroyer.[64]

The leaven of social reform works slowly, but during the last decade of the eighteenth century there were indications that it was beginning to permeate the mass. From Litchfield County, Connecticut, Oliver Wolcott, Sr., wrote to his son regarding a new plan designed "to reform a practice which leads many to poverty, distress and ruin." The result was the formation in 1789 of a voluntary association of forty prominent citizens, who pledged themselves to carry on their respective business interests without the use of distilled spirits, and to serve their workmen only mild beverages such as beer and cider. This association, significant as the first organized abstinence from ardent spirits, prepared the way for the efficient work of Lyman Beecher a generation later.[65] It enrolled in its membership such influential men as Tapping Reeve, Frederick Wolcott, Daniel Sheldon and Benjamin Tallmadge, whose temperance efforts bore fruit during the life-time of their children. A pledge, similar to the Litchfield obligation, was circulated in Nelson County, Virginia, in 1800 and received the signatures of

64 Sermon preached at Templeton, Mass., January 28, 1776, by Rev. Ebenezer Sparhawk. *Ms.* in possession of Dean H. E. Hawkes of Columbia College.

65 Alain C. White, *History of the Town of Litchfield, Conn.,* pp. 157–158, 185–186; G. F. Clark, *History of the Temperance Reformation in Massachusetts,* p. 5; Orcutt, *History of Torrington,* p. 207,

many farmers in the district. The agricultural almanac, that indispensable manual of a century ago, carried to many rural households words of caution in regard to the use of intoxicants.[66] An increasing number of newspaper editors, while advertising in the columns of their publications a choice selection of beverages, found space for sentiments distinctly hostile to their advertisers' business interests.[67] The efforts of the clergy were re-enforced by the work of certain teachers, who were interested in more than the intellectual attainments of their pupils. At Yale Timothy Dwight attempted to persuade the undergraduates to abandon their traditional drinking festivals. His descriptive sermons on the nature, causes and evils of drunkenness constituted a solemn warning that the road to excess began with moderate drinking. In President Dwight's mind, sobriety was associated with the fundamental principles of Federalism, and he sought to enlist the college in the support of both.[68]

Unusual attention was focused on the liquor question during the early years of the national government by the Congressional debates concerning the new revenue system. Madison's proposal to impose a special duty on distilled spirits of foreign origin precipitated a heated argument over the purpose and effect of such a tax. Some, like Boudinot of New Jersey, welcomed it as a discouragement to importation which would ultimately prove beneficial to the morals of the people, but Ames of Massachusetts and Lawrence of New York ridiculed the idea of mingling morality with the collection of revenue. "If any man supposes," said Fisher Ames, "that a mere law can turn the taste of a people from ardent spirits to malt liquors, he has a most romantic notion

[66] G. L. Kittredge, *The Old Farmer and His Almanack*, p. 315.

[67] For example see extracts from the *Wyndham County Herald*, 1797–1800, in Larned, *History of Wyndham County, Conn.*, pp. 390–391.

[68] J. Marsh, *Temperance Recollections*, pp. 10–11.

of legislative power." [69]   That scores of Americans entertained this "romantic notion" was evident from the petitions and memorials forwarded to Congress during the course of the debates.[70]   Out of the mass of conflicting opinions in regard to an excise tax, one petition stood as the expression of a new attitude toward spirituous liquors, which was rapidly gaining popular approval.   On December 29, 1790, the College of Physicians of Philadelphia sent a memorial to the Senate and House of Representatives, which stated that "the habitual use of distilled spirits, in any case whatever, is wholly unnecessary; that they neither fortify the body against the morbid effects of heat or cold, nor render labour more easy or productive; and that there are many articles of diet and drink, which are not only safe and perfectly salutary, but preferable to distilled spirits, for the above-mentioned purposes." [71]

The memorialists placed their hopes in the wisdom and power of Congress to impose such heavy duties that intemperance would be restrained.   In their appeal to the legislative power they were far ahead of their times, but in their refutation of popular misconceptions in regard to ardent spirits they were prophets of the immediate future.   One of their number, Benjamin Rush, already an influential advocate of temperance, was destined to see his theories accepted as the principles of the first temperance society, definitely organized as such, in the United States.

[69] Gales and Seaton, *Debates in Congress*, I, 107 *et seq.*

[70] *Annals of Congress*, II, 1740, 1838, 1791; *Pa. Arch.*, Second series, IV, 19, 22, 30.

[71] *American State Papers, Miscellaneous*, I, 20.

CHAPTER IV

A PHILADELPHIA PHYSICIAN

In 1778, while Washington was perplexed by the problem
of conserving man-power until the arrival of French troops,
the physician-general of the Middle Department of the
Continental Army published a treatise entitled *Directions
for Preserving the Health of Soldiers.* It contained a
warning to the troops under his care against the excessive
use of spirituous liquors. The physician-general at the time
was Dr. Benjamin Rush, a distinguished Philadelphia prac-
titioner, who had already established a reputation as a
medical authority. Fifteen years before he had completed
his preparatory work at Nassau Hall and under the guidance
of Dr. John Redman in Philadelphia had given such promise
of future achievement that his friends had persuaded him
to study in Europe. He spent three interesting and
valuable years after 1766 in England, Scotland and France,
devoting himself conscientiously to scientific research, but
finding time to broaden his interests by association with
Sir Joshua Reynolds, Samuel Johnson, Oliver Goldsmith,
Diderot and the younger Mirabeau. Having received his
degree in medicine from the University of Edinburgh, he
returned to America in 1769 and accepted a professorship of
chemistry in the College of Philadelphia. Academic and
professional duties did not prevent him from taking an active
part in public affairs. His sympathy for the patriot cause
was repeatedly manifested during the events immediately
preceding the Revolutionary War. In 1776 Pennsylvania
sent him to the Second Continental Congress, where he added

his signature to the Declaration of Independence. But his career as a legislator was not prolonged, for in 1777 he resigned his membership in Congress to become physician-general in charge of hospitals in the Middle Department.[1]

In his new position Dr. Rush had an opportunity to study the liquor question from an interesting angle. It was a subject to which he had given much thought while a student at the University of Edinburgh and later while teaching in Philadelphia. As a practising physician, he had taken time to observe carefully the effect of intemperance upon the mental and physical faculties. His treatise addressed to the army contained the conclusions drawn from this study and observation. In it he refuted the beliefs, common to most men of his day, that ardent spirits relieved fatigue, sustained hard labour and protected one against heat and cold. His main theme was that fevers and jaundices, the usual accompaniment of the soldier's life, were aggravated rather than relieved by the use of distilled liquor. He was convinced that certain diseases of the camp were directly traceable to the practice of serving spirit rations to the men. Therefore, he recommended that beer and ale replace the more intoxicating beverages. Although his findings and recommendations effected no change in army policy, they served as a basis for his later writings in more scientific vein.[2]

Retiring from a distinguished public service, Rush gained even greater fame by his original contributions to the theory and practice of medicine. At a time when most scientists and philosophers maintained that the mental faculty was not connected with the physical, he strove diligently to show

---

[1] William Staughton, *An Eulogium in memory of the late Dr. Benjamin Rush, passim; A Memorial containing travels through life of Dr. Benjamin Rush,* L. A. Biddle, ed., pp. 16–57; David Ramsay, *An Eulogium upon Benjamin Rush, passim.*

[2] Benjamin Rush, *Directions for Preserving the Health of Soldiers* (Reprint in *The Military Surgeon,* March, 1908).

the intimate relation between the two. The cure of mental diseases, just beginning to receive attention from the medical profession, interested him more than any other part of his work. By careful analysis of numerous cases brought to his attention, and by shrewd speculation on the nature of nervous disorders, he formulated a hypothesis which seemed satisfactory. He incorporated it in his greatest work, *The Influence of Physical Causes upon the Moral Faculty*, which was a demonstration of the causal relation between physical disability and mental or moral abnormality. This attempt to explain religious hysteria, melancholia and other nervous disorders in terms of some bodily ailment shocked the age in which Rush lived. The Philadelphia physician, however, continued to develop his theory as far as popular prejudice and his own limitations would permit. From a constantly increasing number of cases he gathered evidence which seemed to show that almost every instance of mental abnormality could be traced to a diseased condition of the physical organism. He was equally sure that the mental faculty was responsible for certain apparent physical afflictions.[3]

As an important by-product of this study of mental diseases, Dr. Rush clarified his ideas with regard to the use of spirituous liquors. In 1784 he published a pamphlet, *An Inquiry into the Effects of Spirituous Liquors on the Human Body and Mind*, which contained a clear exposition of the properties of alcohol. From his medical experience he cited cases of disease, nervous affection and mental derangement caused by the excessive use of intoxicants. In each case he outlined in scientific fashion the manner in which the individual was affected. From the specific instance he reasoned inductively to the general proposition that even the moderate use of distilled spirits, if long continued, would

[3] For an excellent discussion of this phase of his work see "Benjamin Rush and Mental Healing" in Woodridge Riley, *American Thought from Puritanism to Pragmatism*, pp. 104–117.

result in serious complications. Hence, he advised his readers to imitate the sober Germans, who relied almost entirely on malt beverages of a harmless character. He believed that temperance would be achieved when ardent spirits were abandoned for beer and light wines. "A Moral and Physical Thermometer" was appended to the *Inquiry*, which indicated that "small beer" led to long life and happiness, that cider and wine, when taken in moderate quantities, produced strength and cheerfulness, while punch and drams opened the way to debtor's prison or the gallows.[4]

At harvest time each year Rush republished and circulated this essay in the hope that farmers might be persuaded to abandon the practice of furnishing liquor as part of the day's wage.[5] Nor was he alone in placing his work before the public. Portions of the essay were copied by newspapers throughout the country, and the compilers of almanacs were glad to include his comments on the alleged medicinal and food value of ardent spirits. So convincing were his conclusions and so ably stated that the tract continued to be the stock in trade of temperance writers long after its first publication.[6]

Dr. Rush was highly gratified by what he considered the immediate and widespread acceptance of his views. He wrote in 1788 to Jeremy Belknap, his associate in numerous philanthropic enterprises, that the essay on ardent spirits was making many converts. Associations were forming throughout Pennsylvania, pledged to discontinue the use

---

[4] *An Inquiry into the Effects of Ardent Spirits on the Human Body and Mind.* This is the title of the 1811 edition. In the *Inquiry* appears a revolting picture of drunkenness. Dr. Rush compares the drunkard to the calf in folly, the ass in stupidity, the skunk in fetor, the hog in filthiness, and the tiger in cruelty.

[5] *Belknap Papers,* III, 403.

[6] *Reminiscences of Neal Dow,* pp. 163–164; John Marsh, *Temperance Recollections,* p. 11; Ebenezer Porter, *The Fatal Effects of Ardent Spirits;* John Watson, *An Alarming Portraiture.*

of liquor during the harvest season. Proprietors of country stores were refusing to buy and sell intoxicants. The Quakers and Methodists were taking the lead in the work of reform in every community where they were numerically strong. In view of the propitious beginning, Rush felt free to call upon his friend to join him in a pretentious campaign of education. He believed that if the force of the press in all sections of the country could be brought to bear upon the problem of intemperance, the evil would be speedily eradicated. To that end he suggested that Belknap supervise the work in New England, while their mutual friend, Dr. David Ramsay of South Carolina, would attend to publicity in the South. He felt sure that the South Carolina physician would welcome the formation of such a triumvirate, and that success would not be long deferred. Indeed, Rush was so sanguine that he prophesied a drunkard in 1915 would be "as infamous as a lyar or a thief, and the use of spirits as uncommon in families as a drink made of a solution of arsenic or a decoction of hemlock."

The enthusiast did not mistake his men. Belknap kept up a constant correspondence with him on the subject, discussing methods and results in New England.[7] The letters of Rush reflected the abounding faith of their author in the ultimate success of the cause. In 1789 he wrote that less rum would be used in New Jersey, Delaware and Maryland than during the previous year. He had succeeded in interesting the Methodist Conference, and was busy persuading the Presbyterians and Episcopalians to take action against the use of ardent spirits. A recent letter to Bishop Carroll of the Baltimore diocese, he believed, would start an association among the Catholics.[8] But Belknap viewed the situation through darker glasses. On July 29, 1789, he wrote to Rush:

[7] *Belknap Papers,* III, 403–404, 416–417, 419–420, 425.
[8] *Ibid.,* III, 435–436.

With respect to spirituous liquors I believe some good has been done, but much more remains to be done. The distilleries here [Boston] are so ready a source of gain, that till the *auri sacra fames* shall cease to be a ruling passion, I fear there will no end be put to them. The demand from abroad, I am told, increases, particularly from the north of Europe, and while the stills are kept going there will be a large home consumption. In an excursion of about 80 miles into the country a few weeks ago, I met many loads of pot and pearl ashes coming down, and on my return the teams which I met were loaded with dry fish, hogsheads of salt and barrels of rum. The thirst for spirits in the back country is so ardent, that in the fall and winter they will sell their wheat for this sort of pay, and then in the spring and summer go 40 or 50 miles after bread.[9]

.Of a sort with this discouraging account was Dr. Ramsay's opinion of conditions in South Carolina. One can understand what was in his mind from the description, which he included in his history of the state, published in 1808. In regard to intemperance, he wrote:

Drunkenness may be called an endemic vice of Carolina. The climate disposes to it, and the combined influence of religion and education, too often fail to restrain it. . . . Several persons are contented with the beverage of nature, and maintain good health and spirits without artificial liquor; but a much greater number drink water only when they can get nothing else. The most harmless substitute that has been found for that pure element is beer. This communicates strength while it quenches thirst, and in its most common forms does not really intoxicate. Unfortunately for Carolinians, cheap fermented liquors do not suit with their climate, especially in the summer when they are most wanted. Recourse is generally had to spirituous liquors; medical theories are made to bend to appetite. Accommodating professional men by their example and advice, recommend it as a corrector of water. Such opinions are readily received and acted upon. The general proposition being once admitted that the

9 *Belknap Papers*, III, 440.

addition of rum, brandy or whiskey is an improvement of water, it is no easy matter to stop at the precise point of temperance.[10]

The pessimism of Belknap and Ramsay did not dampen the ardour of Dr. Rush. He continued to write, whenever he had occasion, and on his professional calls he constantly bore witness against intemperance. Manasseh Cutler, who stopped for a few days in Philadelphia on his way to Ohio, noticed that Rush never failed to remind his patients of the cause of their illness, when he believed that it was due to spirituous liquors.[11] Upon his acceptance of a professorship in the College of Physicians in 1789, he set to work at once to convince his colleagues and students of the soundness of his views, with the result that the faculty joined him in petitioning Congress to use the taxing power as a means of suppressing intemperance.[12] His fame was such, both in Europe and America, that his writings on any subject were welcomed by the reading public. Realizing this, he republished his essay on ardent spirits as often as the editions were exhausted, always believing that the seed of temperance would fall upon good ground and bear fruit.

A copy of one of the numerous editions of the essay finally came into the possession of Billy J. Clark, a physician in the town of Moreau, Saratoga County, New York. A careful perusal of Rush's arguments opened Clark's eyes to circumstances in his own community, which had never before received more than passing notice. As a country doctor, belonging to that circle of public servants whose ministry intimately acquaints them with conditions normally concealed, he could see beyond the particular diseases of his patients to a malady affecting the health of the group. Moreau and the neighbouring town of Northumberland, being

[10] David Ramsay, *The History of South Carolina*, II, 391–392.

[11] W. P. and J. P. Cutler, *Life of Reverend Manasseh Cutler*, I, 281.

[12] See *supra* p. 70.

centres for the seasonal activity of a thriving lumber business, were largely populated by lumber-jacks, who sought compensation for the discomfort and hardship of their employment in generous potations of rum or other spirits. In his professional visits to the families of these men, Dr. Clark was constantly confronted by the disastrous effects of intemperance upon health and morals. Confirmation of Rush's theories in his own experience convinced him that some action was necessary to alter prevailing drinking customs. Accordingly, he sought an ally in his minister, Lebbeus Armstrong, pastor of the Congregational church, and together they worked out what seemed to be a practicable plan of reform. On the evening of April 30, 1808, they called a meeting in the local school-house, which was attended by forty-three of their fellow townsmen. All present were favourably impressed by the plans for an organization to combat intemperate drinking and none refused to sign the constitution of the new society. The membership of the Temperance Society of Moreau and Northumberland was thus pledged to use "no rum, gin, whisky, wine or any distilled spirits, or compositions of the same, except by advice of a physician, or in case of actual disease." It was also agreed that each member would use his influence to restrict the use of liquor among the labouring class of the community.[13]

This was no iron-clad pledge, but in spite of its manifest incompleteness it marked the signers as founders of a new enterprise. Living in a typical community, which regarded ardent spirits as a preventive of disease, which could not build a house, cut down a field of grain, hold a husking, log-rolling, quilting, christening, wedding or funeral without some assistance from alcohol, the society's charter members must have felt considerable misgiving about their experiment. They had agreed, however, to test the new principles for a

[13] Lebbeus Armstrong, *The Temperance Reformation*, pp. 22–23.

period of one year. When the first annual meeting was
held in conformity with the constitutional provision, the
spirit of wonder at the year's success was so pervading that
the gathering became an experience meeting of the revival
type. Everyone was eager to give testimony. As soon as
Mr. Armstrong's prepared address had been delivered, each
member related the effect of the pledge upon his household.
An extract from the statement of Captain Isaac B. Payn,
wealthy farmer and lumber merchant, reveals the dominant
tone:

A hogshead of rum each year [he said] has been consumed in
my business concerns, to say nothing of the wines, cordials and
other liquors consumed by the family, their parties and visiting
friends. After signing the temperance pledge a year ago, instead of a hogshead, I purchased a five-gallon keg of rum, for my
whole business concerns, both farming and lumber, and my reason
for doing this was, because my business required a few excellent
labourers, not one of whose help I could obtain without some
liquor. During the year past, I have exerted the best influence
in my power to reduce the quantity of liquor required by them to
the lowest possible mark. This morning I examined my keg
of liquor, and, as nearly as I could judge, without accurate
measurement, the keg was half full. We have abandoned all
kinds of liquor in the family as a beverage, and the quantity
used among my labourers of the year past, has been reduced
from a hogshead to the half of a five-gallon keg of rum, and my
business was never better performed nor to greater satisfaction.[14]

Captain Payn's surprise that he had been able to carry
on his business enterprises without the use of ardent spirits
was shared by all the members, but it soon changed to a
conviction that the effect of intoxicants on labour efficiency
was the strongest argument that could be presented in
support of temperance. It was the sense of the society that

[14] Armstrong, *op cit.*, pp. 21–22.

this point should be particularly stressed in all educational propaganda. Accordingly, pamphlets and broadsides were prepared for circulation in neighbouring districts, explaining the purpose of the new organization and its claims for support. Farmers were urged to abandon the use of liquor in their work, as there was overwhelming proof that the employer of labour lost money by furnishing his employees with intoxicants. The material for these literary appeals was taken largely from the theories of Dr. Rush and the experience of members of the society. This early work at Moreau was significant because it set the form for future temperance organizations in all parts of the country. The pledge against ardent spirits, partially compromising with existing customs; the constitution, providing for a continuing organization and stated meetings; the appeal to the public through speeches and pamphlets; all became characteristic of the societies of the next generation.[15]

But the enlightening propaganda that issued from Moreau did not effect any sudden change in sentiment throughout the state. Although Sidney Berry, surrogate of Saratoga County, the first president of the society, directed affairs with great skill and established in 1809 an organization in the neighbouring town of Greenfield, the time was not right for any general acceptance of temperance principles. Such support as came to the cause, from a distant section of the state, was unrelated to the Moreau Society. Again, it was the work of Dr. Rush bearing fruit. The pamphlet on ardent spirits had this time fallen into the hands of Lyman Beecher, pastor of the church at East Hampton, Long Island. It made a profound impression on a mind already disturbed by conditions within the parish. Meditation on

15 For details see Ingraham, "The Birth at Moreau of the Temperance Reformation," *New York State Historical Association, Proceedings*, VI, 115–133. Though the pledge placed wine under the ban, ardent spirits were the chief object of the society's attack.

the subject resulted in Beecher's decision that it was his duty to turn the power of his pulpit oratory against existing drinking customs. Much of his past experience entered into this decision, for he could remember that his parents, unlike most of their Connecticut neighbours, had never permitted spirits in their home. As a student at Yale, during the administration of President Dwight, he had been indignant at the intemperate habits of his fellows, rebuking them for the profanity, gambling and licentiousness that went with their drunkenness. The influence of unscrupulous dealers in his parish of East Hampton slowly aroused him to attack the growing evil. Like Dr. Rush he based his denunciation upon the effect of ardent spirits on the body and mind of the drinker, stating with great clarity the horrible consequences which followed even moderate indulgence.[16] Beecher's position was ably seconded by his colleague in the Long Island Presbytery, Nathaniel S. Prime, who opened the meeting of the presbytery on November 5, 1811, with a sermon devoted entirely to an exposition of the pernicious effects of intemperance.[17] These pioneers were but a year ahead of general sentiment in their denomination, for in 1812 the Presbyterian General Assembly, meeting at Philadelphia, appointed a committee to devise ways and means of restricting the use of intoxicants.

So in his last years Benjamin Rush was happy to see the first organization begin its work toward "an extirpation of the use of spirituous liquors," a task to which he had dedicated himself twenty years before. The widespread aid which he had expected from various religious bodies had not been forthcoming, but each year more ministers and

[16] Lyman Beecher, *Autobiography*, I, 25, 43, 177. These sermons were preached between 1806 and 1809.

[17] Nathaniel S. Prime, *A Sermon delivered at the opening of the Presbytery of Long Island*, November 5, 1811. Prime's indebtedness to Rush is acknowledged in the sermon.

physicians were publicly championing his views. In 1813, the year of his death, as if the mantle of leadership were passing from him, a concerted effort was begun by influential New England clergymen to effect the object so near to his heart.

CHAPTER V

SAVING SOCIETY

DURING the decade following the ratification of the Constitution the conservative New Englander came to abhor two things—deism and democracy. He associated both with the excesses of the French Revolution and confused both with Gallic materialism at its worst. The one was the assertion of a heresy in politics, the other the denial of everything orthodox in religion. Each found personification in Thomas Jefferson, for the Virginia statesman subscribed to a philosophy of political equality and boasted of his religious radicalism. He was at least a follower of the deistic school; many said he was an atheist. He had broken the power of the establishment in his native state. He admitted that he was an admirer of the French philosophers, among whom he had lived for five years. He openly confessed his inability to accept the tenets of revealed religion. By the Calvinistic clergy of New England, still powerful in affairs of state, such a man was feared only a little less than he was despised.

The political revolution of 1800, indicating the triumph of Jeffersonian principles, threw the champions of the old order into despair. Dire punishment would be visited upon the nation, they asserted, in consequence of the election of a man who had resorted to all the low tricks of a demagogue. What sort of leadership would be forthcoming from a president who found his support in every common person possessed of the right to vote? His constant catering to the tastes of the masses indicated that he would finally degrade the whole nation. But what else could one expect from an impudent scoffer who lacked all sense of divine guidance? He was no doubt bent upon destroying religion during his presidency. Immorality would then flourish, and the very bonds of society would be loosed.

Although Thomas Jefferson failed to play the rôle of a modern Jeroboam, the staunch defenders of Puritanism insisted that he was responsible for the growth of impiety and immorality, which was evident during his administrations. As his party gained strength in the towns of Massachusetts and Connecticut, a general decline of moral standards became evident. It was manifest in Sabbath-breaking, idle amusements, profaneness and drunkenness. When the "sage of Monticello" was succeeded in 1809 by his fellow-Virginian and political disciple, James Madison, the sober-minded were convinced that unless something was speedily done the Republican party and Republican vices would overrun the last stronghold of Federalism and virtue. It was imperative that strong men come forward to spike up the rafters of the social edifice and prevent its complete collapse.

In Connecticut the leader of political reform and moral regeneration was Lyman Beecher. Having entered upon a pastorate at Litchfield in 1811, he transferred his temperance activities to the new field with the determination that his efforts should effect some changes in local customs. At his first meeting with the Consociation, the assembled clergy enjoyed their usual drinks in such boisterous fashion that he was thoroughly disgusted by what he saw. Of the ministerial conduct, he wrote: "As they could not all drink at once, they were obliged to stand and wait as people do when they go to mill. The side-board with the spillings of water and sugar and liquor, looked and smelled like the bar of a very active grog-shop. None of the Consociation were drunk, but that there was not at times, a considerable amount

of exhilaration, I cannot affirm." [1]   Such a situation moved
Beecher to meditate upon the advisability of persuading his
associates to change their habits.   He went to the General
Association meeting at Sharon in 1812 prepared to suggest
some radical remedies.   When the regular committee reported
that "after faithful and prayerful inquiry" it was convinced
that nothing could be done to check the growth of intemperance, Beecher forced the appointment of a second committee of which he was made chairman.   The report of this
group was couched in no uncertain terms.   It recommended
that steps be taken to restrict the use of ardent spirits and
suggested the following measures: that district assemblies
abstain from the use of ardent spirits at ecclesiastical meetings, that members of churches abstain from unlawful vending
or purchase of liquor, that farmers, mechanics and manufacturers substitute monetary compensation for the ration
of spirits, that voluntary associations aid the civil magistrates to enforce the laws, and that the pamphlet of Dr.
Rush be printed and circulated.[2]

The recommendation in favour of voluntary associations
contained an idea which was the basis for immediate action.
Beecher, like most of the New England divines of his day,
was quite as much politician as preacher.   He thought that
he could see in the deplorable state of public morals the
reasons for the declining prestige of the clergy and the
waning power of the Federalist party.   It was evident that
the lower classes were becoming more arrogant in political
matters and bolder in their defiance of law.   Unless some
organization was effected to resist them, they would vote in
the Republican party with its indiscriminate following of the
irreverent and the vicious.   A society directed against two
outstanding evils, the violation of the Sabbath and the prev-

---

[1] *Autobiography*, I, 245. This Consocation was the district association of Congregational and Presbyterian clergy.

[2] Beecher, *Autobiography*, I, 246–248.

alence of intemperance, seemed advisable from a political standpoint and imperative from the standpoint of public welfare. To this effect Beecher wrote his colleague, Asahel Hooker of New London, on July 28, 1812, suggesting that preliminary arrangements be made in the autumn at New Haven.[3] A few months later Yale College, a centre of Federalist sentiment, was host to a group of gentlemen from various parts of the state, who discussed the propriety of organizing a society for the suppression of drunkenness and kindred vices. In a sermon to this gathering Beecher sounded the keynote of the new movement.

> Our institutions, civil and religious [he said] have outlived that domestic discipline and official vigilance in magistrates which rendered obedience easy and habitual. The laws are now beginning to operate extensively upon necks unaccustomed to the yoke, and when they shall become irksome to the majority, their execution will become impracticable. To this situation we are already reduced in some districts of the land. Drunkards reel through the streets day after day, and year after year, with entire impunity. Profane swearing is heard, and even by magistrates as though they heard it not. . . . But truly we do stand over the confines of destruction. The mass is changing. We are becoming another people.[4]

At the New Haven meeting a committee of twenty-six was appointed to formulate plans for a permanent organization along the lines indicated by Beecher's sermon. The group selected was a notable embodiment of political power and social prestige, containing such distinguished clergymen as Calvin Chapin of Hartford, Heman Humphrey of Fairfield, Asahel Hooker of New London and Timothy Dwight of New Haven. The laity was represented by the most prominent Federalist politicians in the state; John Treadwell and Theodore Dwight of Hartford, Sylvester Gilbert of Tolland,

[3] *Autobiography*, I, 253–254.
[4] *Ibid.*, I, 255–256, 261–262.

Calvin Goddard of Middlesex, Tapping Reeve of Litchfield and Roger Minot Sherman of Fairfield. Throughout the autumn and winter of 1812 Beecher kept up a constant correspondence with his associates on the committee and his ministerial friends in the state, seeking to create an effective public opinion in support of reform. On November 24, he wrote in a letter to his friend, Hooker:

I am persuaded the time has come when it becomes every friend of this state to wake up and exert his whole influence to save it from innovation and democracy. That the effort to supplant Governor Smith will be made is certain, unless at an early stage the rising opposition shall be so great as to deter them; and if it is made a separation is made in the Federal party. . . . If we stand idle we lose our habits and institutions piece-meal, as fast as innovation and ambition shall dare to urge on the work. If we meet with strenuous opposition in this thing we can but perish, and we may—I trust if we look up to God we shall— save the state. I only desire that we may act in his fear, and not be moved in so trying a case by the wrath of man, which worketh not the righteousness of God. . . . Judge Reeve is engaged in the business of organizing the general society, and he told me that it met the approbation of the judges at the Supreme Court. He proposes to convene the committee at Middletown as most central, at some time which will accommodate the greatest number.[5]

The supporters of innovation, "Sabbath-breakers, rum-selling, tippling folk, infidels and ruff-scruff," as Beecher was wont to call them, were not confined to the Republican ranks, but had already begun to bore from within the Federalist party itself. As a part of the campaign against them, the Connecticut Society for the Reformation of Morals began a fight for law enforcement on May 19, 1813. That the new society was inextricably connected with Federalist

5 Beecher, *Autobiography*, I, 257–258, 342.

domination in the state was evident from the personnel of officers and members.   Its first president was ex-Governor John Treadwell, while one of the vice-presidents was Judge Tapping Reeve, who controlled the county of Litchfield. On the executive committee was Thomas Day, secretary of state under John Cotton Smith, while Ebenezer Huntington, Federalist member of Congress, was prominent in the society's councils.   Four of the charter members were Assistants, and five represented the state at the Hartford Convention.[6]   In discussing the purpose of the society at a later date, Lyman Beecher wrote: "It was the anticipation of the impending revolution and the downfall of the standing order that impelled me to the efforts I made at that time to avert it, and to prepare for it in all ways possible.   And one was this association of the 'leading minds' of the laity with us in council, and discussing matters with them. They easily fell in with our views, saw the things as we did, and threw in their influence heartily.   I remember Roger Minot Sherman especially was pleased. 'You have never before,' he said, 'done anything so wisely and so well as this !' " [7]

The leaders of the Republican party in Connecticut quite naturally were hostile to a society formed, it looked, for the purpose of thwarting their political ambitions.   They were quick to see that they were the folk against whom Beecher and his associates were marshalling the forces of respectability.   Therefore, they refused to consider the Moral Society as anything but a clever guise for political intrigue. The idea of reform was merely a cloak for sinister work which could not be done in the open.   They charged the dominant Congregational order with deriving its support from the Charitable Society under Judge Reeve, the Bible

[6] *Connecticut Courant*, Dec. 20, 1814; *Conn. Evangelical Magazine*, June, 1815, p. 225; *Conn. Courant*, Sept. 7, 1813.

[7] Beecher, *Autobiography*, I, 261. For a brilliant summary of the political situation in Connecticut and its relation to moral reform, see Purcell, *Connecticut in Transition*.

Society under the patronage of Governor Smith, and the Moral Society guided by ex-Governor Treadwell. The attacks on Beecher, Reeve, Smith and Treadwell branded those leaders as Federalist politicians masquerading in the rôle of benevolent philanthropists.[8] Such accusations bore a semblance of the truth, but they ignored the fact that there was much real concern over the growth of immorality. Although the members of the Moral Society had taken no pledge in regard to their personal conduct, they were in earnest about the suppression of drunkenness, gambling and general lawlessness. All had agreed that they would use their influence in every way possible to end those vices which were lowering the moral standards of former days.

In the meantime, the Massachusetts clergy were organizing their attack on intemperance. In the summer of 1810 the *Panoplist*, a religious periodical under the editorship of the distinguished layman, Jeremiah Evarts, began to present articles dealing with the cost to the community of the liquor traffic. The October issue contained an essay by the editor, entitled "Arithmetic Applied to Moral Purposes," which aroused considerable interest among the readers of the paper. From his observation of a New England town of less than 2,000 population, Evarts concluded that over $10,000 was spent annually by the inhabitants for ardent spirits, more than the town invested in its churches and its schools. He challenged the wisdom of the expenditure by describing the public improvements which could be financed if the same sum were spent for the good of the community. Similar articles, stressing the economic aspect of the question, met with such response in the state that Evarts' services were much in demand.[9] In June, 1811, the General Association of Massachusetts made him chairman of a committee to co-operate

[8] *Courant*, March 19, 1816.

[9] Tracy, *Memoir of Jeremiah Evarts*, pp. 75–76; *Panoplist and Missionary Magazine*, October, 1810.

with similar committees from the General Association of Connecticut and the Presbyterian General Assembly in devising measures to prevent "some of the numerous and threatening mischiefs that are experienced throughout our country from the excessive and intemperate use of spirituous liquors." [10]   Associated with Evarts were Samuel Worcester, Jedidiah Morse, Abiel Abbott, Benjamin Wadsworth, representing the clergy, and Reuben D. Mussey of Salem and Joseph Storey of Boston, both physicians.   Although their deliberations resulted in no general scheme of reform in conjunction with the other committees, the Massachusetts group issued a call for a state convention to be held at the State House in Boston on February 4, 1813.   The response to the call was extremely gratifying to the friends of law and order, who succeeded in drafting and adopting a constitution, creating the Massachusetts Society for the Suppression of Intemperance.[11]

The object of the organization, as set forth in the constitution, was to "discountenance and suppress the too free use of ardent spirits, and its kindred vices, profaneness and gaming; and to encourage and promote temperance and general morality."   Each member was pledged to "discourage and prevent, as far as maybe, by his own example, and influence, every kind of vice and immorality." [12]   As in the case of the Connecticut Moral Society, the restriction upon the conduct of the members was slight, the obligations could be loosely interpreted, and the membership did not regard the constitution as laying upon them any severe self-denial.   The leadership of the society was distinguished. Of the clergy Jedidiah Morse, Eliphalet Porter and Abiel Abbott were the most active, while Jeremiah Evarts was

[10] *Documents and Records of the Massachusetts Temperance Society,* pp. 1–2.

[11] *Documents and Records of the Massachusetts Temperance Society,* pp. 3–4; *Panoplist and Missionary Magazine,* September, 1812.

[12] *Documents and Records,* pp. 5–6.

the leading layman. With the exception of Abbott they were eminent defenders of the fundamental dogmas of Calvinism against any form of religious innovation. When Unitarianism challenged orthodox Congregationalism, they were prepared to answer the challenge. Morse, already famous by virtue of his books and articles on geography, had established the *Panoplist* in 1806 to answer the critics of Calvinism. Several years later, when most of the churches of Boston save Old South had forsaken orthodoxy, he had borne a hand in the organization of the Park Street Church that the conservative cause might be strengthened. His friend, Evarts, became editor of the *Panoplist* in 1810 and joined him in his various philanthropic enterprises. Eliphalet Porter of Roxbury was an equally determined supporter of what he understood to be traditional Puritanism, but Abiel Abbott, long pastor of a church at Beverly, accepted the intellectual appeal of Unitarianism. The clergymen were well supported by laymen, many of whom were prominent Federalist politicians.

The first president of the society was Samuel Dexter, who had served as a cabinet officer during John Adams' administration, but had later defended the policies of Jefferson and Madison, though he never considered himself a Republican. His interest in temperance reform was shared by Nathan Dane, staunch in his support of Federalist principles. Three members of the society's executive committee represented the state at the Hartford Convention; Timothy Bigelow, William Prescott and Nathan Dane. Among the charter members were Timothy Pickering, a cabinet officer in the administrations of Washington and Adams, who had represented the extreme wing of New England Federalism in his opposition to the Louisiana Purchase, the Embargo and the war with England; Caleb Strong, governor of Massachusetts from 1800 to 1807 and again from 1812 to 1816; and Artemas Ward, whose election to the Thirteenth Congress had been due to his opposition to the War of 1812.

As prominent as the politicians and the clergy were the business men. The first roster of the Massachusetts society contained the names of Samuel T. Armstrong, Amos Lawrence, Robert Rantoul, John Tappan and Elisha Ticknor, well known to the commercial circles of Boston in 1813. Armstrong was a wealthy bookseller, whose fortune gave him an opportunity to spend time and money in the work of the American Board of Commissioners for Foreign Missions and numerous charities. Amos Lawrence's profitable dry goods business was accumulating capital for future investment in the manufacture of cotton cloth. John Tappan was proprietor of a mercantile establishment, which imported from all parts of the world, while Elisha Ticknor, having given up the headmastership of the Franklin grammar-school in Boston, was preparing to establish the first savings bank in the city.[13] Truly the temperance reform was in the hands of the "rich, the well-born and the able." Officers and members alike appreciated the high character of their calling. They were conferring an inestimable boon upon their fellowmen, for they were engaged in the task of saving society from one of its besetting sins.[14]

One of the first circulars sent out by the executive committee stated the mission of the society as it appeared to the leaders:

The design of this institution is not so much to redeem the slaves of intemperance, as to secure from the ignominious bond-

[13] Biographical data are taken from Appleton's Cyclopedia of American Biography and the National Cyclopedia of American Biography. It should be noted in passing that Unitarians as well as orthodox Calvinists were represented in the Massachusetts Society. Many Congregational churches had accepted Unitarianism before 1813.

[14] For lists of officers and members in the Massachusetts Society for the Suppression of Intemperance, see *Documents and Records*, pp. 102–103.

age those who are yet free; not so much to wrest the fatal cup from those who are already brutalized and ruined, as to keep sober those who are sober; to check that general free use of ardent spirits which, though not excessive to intoxication, is yet unnecessary, wasteful and pernicious; to erect a barrier against that wide-spreading flood which so fearfully threatens the dearest interests of individuals, of families and of the Commonwealth. Is not this practicable? Is it not practicable to impress upon the community a deep sense and dread of this great and terrible evil? to combine a salutary influence against it which can everywhere be felt? to render it reputable for laboring people, and those who employ labor, to substitute for daily use, good and wholesome drinks in the place of pernicious liquors; and for all classes of people to refrain from the practice, now so general, of offering ardent spirits to all who come into their houses? If this be practicable, then our design is practicable; let all this be done and our design is well nigh accomplished.[15]

In its attempts to accomplish this design the Massachusetts society worked in close harmony with the Moral Society in Connecticut. Neither deviated much from the methods earlier adopted by the temperance group in Moreau, though their operations were on a considerably larger scale. Convinced that their first task was that of enlightenment, they relied upon the printed page to accomplish their purpose. The reports submitted at the stated meetings were prepared for publication, and periodic appeals were sent to employers of labour urging them to abandon the use of spirituous liquors in their enterprises. Pamphlets, containing sermons and addresses, set forth the causes of intemperance and portrayed the dire effects upon the individual and the group. One of the most popular of these tracts was from the pen of Mason L. Weems, whose chief claim to fame rests upon his fanciful biography of Washington. He had been successively an Episcopalian clergyman, travelling book agent

[15] *Circular Addressed to the members of the Massachusetts Society for the Suppression of Intemperance* (1814).

for Matthew Carey, the Philadelphia publisher, and hack-writer for numerous religious journals, but in his later years he became an ardent expounder of moral truth. His highly imaginative writings against duelling, drunkenness and murder were in great demand and furnished excellent material for societies interested in moral reform. *The Drunkard's Looking Glass, reflecting a faithful likeness of the drunkard in sundry very interesting attitudes* appealed to both young and old and was used by the temperance organizations, though the woodcuts which ornamented and explained its pages must have served to pique the curiosity of its youthful readers, rather than to warn them against evil.[16] Not having a periodical exclusively devoted to their interests, the early societies relied upon the religious journals to carry articles demonstrating the social consequences of the use of ardent spirits.[17]

These printed appeals, re-enforced on occasion by personal visitation, enabled the state societies to establish local auxiliaries throughout Massachusetts and Connecticut, the members of which were pledged to discourage by precept and example such devastating sins as Sabbath-breaking, gambling and tippling. The auxiliaries, independent of the central societies in matters of policy, reported annually their increases in membership and the progress of temperance sentiment in their respective communities. The tabulation of these reports indicated no striking change in the popular attitude toward spirituous liquors, but revealed a steadily growing interest in the liquor problem. Pulpit and press had carried the movement of reform far beyond the confines of Connecti-

[16] M. L. Weems, *The Drunkard's Looking Glass* (6th edition, 1818).

[17] Besides the *Panoplist,* already mentioned, the following journals were of assistance to the reformers: the *Religious Remembrancer* (Philadelphia, 1813), the *Recorder* (Boston, 1816), the *Christian Herald* (New York, 1816), and the *Christian Disciple,* a Methodist weekly founded at Boston in 1819. *Panoplist* for February, March and May, 1813 contains statements of the punishment meted out to drunkards in this life and hereafter.

cut and Massachusetts. Societies had been organized in
Rhode Island, New Hampshire, Vermont, Maine, New York
and Pennsylvania. From regions so distant from the source
of the movement as South Carolina, Ohio and Illinois came
reports of efforts to enforce a higher standard of morals.
The countless thousands, who went out from the towns and
farms of the East to follow the well beaten trails across the
mountains, carried with them the principles and organizations of the reform.[18] Of the situation in the western country Thomas Hinde, one of the founders of Mt. Carmel,
Illinois, wrote to a friend in the East:

Before the commencement of the war in 1812, it appeared to
me, that the cause of intemperance had reached its zenith. It
was as much as the sober, moral and religious citizens could
sustain, to bear up under the evil works and abominable prac-
tises; but when the war was declared and the recruiting officers
were sent out, they swept the towns generally throughout the
west of nearly all those pests of human society. . . . In 1815
I belonged to an association of different orders of the religious
and of moral persons, that formed the first temperance society
I ever heard of; this was, however, termed a society for the
suppression of vice and immorality. The temperance department was committed to the care of my inexperienced hands; I
have now the whole proceedings, as published, preserved in a
book. This organization was most miserably prosecuted, but it
did much good. My worthy friend, Rev. Robert G. Wilson,
president of Ohio University, was our champion on that occasion; he was firm and inflexible on all occasions, whether in
the cause of religion, morality or temperance.

[18] Evidence of the increasing interest in moral reform may be found
in *Connecticut Courant*, June 28, 1815; *Annual Report of the Massa-
chusetts Society for the Suppression of Intemperance* (1820); Nathaniel
S. Prime, *Address to the Cambridge Branch of the Moral Society of
Washington County, N. Y.* (1815); *Journal of the American Temperance
Union*, February, 1837; *Reminiscences of Neal Dow*, pp. 184–194;
Morrison, *History of Windham, N. H.*, pp. 233–234; Barry, *History of
Hanover, Mass.*, pp. 173–174.

Out of this plan of a "Moral Society" grew a plan on which this town was established, as the first town established on temperance principles on earth! We never have had any intemperance amongst us scarcely in any way, except by interlopers and stragglers. The town was laid out about 1818, and the settlements commenced in 1820; and I do not know in any part of the United States in the same length of time, where as many of the first settlers are alive and in health, notwithstanding the encountering of much sickness and many deprivations in settling a new country. The impetus thus given has a wonderful bearing on the minds of the community.[19]

The years, which marked so auspicious a beginning for the little Illinois community, brought to the country as a whole industrial depression, unemployment and widespread destitution. Inevitable readjustments following the War of 1812, aggravated the disasters occasioned by poor banking methods; they caused importers, manufacturers, landed proprietors, farmers, and all dependent on these classes, to share in the general distress. Foreclosures were frequent; bankruptcies in mercantile circles attested the scarcity of money and the stagnation of trade. The closing of factories increased the idle class and threw men into prison because of their debts. The resources of charitable institutions were taxed to the utmost in an attempt to care for the unemployed and the families of unfortunate debtors. But despite these efforts the pauper and criminal classes steadily grew.

Conditions could scarcely have been more favourable for the growth of temperance sentiment. Everywhere crime, pauperism and drunkenness prevailed to such an extent that the public welfare demanded an investigation of the forces which burdened society with undesirables. Charity organizations in New York, Philadelphia, Baltimore and Boston reported that the use of spirituous liquors was one of the

[19] Letter to E. C. Delavan, January 4, 1836. Printed in *Journal of the American Temperance Union*, February, 1837, p. 8.

most important factors in the growth of the criminal and pauper classes.[20] The Society for the Prevention of Pauperism, organized in New York in 1817, called attention in its first annual report to more than 1600 licensed groceries in the city which dispensed liquor in small quantities to anyone of any age.[21] At the same time the Massachusetts Society for the Suppression of Intemperance began to devote its annual reports and circulars to a discussion of the relation between intemperance and pauperism. Special emphasis was placed upon the fact that the majority of the inmates of poor-houses and work-houses were habitual drunkards and that at least two-thirds of those who received "outdoor relief" were addicted to the use of ardent spirits. As a remedy the society suggested that all public spirited citizens insist upon a scrupulous enforcement of the laws regulating the issuance of licences and the selection of retail dealers. Lengthy appeals were sent to employers, containing an exposition of the effect of intemperance on business prosperity and an estimate of the sum annually wasted on intoxicants by the labouring classes.[22] Newspapers carried remonstrances against unlicensed dram-shops, tippling-houses and corner groceries, which were fast destroying good morals and religion. The New York Society for the Promotion of Internal Improvements circulated in 1819 Judge Thomas Hertell's essay, *An Expose of the Causes of Intemperate Drinking*, which advocated total abstinence from all that intoxicates as the true basis of temperance. Though Hertell's doctrine of total abstinence was far too radical for his day, he admirably stated the fears of those who

[20] *American Daily Advertiser*, May 10, June 20, March 21, 1817; *New England Palladium*, January 31, 1817; *Albany Gazette*, June 13, 1817. Cited in McMaster, *History of the People of the United States*, IV, 526–532.

[21] *First Annual Report of the Managers of the Society for the Prevention of Pauperism in New York* (1818).

[22] *Annual Report of the Massachusetts Temperance Society*, 1818, 1819, 1821.

believed that no society so deeply attached to the use of spirituous liquors could long endure. It was a gloomy picture he painted of the existing demoralization and the inevitable disaster to follow, unless intemperance was speedily checked by an aroused public opinion.[23]

Hertell was no alarmist. Neither were the people who, rejecting his prescription, nevertheless agreed with his diagnosis. Indeed, the friends of temperance were guilty of little exaggeration when they characterized their fellow-countrymen as a race of hard drinkers. This judgment was substantiated on numerous occasions by foreign travellers, always quick to relate anything which impressed them as a peculiarity of the New World. The Frenchman, Michaud, in his journeys through the western counties of Pennsylvania during 1802 and 1803, noted a general passion for ardent spirits that frequently resulted in horrible excesses, since whisky, rum and brandy were always available.[24] John Melish, in more charitable spirit, attributed the generous use of strong liquor to the effect of the hard labour required in clearing the land and to the excessive heat of the summer months, which made it dangerous to drink cold water. As there could be no cider in a new country, he reasoned, and since malt liquors would not keep, ardent spirits were the only practical beverages for the pioneer. The passing years would bring a more temperate use of milder beverages. His opinion was somewhat altered, however, after he had watched the flatboats on the Ohio River, laden with hundreds of barrels of whisky, cider, peach brandy and cherry bounce. Any general reform was unlikely so long as the drinking customs of the people were intimately associated with the

[23] Thomas Hertell, *An Expose of the Causes of Intemperate Drinking* (1819).

[24] F. A. Michaud, *Travels to the West of the Allegheny Mountains*, II, 32, 40.

sources of their economic prosperity.[25] Trade considerations were important in all parts of the country. In 1807 the English traveller, Charles Janson, was astonished that Boston supported only two breweries, but distilled large quantities of rum in forty establishments. Everywhere he went in New England the distilleries were busy supplying spirits for use in interstate and foreign commerce.[26] In 1819 almost every town of one thousand population in Connecticut and Rhode Island had its own gin or rum distillery. Hartford County was proud of its twenty-one plants, which furnished a market for the farmers' grain and wood. In Rhode Island, Newport, Providence and Bristol retained their old supremacy, having, respectively, eight, five and three large establishments.[27] The taverns, groceries, chandlers' shops and grog-shops, retailing at two-pence a glass, were abundantly supplied with a cheap grade of ardent spirits.[28]

The centre of production was rapidly shifting westward, however, as grain and fruit replaced molasses in the industry. In 1810 it was estimated that 14,191 distilleries produced over 25,000,000 gallons of spirits, ninety per cent of which was distilled from fruit and grain.[29] Ten years later the fragmentary reports on manufactures in the returns of the fourth census indicated that New York, Pennsylvania, Ohio and Tennessee had more capital invested and employed more men in the production of ardent spirits than any other states in the Union. Especially significant were the comments of the officials, who forwarded the census returns, to the effect

[25] John Melish, *Travels in the United States of America*, II, 51–52, 156–157.

[26] C. W. Janson, *The Stranger in America*, pp. 28, 30, 299–300.

[27] J. C. Pease and J. M. Niles, *A Gazetteer of Connecticut and Rhode Island, passim.*

[28] H. B. Fearon, *A Narrative of a Journey*, pp. 28–29.

[29] Adam Seybert, *Statistical Annals*, pp. 463–464.

that it was useless to consider distilling a distinct industry, since it was carried on generally throughout the rural districts.[30]   Such a situation might well alarm the reformers in view of the fact that statistics kept by the Treasury department between 1813 and 1817 listed the domestic consumption of ardent spirits as ninety per cent of the total production.

Serious as conditions were, temperance organizations were credited with no outstanding achievements.   A vital element seemed to be lacking in the reform movement.   The leaders were inspired with the benevolence of the philanthropist rather than the conviction of the moralist.   Although they were not unmindful of the desirability of modifying their own conduct, their chief concern was to save the other fellow from disaster.   They preferred to compromise with existing customs rather than to alienate possible support by too militant an attitude.   They were temperate in their temperance.   Sincerely believing in the merits of their cause, they had not yet accepted it as the paramount concern of their lives.   As a result, the reform failed to secure fast hold on any considerable group of devotees.   Not until a later day did the reformers fully realize that it requires something of the spirit of the zealot to arouse mankind.

[30] Gales and Seaton, *Digest of Manufactures, Fourth Census of the United States.*

CHAPTER VI

THE CHURCH MILITANT

"IDEAS," says Romain Rolland, "have never conquered the world as ideas, but only by the force they represent. They do not grip men by their intellectual contents, but by the radiant vitality which is given off from them at certain periods in history. . . . The loftiest and most sublime idea remains ineffective until the day when it becomes contagious, not by its own merits, but by the merits of the groups of men in whom it becomes incarnate." For several years groups of philanthropists in various parts of the country had been toying with the idea of moderation in the use of liquor. Its intellectual appeal interested them. They were anxious to test its value as a corrective of certain social evils, but they were not deeply concerned about the success of the experiment. They were far from feeling that zealous devotion which characterizes the true reformer. In spite of their lack of enthusiasm, however, the idea of temperance, which they sponsored, was gradually entering upon its period of "radiant vitality." It was being appropriated by groups able to transfuse into it the power which grips men. It was becoming incarnate in the organizations of evangelical Protestantism.

Shortly after 1815 the evangelical sects in the United States manifested unusual activity. Religious journals were filled with accounts of the renewed interest in the Scriptures, the formation of Bible study groups, and the organization of prayer societies throughout the nation. After a season of

101

general indifference to the claims of revealed religion, the people seemed to be returning to their former faith. Communities from Maine to Georgia and from Kentucky to Maryland reported enthusiastic revival meetings, till it appeared as if the Great Revival of 1801 in the western country was to be reproduced on a national scale. As the late war had freed the nation from the political complications of European diplomacy, so the revival movement was purging it of the religious heresies born of the French Revolution. Some regarded the numerous outbursts of religiosity as miraculous dispensations, others found in them only the natural result of the era of reaction. Now that the country's foreign difficulties were settled, attention was being focused upon domestic problems, and religious leaders were undertaking in earnest the diffusion of the word of God.[1] Whatever the cause of the religious emotionalism, there can be no doubt that the country was profoundly stirred. Secular papers reported in detail the progress of revival sentiment, not only in their own localities but also in distant parts, while religious periodicals had little for their readers but the glorious news of the "workings of the hand of God." [2]

Popular interest in the revivals was a powerful incentive to home missionary activity. Communities noted for their religious fervour were eager to share their blessings with less fortunate districts. As the westward migration carried thousands into the trans-Appalachian region, Methodist and Baptist circuit riders pressed ever forward close to the fringe of settlement, while Congregational and Presbyterian clergymen established churches wherever congregations

[1] *Connecticut Courant,* January 16, February 20, 1816.

[2] The religious intelligence column in the *Courant,* for example, dates from the autumn of 1815. For accounts of revivals see: *Courant,* February 20, 1816; *Connecticut Journal,* files for February–May, 1819; *Boston Recorder,* March 25, April 8, 22, May 13, 1820, June 9, 16, 1821, January 12, 1822; *Religious Intelligencer,* files for 1817–1818.

could be gathered together. Often these home missionaries maintained a close connection with the older churches of the East, and their reports to mission boards or fellow workers in the denomination inspired an increased devotion to the cause of evangelization. The most active workers, whether preaching in the frontier communities or directing the missionary enterprise from eastern cities, were not slow to realize that one of the greatest obstacles in their way was the excessive use of ardent spirits. James B. Finley, a pioneer among Methodist preachers in the Ohio valley, regarded alcohol as the most powerful enemy he had to encounter. Wherever his mission took him, he enforced upon the people to whom he ministered the Wesleyan rule against the use of ardent spirits as a beverage. He encountered strong opposition, because of his temperance principles, but an invariable accompaniment of his camp-meetings was the passing of intemperance from the community. There was no chance, he believed, for the word of God to take root among people who drank to excess.[3] His contemporary, Peter Cartwright, an outstanding evangelist and militant preacher, was likewise determined that his efforts should not be nullified by the ravages of ardent spirits. He was perfectly willing to resort to physical violence, if necessary, to persuade drunken rowdies that they were not welcome at his camp-meetings. In the Kentucky and Tennessee Conferences, before he was transferred to Indiana, he won whole congregations to the temperance standard and held backsliders in line by enforcing a rigorous discipline.[4]

Cartwright and Finley were representative of scores of clergymen, in the East as well as West, who were associating temperance work with their pastoral ministrations. The

[3] *Autobiography of James B. Finley*, W. P. Strickland, editor, pp. 248–249, 299.

[4] *Autobiography of Peter Cartwright*, W. P. Strickland, editor, pp. 182–185, 212–214.

western evangelists, probably because they came in contact more frequently with flagrant excesses, were often instrumental in arousing their eastern brethren to renewed efforts. It was James Axley of the Tennessee Conference, for example, who led the fight for more stringent rules in the Methodist Episcopal Church. With the support of his western associates Axley finally secured favourable action from the General Conference in 1816 on his resolution that any local preacher found guilty of distilling or retailing spirituous liquor should forfeit his licence. Clergy in Congregational and Presbyterian churches were manifesting greater interest in the fortunes of the moral and temperance societies, endeavouring to supplant apathy with enthusiasm, to provide a definite objective, and to inspire the members with faith in the ultimate success of the cause.[5]

Once again the leadership was assumed by New England. The sermons of Timothy Dwight at New Haven were widely heralded as a new phase of the movement, since the President of Yale attacked not intemperance, but temperate drinking. At the same time Calvin Chapin, pastor at Rocky Hill in the Connecticut valley, made a missionary tour of the Western Reserve in 1825 and was deeply impressed by the evidence of intemperance which he found in the western country. His views of the situation were expanded into a series of articles, the first of which appeared in the *Connecticut Observer* for January, 1826. Chapin took for his text, "Abstinence from ardent spirits is the only certain preventive of intemperance." He was interested in proving that total abstinence was not only possible but also desirable. Too many of his neighbours and parishioners, he thought, clung to the belief that the use of ardent spirits was necessary

[5] *Journals of the General Conference of the Methodist Episcopal Church*, I, 117, 168; *Religious Intelligencer*, II, 383, IV, 815; *Conn. Journal*, August 20, 1822.

for the preservation of health and that abstinence was apt
to result in sudden physical decline. In refutation Chapin
cited to his readers the fact that he and some of his friends
had "abstained" for several years with noticeable benefit to
their minds and bodies. What had been done by a few
could be done by others. The experiment had convinced him
that the friends of temperance need no longer compromise
with popular misconceptions in regard to intoxicants.
Nothing less than *total abstinence* from the use of *ardent
spirits* could henceforth be the objective of the reform.[6]

While Chapin's articles were arousing both favourable
and unfavourable comment, Lyman Beecher was preparing
for publication a new and complete statement of his attitude
toward the liquor question. He had witnessed the political
revolution of 1818 in Connecticut, which had overthrown the
established order without dire calamity to the Commonwealth, and he was willing to separate the idea of reform from
that of party alignment. Besides, he had been active in the
revivals in New England with the result that he saw more
clearly than ever the dangerous foe confronting religion in
the guise of intemperance.[7] With all the power of his
pulpit oratory he renewed his denunciation of an old enemy.
Six sermons, preached before the Litchfield congregation in
the autumn of 1825, were published the next year for general
circulation. They constituted in their particular sphere as
significant a piece of special pleading as was later his
daughter's famous novel in support of abolition. Reprinted
during the next decade by almost every temperance organization of consequence, the sermons were as widely read
and exerted as great an influence as any other contribution

[6] E. P. Parker, *An Appreciation of Calvin Chapin*, pp. 9–11; *Permanent Temperance Documents, Fourth Report*, pp. 14–15; *The History of Ancient Wethersfield, Conn.*, H. R. Stiles, editor, I, 857.

[7] Beecher, *Autobiography*, II, 34–35.

to the literature of the reform.[8] From his pulpit Dr. Beecher sought to define the term temperance, so loosely and variously used in all discussions of the liquor question. In his mind there was a vital distinction between intemperance and intoxication. "So long as men suppose," said he, "that there is neither crime nor danger in drinking, short of what they denominate drunkenness, they will cast off fear and move onward to ruin by a silent, certain course, until destruction comes upon them and they cannot escape. . . . Let it therefore be engraven upon the heart of every man, that the daily use of ardent spirits, in any form, or in any degree, is intemperance." [9] Having thus defined his position, he proceeded to analyse the causes of the widespread use of intoxicants. They seemed to him to be deeply rooted in the social customs of the time, and he believed that they could not be removed unless every community was filled with a sense of the danger involved in moderate drinking. Intemperance he regarded as a disease, beginning in the germs of temperate drinking and becoming finally as deadly as a plague. The only practical remedy for the malady was immediate and entire abstinence. For the idea of gradual emancipation from the use of intoxicants Beecher had the utmost contempt. "Wine has been prescribed," he admitted, "as a means of decoying the intemperate from the ways of death. But habit cannot be thus cheated out of its domain, nor ravening appetite be amused down to a sober and temperate demand. If it be true that men do not become intemperate on wine, it is not true that wine will restore the intemperate, or stay the progress of the disease." [10] This was strong

8 *Mass. Spy,* July 10, 1833; Edwin Emory, *History of Sanford, Maine,* p. 234; Andrew Young, *History of Warsaw, N. Y.,* p. 150; E. C. Blackman, *op. cit.,* p. 560; Joseph Cochran, *History of Mifflin County, Pa.,* I, 194–195; *Permanent Temperance Documents, Fourth Report,* p. 16.

9 Beecher, *Six Sermons,* pp. 11, 39.

10 *Ibid.,* pp. 7, 64.

doctrine, but it indicated how far the new movement was reaching beyond the grasp of the old. In his discussion of practical methods Beecher recommended a campaign of education to correct erroneous opinions with regard to the medicinal properties of ardent spirits. Next in point of importance was the formation of voluntary associations pledged to total abstinence from distilled liquors. He also advised that an effort be made to enlist the official bodies of all denominations of Christians in a general condemnation of the liquor traffic. Filled with a vision of the high calling of his country in international affairs, he issued solemn warning that intemperance would in time prevent the realization of that destiny. He spoke with conviction when he said:

Intemperance is the sin of our land, and with our boundless prosperity is coming in upon us like a flood; and if anything shall defeat the hopes of the world, which hang upon our experiment in civil liberty, it is that river of fire, which is rolling through the land, destroying the vital air, and extending around an atmosphere of death. . . . In our view, and in our practice as a nation, there is something fundamentally wrong; and the remedy, like the evil, must be found in the correct application of general principles. It must be an universal and national remedy. What then is this remedy? It is the banishment of ardent spirits from the list of lawful articles of commerce, by a correct and efficient public sentiment; such, as has turned slavery out of half of our land, and will yet expel it from the world.[11]

[11] For evidence confirming Beecher's opinion of the prevalence of intemperance see the accounts of foreign and native travellers. Coke, *A Subaltern's Furlough*, I, 212; I. Finch, *Travels in the United States of America and Canada*, p. 13; B. Hall, *Travels in North America*, I, 125–126; I. Holmes, *An Account of the United States*, p. 352; Adam Hodgson, *Letters from North America*, II, 249–250; Peter Neilson, *Recollection of a Six Years' Residence in the United States*, pp. 67–69; Anne Royall, *Sketches of History, Life and Manners in the United States*, pp. 100, 158–159.

The first response to Beecher's powerful appeal came from Massachusetts, where several of his associates on the American Board of Commissioners for Foreign Missions decided that the time had come for definite action. One of their number, Justin Edwards, pastor of the Park Street Church, Boston, wrote to his friend, William A. Hallock of New York:

We are at present fast hold of a project for making all people in this country, and in all other countries, temperate; or rather, a plan to induce those who are now temperate to continue so. Then, as all who are intemperate will soon be dead, the earth will be eased of an amazing evil. This you will see at once, is a great plan, to execute it thoroughly will require great wisdom and strength.[12]

For some time Edwards had been turning the project over in his mind and discussing it with influential members of his congregation. From them and from his colleagues in the American Tract Society he had received enough encouragement to warrant the calling of a state convention to consider ways and means of fighting intemperance. The convention met at Boston on February 13, 1826, and enthusiastically adopted a constitution for the American Society for the Promotion of Temperance. The sixteen signers of the document, few in number but representing powerful forces in the state, formed the temporary membership of the new group. They were, Leonard Woods, William Jenks, Justin Edwards, Warren Fay, Benjamin Wisner, Francis Wayland and Timothy Merritt of the clergy, and Marcus Morton, Samuel Hubbard, George Odiorne, John Tappan, William Reed, William Ropes, James Chaplin, Enoch Hale and S. V. S. Wilder of the laity.[13]   Five of their number were active

12 W. A. Hallock, *A Sketch of the Life and Labors of Justin Edwards*, p. 195.

13 Hallock, *op. cit.*, pp. 196–197; *Permanent Temperance Documents, Fourth Report*, pp. 11–12.

in the work of the Board of Commissioners for Foreign Missions, and the new society was modelled closely after that organization.[14] Though the initial membership was confined to citizens of Massachusetts, additional members were to be selected from the friends of temperance in all parts of the nation that the movement might become national in scope. The society's executive committee was to attempt to co-ordinate and direct the activities of all temperance workers.[15] The clergy were the moving force in the early stages of organization, Edwards, Wayland, Wisner and Woods being especially active.

Leonard Woods, professor of theology at Andover Seminary, combined an intense religious zeal with a large capacity for human friendships. The charm of his personality transformed his admiring pupils into his devoted followers and gave him an opportunity to commit his fellows to every good cause. It was in the class-room at Andover that he met Justin Edwards and recognized in the young student of theology the qualities of a leader. Between teacher and pupil there developed a deep friendship, cherished during later years as the two men found mutual interests in the Massachusetts Bible Society, the American Tract Society, the foreign missionary enterprise and finally the temperance movement. Edwards' connections in Boston enabled him to enlist the interest of two of his colleagues in the ministry. Francis Wayland, later to be distinguished as the great president of Brown University, was pastor of the First Baptist Church, while Benjamin Wisner brought to the support of Edwards' project the prestige of the historic Old South Church.[16]

[14] *Report of the American Board of Commissioners for Foreign Missions* (1825).

[15] *P. T. D., Fourth Report*, pp. 12–14.

[16] Hallock, *op. cit.*, pp. 197–8.

Although the clergy were the efficient element in the new society, they entrusted the business administration to the laymen. The executive committee of seven contained only two ministers, Woods and Edwards. The members chose Marcus Morton for the first president. He was a politician with interests that extended far beyond the range of his political activity. He had represented his district in Congress for three terms, had served for one year on the state executive council and in 1824 had been elected lieutenant-governor. At the time the American Temperance Society was formed he was an associate justice of the Massachusetts Supreme Court.[17] Associated with Morton on the executive committee were Samuel Hubbard, John Tappan and S, V. S. Wilder. Hubbard, like Morton, was a lawyer who did not allow his legal practice to occupy all of his time. He had served for several years on the Board of Commissioners for Foreign Missions, where Tappan and Wilder had been his colleagues, and through their influence he had come to regard intemperance as a great obstacle to the progress of home and foreign missionary enterprises. Wilder's reputation as a friend of missions was international, for his connection with large mercantile establishments in Boston and New York necessitated long periods of residence in European countries. He was one of the directors of the American Bible Society and the founder of the Protestant Bible Society of Paris. To the temperance cause he brought the same interest and enthusiasm which characterized his business and missionary activities.[18] Tappan had been a charter member of the Massachusetts Society for the Suppression of

[17] Morton was elected governor of Massachusetts in 1839, served under Polk as collector of the port of Boston, but left the Democratic party in 1848 because of his anti-slavery sentiments.
[18] *First Ten Annual Reports of the American Board of Commissioners for Foreign Missions;* H. O. Dwight, *The Centennial History of the American Bible Society,* p. 58.

Intemperance and he was eager to see the work extended throughout the country by an organization which could formulate and enforce uniform methods and policies.[19] With so distinguished and earnest a leadership the American Temperance Society gave promise of carrying its campaign far beyond the limits reached by any previous temperance group. Success was foreshadowed in the first official pronouncement of the executive committee issued on March 12, 1826. The statement read:

The American Society for the Promotion of Temperance has, after devout and deliberate attention to the subject, resolved in the strength of the Lord, and with a view to the account which they must render to Him for the influence they exert in the world, to make a vigorous, united and persevering effort, to produce a change of public sentiment and practice, with regard to the use of intoxicating liquors. For this purpose they deem it of primary importance that they should obtain an adequate fund for the support of a man of suitable qualifications, in the office of secretary, who shall devote himself to the service of the society, and in the various ways pointed out in the constitution labor to promote its object.[20]

One detects here the most significant characteristics of the temperance reform at this period in its development. In the first place, its supporters were under a divine compulsion to wage a ceaseless war against intemperance; secondly, they had resolved to wage this war by sending out missionaries to preach a new gospel. The cardinal point in the new gospel was the doctrine of total abstinence from the use of ardent spirits as a beverage. As an initial step in the campaign, Justin Edwards was appointed secretary that he might devote his entire time to furthering the society's interests. He proceeded to justify his appointment by

[19] *Supra* p. 92.
[20] Clark, *op. cit.,* p. 21.

raising $7500 during the autumn of 1826 for the support of another agent.[21]   Nathaniel Hewitt, pastor at Fairfield, Connecticut, was selected to assist Edwards, and the two men spent almost a year on an itinerary that took them through New England and most of the middle Atlantic states.   They had for their reward the satisfaction of reporting that six state and two hundred and sixteen local societies had become auxiliary to the national organization.   In the system of creating auxiliaries to the central society they copied the plan of the American Bible Society, which had been extremely successful in extending its work to all sections of the country. The membership of every auxiliary was required to sign the pledge of total abstinence.[22]

The phenomenal success of Edwards and Hewitt was made possible by the revival of old societies, which had been dragging out an uneventful existence for a decade, and by the response of religious bodies to the temperance appeal. Everywhere the agents worked through the churches.   In 1827 Hewitt addressed the General Assembly of the Presbyterian Church at its meeting in Philadelphia with the result that resolutions were passed instructing the various presbyteries to co-operate in every possible way with the American Temperance Society.[23]   Likewise, the New York Synod of the Dutch Reformed Church resolved that ministers and congregations be urged "to abstain entirely from the use of spirituous liquors, and to promote, by precept and example, the cause of strict temperance." [24]   In 1828, the Methodist General Conference, in answer to petitions from many of the district conferences, advised all communicants to abandon the manufacture and sale of ardent spirits and to

[21] Hallock, op. cit., p. 228.

[22] Annual Report of the American Temperance Society (1829).

[23] Marsh, op. cit., p. 39; P. T. D., I, 242; N. Y. Observer, June 12, 1830.

[24] N. Y. Observer, June 5, 1830.

discontinue the practice of giving liquor to employees.[25] During the next five years other Protestant sects fell into line. The General Associations of Congregational churches in Maine, Massachusetts, Connecticut and New Hampshire went so far as to brand the traffic in intoxicants as immoral and inconsistent with a profession of the Christian religion.[26] In the southern states Baptist churches were often the centres from which temperance sentiment radiated, but the activity of the denomination was not confined to any one section of the country.[27] Lutherans and Episcopalians were accused of being indifferent to the reform, and they probably were not so enthusiastic as their Methodist and Baptist friends, but advocates within their ranks could point to distinguished individuals and numerous congregations that were deeply interested. The *Southern Churchman* cited Bishops Otey and McIlvaine as prominent Episcopalians who had espoused the temperance cause.[28]

As the leadership and membership of the temperance societies came largely from the churches, so the appeal of the movement was apt to be religious. The reform took on the attributes of a huge revival. Temperance workers were evangelists preaching a new gospel, and they stated its dogmas in the pulpit phraseology of the day. Persons who responded to the powerful appeal and signed the pledge were known as "converts." For the programs of the societies into which the "converts" were gathered the evangelical prayer meeting served as a model. Appropriate verses,

---

[25] *Journals of the General Conference of the Methodist Episcopal Church*, I, 359, 384.

[26] *Mass. Spy*, June 1, 1831; *P. T. D.*, I, 241–244.

[27] *Georgia Journal*, June 5, 1830; *Boston Christian Herald*, Oct. 26, 1831; *Western Carolinian*, March 15, 1834. Exception should be made in the case of the Primitive Baptists or "Hard-shells," who were as opposed to temperance propaganda as to missionary enterprise in their denomination. See J. B. Jeter, *A Memoir of Abner Clopton*, p. 175; Scomp, *King Alcohol in the Realm of King Cotton*, p. 286.

[28] Quoted in the *Pa. Temperance Recorder*, May, 1835, p. 23.

set to familiar gospel tunes, were sung with all the fervour of religious exaltation. The emotional appeals of the speakers and the "testimony" of the pledge-signers strongly suggested the revivals of the evangelical sects. Indeed, the most effective propagandist for temperance was usually the Protestant clergyman who devoted a large proportion of his sermons to denunciation of the liquor traffic, indicting intemperance as the great barrier in the way of the church militant as it marched on to become the church triumphant.[29]

Unfortunately, it is not possible in complex social movements to isolate single factors and evaluate their relative importance. If such an analysis could be made of the temperance reform, the results would probably reveal the fact that the greatest force possessed by the reformers was their explanation of the manner in which the use of ardent spirits frustrated the accomplishment of the church's mission. Since the church of Christ had been established on earth for the purpose of saving souls, there could be no doubt that its purpose was thwarted by any influence which consigned human beings to perdition. Therefore, intemperance, plainly marking its victim as unfit for salvation, was the hideous enemy of organized religion. On this point the *Temperance Manual* was scarcely in accord with the Calvinistic doctrine of election. It said:

The Holy Spirit will not visit, much less will He dwell with him who is under the polluting, debasing effects of intoxicating drink. The state of mind and heart, which this occasions, is to Him loathsome, and an utter abomination. Not only does it darken the understanding, sear the conscience, pollute the affections, and debase all the powers of the soul; but it counteracts the merciful designs of Jehovah, and all the overflowing kindness of an infinitely compassionate Saviour, for its deliverance; binds the soul in hopeless bondage to its destroyer; awakens the "worm

[29] *Temperance Recorder*, files for 1832 and 1833.

that dieth not, and the fire which is not quenched," and drives the soul away in despair, weeping and wailing, to be punished with everlasting destruction from the presence of the Lord and the glory of His power.[30]

Having fallen victim to the consummate work of Satan for human destruction, the drunkard was beyond the reach of God's saving grace. He could never inherit the Kingdom of Heaven. Here, then, was an enemy that must be destroyed, else the church would never be successful in its effort to redeem the world.[31]

Temperance advocates were well aware of the value of an alliance with organized religion. In season and out they stressed the divine origin of their reform and the religious character of their propaganda. Gerrit Smith, with the same enthusiasm which he manifested for the cause of abolition, characterized the temperance reformation as the work of the Holy Spirit. He regarded it as the preliminary to a general acceptance of the principles of Christianity. Well had it been named the John the Baptist of the Gospel![32] To Lebbeus Armstrong, who had laboured diligently since the formation of the first society at Moreau, temperance seemed to have been sent by Providence for the salvation.of men. It had been foretold by the prophets of old and was a part of God's plan for blessing the world. From the beginning the movement had been attended by signal manifestations that some supernatural agency was controlling it. Every sign pointed to the hand of God working through men to exterminate the use of ardent spirits and drive the curse of intemperance from its strongholds.[33]

[30] *Temperance Manual* for 1836, p. 9.

[31] L. Armstrong, *An Address to the Temperance Society of Malta, New York* (1834); Samuel Spring, *The Only Safe Expedient.*

[32] *American Quarterly Temperance Magazine,* November, 1833, p. 356.

[33] Armstrong, *The Temperance Reformation,* pp. 24–25, 243.

Since the cause was divinely inspired, the duty of the Christian church was plain. In every communion official action should brand as immoral the manufacture, sale and use of distilled liquors; and this pronouncement of truth should be enforced by a severe discipline.[34]   Since even the moderate use of ardent spirits was but the beginning of intemperance, total abstinence must be required from the church member that he might not, by falling into the plight of the drunkard, shut himself off from the power of the church to save.[35]

In the campaign to commit Protestant sects to these propositions the chief attacks were directed against church members who received their livelihood from the liquor traffic. The executive committee of the American Temperance Society emphasized in its official circulars the immoral character of the trade, the evident conflict with Christian principles and the moral responsibility for the crimes which drink occasioned.   The committee knew of no principle of the Gospel that would justify Christian churches permitting their members to continue in a business which filled the poorhouses and fostered every manner of crime.   From all parts of the country reports indicated that the greatest obstacle in the way of temperance reform, the success of the Gospel, and the salvation of men was the example of church members who still sold ardent spirits.   If the church continued to connive at their offence by refusing to discipline them, it would be forced to assume full responsibility for the evils of intemperance.   There could be no evasion.   A sect which compromised with sin must bear the guilt of the sin which it condoned.[36]   So the issue after all was Cain's immortal question, "Am I my brother's keeper?"   No church dared answer that question by insisting that so long as its members

[34] *Ibid.*, pp. 56–57; *Am. Quart. Temp. Mag.*, November, 1833, pp. 343–347.
[35] *Journal of Humanity*, March 10, 1831.
[36] *P. T. D., Fifth Report*, pp. 153–154.

remained sober and honourable, it mattered not how they earned their living. Each congregation was accountable not only for its own conduct, but also for the influence of its conduct upon others. If it offered fellowship to those who used, produced and distributed ardent spirits, it was directly concerned with the pauperism, disease and crime which were inevitable results. How could any sect speak of a Christian dram-shop? Such an idea was doubtless a choice gem in the phrase-book of Satan. The church did not deny that the dram-shop was the recruiting rendezvous of Hell. How, then, could a Christian be the recruiting officer? [37]

Such was the burden of the exhortations addressed to the various church bodies in an attempt to enlist organized religion in the campaign against intemperance. It was a challenge to all denominations of Christians to brand the liquor traffic as a business irreconcilable with the standards of Christian morality. Among the Methodists Wilbur Fisk, principal of Wesleyan Academy in Massachusetts, believed that the interests of his church would best be served, if he could persuade it to purge its membership of all who refused to renounce the use of ardent spirits. Some Methodist conferences were persuaded to restore Wesley's original rule on the subject and regulate their discipline accordingly.[38] Dr. Fisk was responsible for the conversion of Dr. Nathan Bangs, editor of the *Christian Advocate*, who immediately devoted the columns of that Presbyterian periodical to the work of reform. The agents of the American Temperance Society, travelling through all parts of the country, never failed to stress the Christian's duty to enlist in the warfare against a system which flouted every religious and moral principle. The publicity department of the national or-

[37] G. Prentice, *Wilbur Fisk*, p. 190.

[38] Prentice, *op. cit.*, pp. 184–192; *Journal of the Indiana Annual Conferences of the Methodist Church* in W. W. Sweet, *Circuit-Rider Days in Indiana*, pp. 147, 197–198, 325.

ganization kept constantly before church members the effect of intemperance upon the progress of organized religion.[39] Statistics were compiled to prove the point. A tabulation of the records kept by Congregational and Presbyterian churches in New England, New York, Pennsylvania and Ohio showed that during the half-century following 1780 over fifty per cent of the disciplinary troubles, resulting in excommunication, were caused by drunkenness.[40]

This propaganda was not wasted upon the churches, for in many localities the arguments of the temperance leaders were productive of definite action. Some congregations made total abstinence from the use of ardent spirits a necessary qualification for membership. Methodist and Baptist conferences, Presbyterian and Reformed synods passed resolutions, commending the temperance reformation, encouraging ministers to support the movement and exhorting church members to abstain from all connection with the liquor traffic.[41] Camp meetings in the South and West were turned into seasons of pledge-signing, and converted drunkards were admitted into Christian fellowship as evidence of the power of temperance principles to save souls.[42] From every section came reports of the increased activity of the clergy, who were beginning to realize that their efforts to spread the Gospel were nullified by the intemperate habits of the people among whom they laboured. In 1835 there were more than 3000 ministers on the records of the

[39] *P. T. D., Fifth Report*, pp. 129–131; *Journal of Humanity*, November 4, 1830.

[40] I. R. Barbour, *A Statistical Table showing the influence of intemperance upon the church.* The records of ninety-four congregations revealed 469 excommunications between 1810 and 1830 of which 256 were caused by intemperance.

[41] *Journal of Humanity*, Nov. 18, 1830; *N. Y. Observer*, Dec. 4, 1830; *Am. Quart. Temp. Mag.*, May, 1833; T. S. Griffiths, *A History of Baptists in New Jersey*, pp. 510–511.

[42] *Christian Advocate*, Oct. 31, 1828; *P. T. D.*, I, 86–87.

national society as signers of the abstinence pledge.[43]   To the enthusiasts in the reform this co-operation of the religious organizations meant not only the triumph of temperance principles, but also the dawn of the millennium for the church.   The editor of the *Temperance Recorder* phrased the general rejoicing in these words:

Ages have gone by since the fact was revealed in the predictions of inspired men, that there shall ere long dawn upon the church, while her residence is yet on earth, a day of triumph and jubilee—a period in which her light and glory shall fill the world. . . . Who that looks abroad upon the world and surveys the moral machinery that is now in operation, can doubt that we are fairly brought to this cheering and triumphant conclusion? And who that looks at the progress and present state of the temperance cause—at the strength which it has gained in this nation, and at the increasing rapidity and majesty with which it moves forward—who can let his eye rest upon all this, without being full in the conviction that this very cause is at once the harbinger of the millennium and destined to be one of the most efficient means of its introduction.[44]

But this glowing tribute did not represent the sentiment of all the religious forces of the country.   Protestant sects were far from unanimous in their estimate of the temperance movement.   Some congregations, like that of the Dutch Reformed church at Breakabeen, New York, openly denounced the reform and forbade their members to participate in it.[45]   Certain Primitive Baptist churches in Tennessee actually excommunicated members who were guilty of joining a temperance society.[46]   Complaints were numerous that in Georgia faithful workers were hindered by the hostility

[43] *Pa. Temp. Rec.*, May, 1836, p. 40.
[44] *Temp. Rec.*, March 6, 1832.
[45] *Ibid.*, June 5, 1835.
[46] *N. Y. Evangelist*, June 14, 1834; *Journal of the American Temperance Union*, May, 1837.

of ministers who not only set a poor example by their personal conduct, but also ridiculed temperance principles from their pulpits. In Virginia and the Carolinas Abner Clopton found that his most difficult problem was to enlist the support of the more conservative Baptist clergymen.[47] Sectarianism was another shibboleth of church members who were unwilling to sign the pledge. They charged the reform with being a cloak for the activity of certain sects which were busily engaged in gathering the membership of temperance societies into their own ranks. Some colour was given to this charge by the preponderance of Methodist influence in certain communities, but the reformers indignantly denied that they had any interest in denominational rivalries. They pointed to the fact that representatives of every sect were found among the friends of temperance as proof that no particular group occupied a preferred position. None were excluded, and none were discriminated against. The man who professed no religious belief was as important a recruit as the most devout Christian. Catholic and Protestant were equally welcome as leaders or workers in the ranks.[48]

But in the minds of some Christians sectarianism was not the most serious accusation that could be brought against the zealous reformers. The entire philosophy of the temperance movement was founded upon a heresy, namely, that secular organizations could accomplish results which could not be achieved through the agency of the church. This view was ably expressed by Bishop John H. Hopkins of Vermont in his book on *The Primitive Church*. Because of his interest in the æsthetic and mystical aspects of religion, Bishop Hopkins had given up a profitable manufacturing

[47] *Georgia Journal,* June 5, 1830; Jeter, *Memoir of Abner Clopton,* p. 175.

[48] *Journal of Humanity,* Nov. 4, 1830; *N. Y. Evangelist,* April 14, 1832.

business in Pittsburgh in order to enter the priesthood of the Protestant Episcopal Church. A musician, artist and architect of considerable ability, he found in his church a means of satisfying his love of beauty. In the dogmas and methods of evangelical Protestantism he saw nothing to admire, for the emphasis seemed to be placed upon the good rather than the beautiful. Perhaps, it was this fact that first aroused his hostility to the temperance movement, which was so definitely evangelical in its methods. At any rate, he attacked it with as much zest as he criticized abolitionism. To him there was nothing mystical about the reform. It was not the work of the Holy Spirit, but a clear case of men ascribing to secular organizations the ability to change social customs so completely as to produce a spiritual regeneration. It was an attempt to set aside religious influences as worthless and substitute for them man-made societies which sought to hallow their work by the claim that they were divinely sanctioned. It was a monstrous negation of the fundamental principle of Christianity that the church of Christ alone can save men's souls.[49]

The people who took Bishop Hopkins' work seriously were interested to read in 1836 an anonymous publication called *Protestant Jesuitism*. They would have been more interested had they known that its author was at the time a travelling correspondent for the *New York Observer*, a religious weekly constantly friendly to the temperance reform. For the author of *Protestant Jesuitism* was Calvin Colton, later famous as the biographer of Henry Clay and the editor of the Whig statesman's public and private papers. Colton had graduated from Yale College and Andover Theological Seminary, had served as a home missionary for three years in New York state and had then accepted a call from the Presbyterian church at LeRoy, New York. When

[49] Hopkins, *The Primitive Church; The Life of John Henry Hopkins*, By One of His Sons, pp. 169–170.

he was forced to resign from the ministry, because of a failing voice, he turned to journalism and became a successful writer of special articles on religious subjects. For the *Observer* he travelled widely, spending several years in Europe. It was during this time that he abandoned his Calvinistic theology and decided to take orders in the Protestant Episcopal Church. He seems to have been temperamentally prejudiced against all reformers, for his hostility toward the temperance workers was only exceeded by his hatred of the abolitionists.[50]   Through many of his writings runs a strain of protest against the attempts of non-political organizations to secure political power for the purpose of effecting moral or religious reforms. This was the basis of his attack on the anti-slavery societies, as it was the theme of his denunciation of the temperance conspiracy.

Colton placed the mark of his approval upon an idea which had caused the reformers much trouble. He charged that a group of determined people, representing various Protestant sects, had inaugurated a campaign to dominate public opinion through a well-organized minority. Pretending that they were eager to advance the cause of Christianity, they were really planning to usurp for themselves the influence of the Christian church. Under the guise of moral reform they were carrying out their sinister purpose to destroy the liberties of the American people.[51]   Their methods betrayed them. By an inquisitorial system, which left the individual neither the keeping of his own conscience nor the use of his own judgment, they compelled the acceptance of their doctrines. The manner of obtaining signatures

[50] Colton, *Abolition, A Sedition, passim;* Colton severed his connection with the *Observer* shortly after he published *Protestant Jesuitism.*

[51] Some claimed to see in the temperance organizations an attempt to unite church and state by using the force of organized religion to compel the state to take action against the liquor traffic. *Journal of Humanity,* October 14, 1829, p. 83; *Reasons for not joining the Temperance Society,* By a Clergyman (1836); E. C. Blackman, *op. cit.,* p. 565.

to the pledge was particularly artful and cunning, for signers were cleverly led to the altar and there compelled to humble themselves before the public. The principle of the movement was coercion not reform. The individual was prostrated by the force of an overpowering bigotry and became an unwilling servant of zealots whom he really despised.[52]

Though the temperance forces might smile at such a description of their methods and purposes, they realized that many were only too ready to believe Colton's accusations.[53] Church members explained their refusal to abstain from the use of ardent spirits by professing to see the sinister design of the temperance movement. Christians continued to engage in the liquor traffic, maintaining that the campaign against their business was an unholy effort of a fanatical minority to deprive them of their liberty and property. These charges, a curious compound of sincerity and hypocrisy, constituted a counter-offensive which the reformers could not ignore. They met it usually by vigorously reaffirming their belief in the divine origin of their cause and its prophecy of the millennium. Chancellor Walworth of New York well voiced their faith:

As you value the souls of your fellow-men, and the dying love of Him who came to seek and to save, and who went about doing good, let me entreat you to persevere in this benevolent and glorious work, until "total abstinence" shall be inscribed upon the banner of every state and nation of this world. Then, and not till then, shall the peaceful reign of the kingdom of the Messiah commence and be extended to the ends of the earth.[54]

The temperance idea had indeed become incarnate in its faithful supporters.

[52] Colton, *Protestant Jesuitism*, pp. 50–92.
[53] In 1842 A. S. Davis of Hanover, Pa., issued *A Loud Call to the Citizens of the Nation* in which he revived the charge that the temperance societies were attempting to unite church and state.
[54] *Mass. Spy*, Aug. 24, 1836.

CHAPTER VII

ORGANIZING FOR VICTORY

THE temperance reformers were propagandists who neither feared nor denied the designation. They willingly admitted that they were in the business of creating a public opinion which in time would substitute a better standard of conduct for the existing one. Two pictures were constantly in their minds, one of a nation doomed to destruction because of the ravages of strong drink, the other of a nation happy and prosperous under a regimen of temperance. To translate into terms of everyday life the promise of the latter picture was their objective; success depended upon their ability to make others see the situation as it appeared to them. They must, therefore, unite in permanent organizations all those who considered abstinence from the use of ardent spirits of primary importance in the control of human relations. This would give them an effective means of voicing opinions favourable to their purposes.

The problem of persuading the unconvinced was handled with an evident understanding of human nature. The mind of man, reasoned the reformers, is so constituted that it may be more effectually reached by forbearance and mild suggestion than by severity. This is particularly true when the purpose is to induce men to change their usual course of conduct and to adopt new principles of action. Many people have a pronounced pride of opinion, an unwillingness to lay aside long cherished sentiments and an aversion from breaking firmly fixed habits, which cannot be overcome by frontal attacks. They must be convinced of the advisability of the suggested change by arguments which recognize some merit in the former practice, but urge its abandonment for the sake of something better. Accordingly, during the first years of the American Temperance Society's work, propaganda was couched more often in terms of mild criticism than in those of bitter invective.[1]

The philosophy underlying the reform was essentially of the eighteenth century, for its central idea was the perfectibility of man. The infinite capacity of mankind for self-improvement, said the temperance leaders, made it possible to correct conduct and to elevate moral standards by means of intellectual appeals. In fact, error was virtually harmless, as Jefferson had said, if reason was free to combat it. Since men were rational creatures, it would not be difficult to persuade them that self-control was desirable and that it could best be insured by abstinence from anything that tended to encourage excess. Such persuasion would require a widespread diffusion of knowledge through an energetic educational campaign. The duty of the temperance societies, therefore, was to direct the thoughts of intelligent people in such fashion that they would understand the effects of intemperance and the practicability of abstinence as a remedy. The principal instruments through which this could be accomplished were voluntary associations of abstainers, constant admonitions from Christian pulpits and informing appeals in the religious and secular press.[2] That the result of a concerted campaign would be the gradual discrediting of existing ideas with regard to the use of intoxicants, the reformers never doubted. They were confident that, since sin was due to ignorance, knowledge would turn men from vice to virtue.

Indeed, the decade following the formation of the American

[1] *Temperance Recorder*, April 3, 1832, pp. 9–10; *Journal of Humanity*, November 18, 1830, p. 101.

[2] *Journal of Humanity*, January 24, 1829, p. 17; *Pa. Temperance Recorder*, March, 1835.

Temperance Society in 1826 was a period of optimism. High hopes were entertained that the temperance idea would become so popular that it would effect a revolution in manners and morals. Favourable sentiment was evident in all parts of the country, sometimes a direct result of the work of the national society and its auxiliaries, but more often an independent manifestation of the opinion of a particular community. Writers in temperance periodicals were prone to regard this popular concern over intemperance as a result of the principle and practice of self-government. Rulers by divine-right and hereditary nobles might tolerate with impunity depraving indulgences which kept the great mass abject, but when the many came into political power a more rigorous social control was necessary for the success of republican institutions.[3] Though this explanation may have been more ingenious than valid, the fact remained that the poorer classes in the community were manifesting an unwonted interest in social problems, an interest which the temperance forces were quick to convert into organized effort for reform.

In an attempt to establish uniform procedure throughout the country the national society suggested that all local groups, regardless of their origin, adopt the same pledge and become auxiliary to their state society. For a model pledge it recommended:

We, the subscribers, residing in the state of............, county of............, town of............, believing that the drinking of ardent spirits is, for persons in health, not only unnecessary but injurious; that its use is the cause of forming intemperate appetites and habits; and while it is continued, the evils of intemperance can never be prevented: do therefore agree, that we will not, except as a medicine in case of bodily in-

[3] *Am. Quart. Temp. Mag.*, February, 1833, p. 28; November, 1833, p. 326. See also Lyman Cobb, *Juvenile Reader, No. 3.* p. 187, published at Chambersburg, Pa., in 1836.

firmity, use distilled spirits ourselves, or procure them for use of our families, or provide them for the entertainment of our friends, or for persons in our employment, and that in all suitable ways we will discountenance the use of them in the community.[4]

This pledge was not generally used by the societies, for many never became auxiliary to the national organization, and of those that did a majority preferred to work out their own ideas of a proper obligation.   As the number of societies increased, central control became less practicable, and each state was advised to take care of its own work.   In some sections the state organization was an efficient force; in others it was merely an annual convention of delegates from county and local societies.   New York, Massachusetts and Connecticut possessed strong central societies which dominated activities in the entire state, but there were many local groups even in these districts that did not recognize any outside control.   In the South and West there was little indication of a federation of the temperance forces, the result being that much power was lost through the failure to co-ordinate efforts.   This lack of organization on a large-scale meant also that records of the movement were kept either poorly or not at all.   Where the state society wielded an effective control, the auxiliaries sent in annual reports, but elsewhere achievements went unheralded, unless some enterprising member sent news items to the temperance periodicals.   The paucity of statistics and the enthusiasm of devoted statisticians caused many compilations to represent an earnest hope rather than an accurate enumeration.[5]

Although a minority of the temperance forces were affiliated with the American Temperance Society, that organization served as a clearing-house for the friends of the reform. Its annual reports attempted to present a survey of con-

[4] *Temperance Recorder,* May 1, 1832, p. 17.
[5] *P. T. D.,* I, 161, 342.

ditions throughout the United States. In 1829 approximately 1000 societies were listed with a membership of more than 100,000. Two years later the movement had doubled in strength, for the records showed 2200 distinct groups totalling 170,000 members.[6] Nineteen state societies were sharing the responsibilities of the nation-wide campaign. Agents were at work in all parts of the Union, for the missionary motive was so strong that workers were constantly seeking out communities where the temperance message had not been heard. New York, Massachusetts and Pennsylvania were unusually generous in devoting funds to the maintenance of agents in the newer states of the South and West.[7] But the work at home was not neglected for the sake of fields afar off. Each state society was urged to encourage the formation of county units which would regulate the activities of the smaller groups. As the officers of the county societies would be ex-officio members of the executive committee of the state society, unity of action could thus be secured. In New York the suggestion was most carefully worked out through a federation based upon the school district associations and culminating in the state organization, which gave every society in the state an opportunity to make its influence felt.[8] The system was well designed to preserve at least the semblance of uniform methods, in spite of the inevitable diversity resulting from rapid expansion. In order to foster a consciousness of similar purposes, the executive committee of the national society recommended in 1832 that in all cities, towns and villages throughout the country meetings be held on February 26, the anniversary of the formation of the American Temperance Society. The suggestion was adopted the next year, and from Maine to Louisiana simultaneous gatherings cele-

6 P. T. D., I, 28, 38.

7 Ibid., I, 236.

8 Temperance Recorder, March 6, 1832, pp. 1–2.

brated the progress of the reform.[9]   Official estimates of
the time placed the number of societies at 4000 with more
than 500,000 active members, a fact which, in the opinion
of the reformers, warranted national rejoicing.[10]

An analysis of the records for 1831 reveals the numerical
preponderance in the reform of New Englanders and their
widely scattered descendants.[11]   Although less than one-
sixth of the people of the United States at that time lived in
the six states north-east of the Hudson, they had formed
more than one-third of the temperance societies with nearly
one-third of the total membership.   Furthermore, a significant relation between the expansion of New England and the
growth of temperance sentiment was apparent from the
geographical distribution of the societies in New York and
Ohio.   Of the 700 organizations in the former state, em-
bracing fully fifty per cent of the temperance forces in the
entire country, a majority were located in districts which
had received the largest immigration from New England.   A
survey of the most pronounced temperance counties shows
a solid belt, beginning with Broome County on the Pennsylvania line and running north-west through Tioga, Cortland,
Tompkins, Yates, Ontario, Monroe and Genesee.   Histor-
ically, this section belonged in large part to the two tracts
ceded, as real estate, by New York to Massachusetts in 1786.
Genesee, Ontario, Monroe and Yates were included in the
more than six million acres, known as the "Genesee Country,"
which Massachusetts sold to Oliver Phelps and Philip Gor-

[9] *P. T. D.*, I, 232–233; *The Georgian* (Savannah), March 2, 1833.

[10] *P. T. D.*, I, 161.

[11] The figures reported in 1831 are used because they represent the
most accurate enumeration ever made by the early societies.   There are
undoubtedly omissions, particularly in the southern and western states,
but the relative strength of the reform in the various sections seems
to be truly represented.   The lists are given in the *Journal of Humanity*
files for 1831, to which I have added societies from other available
records.

ham, while Tioga and Broome were embraced in the tract sold to John Brown and others.[12]   Both the Brown and Phelps-Gorham purchases became replicas of New England during the decades between 1810 and 1830, and their inhabitants proved ready converts to the temperance gospel.   In Ohio a similar situation existed.   One-quarter of the societies in the state were located in that second New England which had been planted in the Western Reserve lands of Connecticut. Portage County alone, peopled largely by families from Massachusetts, Connecticut and western New York, contained ten organizations active in reform work.   Two other sections of New England settlement were important strongholds of the temperance forces, the Marietta district along the Ohio River and the villages near Granville and Worthington in the centre of the state.[13]   In Pennsylvania a majority of the societies were supported by the descendants of Welsh and English Quakers and Scotch-Irish Presbyterians. The latter were chiefly responsible for the fact that within the two westernmost tiers of counties lived more than thirty per cent of all Pennsylvanians who had signed the pledge.

South of the Mason-Dixon line and the Ohio River there were only 15,000 pledged to abstinence from distilled spirits, less than ten per cent of the abstainers in the whole country. Of this number at least half were members of societies in Virginia and Georgia, where the southern phase of the movement had its origin.   There had been no causal relation between the temperance organizations in New England and New York and the beginnings of reform in the states of the

<hr />

[12] O. Turner, *Phelps-Gorham Purchase*, p. 40; Lois K. Mathews, *Expansion of New England*, pp. 155–169.

[13] See map opposite. The geographical location of the various temperance societies has been determined from the early records. Each dot represents the existence of *five* societies within a radius of less than twenty miles. For data on the expansion of New England see Mathews, *op. cit.*, pp. 178–181.

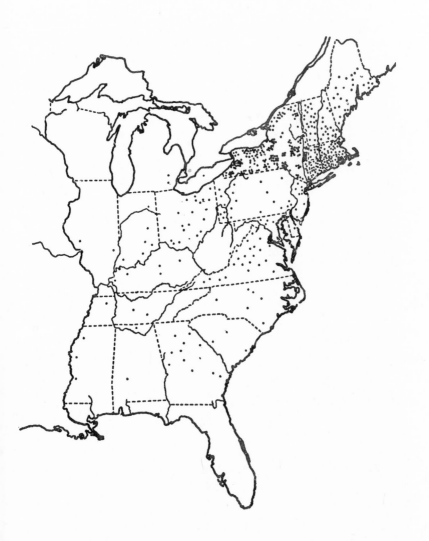

seaboard South, but many of the southern societies had affiliated with the national society before 1831. When Abner Clopton, an influential Baptist preacher in Virginia, began to organize the temperance work in his own state in 1826, he had not heard of the formation of the American Temperance Society a few months earlier in Boston, and his efforts were entirely independent of what was being done in other parts of the nation. His success in persuading the Baptists and Methodists to interest themselves was responsible for the spread of Clopton societies throughout the western part of Virginia, whence they finally secured a foothold in the Carolinas and Georgia. Adiel Sherwood, Clopton's most zealous disciple in Georgia, maintained that in his state temperance reform was growth of the southern soil and owed little to the northern societies.[14] Although this was in a sensé true, Georgia and Virginia with the rest of the southern states profited much by the missionary work done through the New York and New England societies. Sherwood, himself, a native of New York who had studied theology in 1817 under Leonard Woods at Andover, was no stranger to temperance sentiment in New England.

The fact that temperance groups in different parts of the country did not owe their existence to a common source caused some to fear for the unity and harmony of the movement. Besides, many workers were convinced that individual efforts were not properly supervised and that the public was not aware of the magnitude of the enterprise. It seemed advisable, therefore, to focus attention on the strength and co-operation of the various groups through the medium of a national convention. The executive committee of the American Temperance Society issued a call for a meeting

[14] Jeter, *A Memoir of Abner Clopton*, pp. 171–173; Scomp, *op. cit.*, pp. 236–240. New York ranked first among the states in the percentage of total population enrolled in temperance societies. Next in order came Connecticut, Vermont, Rhode Island, Massachusetts, Maine, New Hampshire, Georgia, Virginia, and Ohio.

of delegates from all county and state societies to be held in Independence Hall, Philadelphia, on May 24, 1833. The response surprised the most optimistic, for more than four hundred representatives of organizations in twenty-one states attended the sessions. Chancellor Reuben Walworth of New York presided with such grace and wisdom that harmony was preserved in spite of the variety of opinions voiced by the delegates. A steering committee, controlled by representatives of New York and Massachusetts, outlined matters for discussion and suggested a plan for a permanent body which would formulate the policy of the temperance forces in the future.[15]

On the floor of the convention several important questions were settled to the satisfaction of a majority of the delegates. While the type of pledge was under discussion, a small group of conservatives challenged the soundness of the abstinence principle, and a radical minority desired to place fermented liquors as well as ardent spirits under the ban. The sentiment of the majority, however, was strongly in favour of retaining without amendment the pledge of "total abstinence from the use of ardent spirits." Not so easily settled was the question of the proper attitude to be adopted toward the liquor traffic. The debate, which at times waxed acrimonious, was precipitated by the introduction of a resolution declaring the traffic in distilled spirits to be morally wrong and deserving of the severest condemnation. Opposition came from several quarters. Some maintained that such a pronouncement would alienate many from the cause, since it would be considered an unnecessary impeachment of the "pious dealers" of former days. Others insisted

[15] The committee was composed of such able and distinguished philanthropists as Reuben Walworth, Gerrit Smith, Edward C. Delavan and Hugh Maxwell of New York, Justin Edwards and John Tappan of Massachusetts, Timothy Pitkin of Connecticut, Peter D. Vroom of New Jersey, Roberts Vaux of Pennsylvania, and D. W. Lathrop of Ohio.

that denunciation would only serve to arouse the bitter hostility of those engaged in the business and would persuade none to abandon the traffic. In spite of objections, however, the convention finally adopted the resolution, justifying its action on the ground that a definite statement might deter honourable men from engaging in a disreputable business.[16]

The creation of a national organization was effected without any difficulty. On recommendation of the special committee the delegates decided that the United States Temperance Union should be formed on a federation basis, the membership to consist of the officers of the American Temperance Society, the officers of the twenty-three state societies and representatives from as many local societies as desired to join. The work of the Union was to be placed in the hands of a president and executive committee selected by the members, who should serve as the final authority in all matters pertaining to the spread of temperance propaganda. Every society in the country was urged to become affiliated with the Union in order that the full strength of the movement might be represented. For the first president of the new organization the members chose that conscientious and benevolent aristocrat, Stephen Van Rensselaer, whose offer to publish and distribute 100,000 copies of the proceedings of the convention had been accepted with enthusiasm. By reason of his large estates in New York, General Van Rensselaer was one of the richest men of his day, and he devoted a generous proportion of his income to philanthropic enterprises of an educational and moral character. He was assured able assistance in the new work by the selection of Judge William Jay of Westchester County, New York, as chairman of the executive committee. Judge Jay was well-known in all parts of the country for his ability as a jurist and his activity in a wide variety of reform movements. He had joined Elias Boudinot and others in forming

16 *P. T. D.*, I, 342; Marsh, *op. cit.*, p. 37.

the American Bible Society in 1810, had been prominent in the organization of the New York City Anti-Slavery Society, and had contributed constantly to the literature of protest against duelling, gambling, Sabbath-breaking and intemperance. Though his interests were many, he had proved in the temperance organizations of his own state that he was willing to give a large share of his time to that particular cause. His associates on the executive committee, chosen with regard to the sectional strength of the reform, were from New England and Pennsylvania. Massachusetts was represented by Harrison Gray, the Boston publisher and bookseller; Connecticut by Cyrus Yale, long pastor of the Congregational Church in New Hartford; New Hampshire by Richard Boylston [17] of Amherst, whose interest in temperance was a by-product of his efforts to improve conditions on American farms; and Pennsylvania by Samuel Agnew, a popular physician of Lancaster, who voiced the opinion of many of his profession in regard to the use of distilled liquors.[18]

It was not an accident that the officers of the Union were men who had been successful in business and the professions, for the temperance forces consciously strove to gain prestige for their cause from the prominence of their official leaders. In New York, for example, the personnel of the state society's roster of officers was unusually impressive. The president was Judge Reuben H. Walworth, one of the leading lawyers of Saratoga County, then serving the state as chancellor. The vice-presidents, representing the most important districts, were Judge William Jay of Westchester County; David Buell, Jr., of Troy, vice-president of Rens-

[17] Richard Boylston in 1836 became editor of the *Farmer's Cabinet,* a periodical devoted to the promotion of scientific methods of agriculture.

[18] The secretaries or agents of the Union were John Marsh and Isaac S. Lloyd of Pennsylvania and Thomas Brainard of Ohio. Marsh, *op. cit.,* pp. 37–38; *P. T. D.,* II, 14.

selaer Institute; Henry Huntington, wealthy merchant of Rome and president of the Utica Bank; Henry Dwight, president of the Bank of Geneva; Judge Ashley Sampson of Rochester; Ben Johnson, leader of the Tompkins County bar; and the venerable John Watts of New York City, founder of the Leake and Watts Orphan House and president of the New York Dispensary. The management of the society's work was entrusted to Edward C. Delavan of Albany, a wealthy merchant who had amassed a fortune in the wholesale hardware business.[19] The New York leadership was typical of that elsewhere in the nation. In Pennsylvania Roberts Vaux, the Quaker philanthropist and reformer,[20] was succeeded in the presidency of the state society by Matthew Newkirk, whose drygoods business in Philadelphia had brought him a substantial fortune. His means enabled him to become one of the foremost railroad builders of his day, a benefactor and trustee of Princeton, and a generous contributor to the financial support of temperance work. Newkirk's most influential associate was Thomas P. Cope, founder of the famous Philadelphia importing house and manufacturer of cotton goods. Like Newkirk he invested a part of his fortune in railroads, and his Liverpool packets were an important part of the American merchant marine during the decade of the forties.[21]

New Jersey possessed an able and efficient leader in Theodore Frelinghuysen, who became president of the state society while he was in the United States Senate. Though his political and educational interests took much of his time and energy, he remained faithful to the temperance reform

[19] *Annual Report, New York Temperance Society* (1830).

[20] Thomas M. Pettit, *Memoir of Roberts Vaux* contains an account of Vaux's work in behalf of public education, prison reform, care of the insane, and institutions for the deaf and dumb.

[21] Data in regard to Newkirk and Cope may be found in *Biographical Encyclopedia of Pennsylvania of the Nineteenth Century.*

throughout his lifetime.[22]   Nor was he the only public official prominent among the reformers during the decade of
the thirties.   In Ohio the state society was presided over
first by Governor Allen Trimble, who was succeeded by Governor Robert Lucas, while in Maine Governor Robert P. Dunlap secured recognition for his state in the national councils
of the movement.[23]   Judge Willard Hall of the United
States District Court and Senator Arnold Naudain directed
the Delaware society for the greater part of a decade.   In
the neighbouring state of Maryland Judge Stevenson Archer
of the Court of Appeals was responsible for the most successful years.[24]

As every responsible leader realizes the value of attaching
to his following people of consequence in the community, so
the temperance workers understood the importance of en-
rolling in their societies men whose achievements commanded
respect.   This was the idea underlying the campaign begun
in 1832 to organize legislative temperance societies.   The
members of Congress and state legislatures were to be
brought together, not for the purpose of securing legislation
against the liquor traffic, but rather that the example of the
law-makers might be used to influence their constituents.
With this end in view a preliminary meeting was held in
Washington, D. C., during the spring of 1832, at which
plans for a Congressional society were discussed.   The enthusiasm of Senator Frelinghuysen, who was largely responsible for the gathering, was shared by Senator Felix Grundy

22 L. Q. C. Elmer, "Reminiscences of New Jersey," *New Jersey Historical Society, Collections*, VII, 440–456. Frelinghuysen was Chancellor of New York University, vice-presidential candidate on the Clay
ticket in 1844, president of the Board of Commissioners for Foreign
Missions (1841), American Bible Society (1846), Rutgers College
(1850).

23 *P. T. D.*, II, 14.

24 For lists of officers of state societies see *Journal of the American
Temperance Union*, January, 1838.

of Tennessee and the Secretary of War, Lewis Cass. Daniel
Webster, never known as a foe of alcoholic stimulants, was
persuaded to offer the resolution that some sort of organization be effected to combat the evils attendant upon the
use of distilled spirits.[25] Definite action was postponed until February 26, 1833, when the American Congressional
Temperance Society was formed for the purpose of discoun-
tenancing *the use of ardent spirit and the traffic in it, by
example and by kind moral influence.*[26] Secretary Cass,
who at the time was receiving much commendation for his
order of November, 1832, removing ardent spirits from the
regular army ration, was chosen president. To assist him
an executive committee was selected composed of Senators
Theodore Frelinghuysen of New Jersey and Arnold Naudain of Delaware, and Representatives John Blair of Tennessee, George N. Briggs of Massachusetts and Eleutheros
Cook of Ohio.[27] Representative Cook voiced the appeal to
national pride in his boastful assertion that Americans had
given mankind the first example of the benefits of temperance
and were, therefore, peculiarly obligated to carry on the
work. The nations of the world, he believed, had caught the
significance of the example set for them and were engaged
in imitating it. Certainly it would be a national disgrace, if
the United States, after raising hopes so high, should fail
to continue its moral leadership.[28]

[25] *Documents and Records of the Massachusetts Temperance Society,*
pp. 36–37; Marsh, *op. cit.,* pp. 31–33.

[26] *Proceedings of the Convention for the Promotion of the Cause of
Temperance,* p. 47.

[27] The honorary vice-presidents were: Senators Samuel Bell of New
Hampshire, Gideon Tomlinson of Connecticut, William Wilkins of
Pennsylvania, Thomas Ewing of Ohio, Felix Grundy of Tennessee, John
Tipton of Indiana, and Representatives John Reed of Massachusetts,
Lewis Condict of New Jersey, David Wardwell of New York and James
Wayne of Georgia.

[28] *Proceedings of the Convention for the Promotion of the Cause of
Temperance,* p. 48.

The temperance forces welcomed the opportunity to capitalize political prestige for the spread of their doctrines. Lewis Cass was hailed as the great exemplar of total abstinence. Of his career one enthusiast wrote:

Notwithstanding the numerous and diversified temptations and exposures of a frontier life, he passed through a distinguished career of usefulness without having ever tasted ardent spirit. In his numerous journeys as a commissioner for the United States, in the damp and chilling climates of the northwestern lakes, and through the swamps, fens and miasmatic tracts of the Mississippi, his uniform abstinence from spirituous drinks, had made him a model of temperance, before temperance societies had been heard of in those remote solitudes.[29]

With such a leader the Congressional Temperance Society seemed destined to wield a powerful influence.[30]   It was expected that lesser politicians would imitate the example of the national legislators and organize legislative temperance associations in their respective states.   This was exactly what happened, but the movement originated in the work of individual reformers and not in any missionary work done by the Congressional society.   Massachusetts was the first state to take action.   On March 15, 1833, a legislative temperance society was formed at Boston with ex-governor Levi Lincoln as president.[31]   Within a few months fully half the members of the Ohio and Kentucky legislatures pledged themselves "to abstain from drinking ardent spirit." [32]   During the next two years legislative temperance societies became the rule rather than the exception.   Their number indicated that many politicians, witnessing the change in customs and the growing popularity of abstinence, believed there was

[29] *Am. Quart. Temp. Mag.*, May, 1833, p. 120.
[30] Cass remained president until 1837, when the society was reorganized under the leadership of Felix Grundy of Tennessee.
[31] *Mass. Spy*, March 27, 1833.
[32] *P. T. D.*, I, 345–346.

nothing to lose and probably something to gain by accepting the standards of the reformers.

By the middle of the decade the temperance cause had a following that was well-organized and determined to win its objective. Every state was enrolled in the movement. From the incomplete returns of the state societies in 1834 statistics had been compiled showing more than 5000 local groups with a membership of approximately 1,000,000, an increase in three years of five hundred per cent.[33] There was additional joy in the fact that these organizations had at their disposal the means of carrying on an educational campaign. In spite of inadequate funds and general indifference, the friends of temperance had succeeded in establishing a press of their own which served to carry propaganda into all parts of the nation. The first issue of the *National Philanthropist*, printed at Boston on March 4, 1826, under the editorship of Rev. William Collier, was followed by a score of similar publications, many of which were influential though short-lived.[34] The American Temperance Society established the *Journal of Humanity* at Andover, Massachusetts, in 1829 and supported its publication until February, 1833. In 1836 there were eleven weekly and monthly journals devoted solely to the interests of temperance, while many religious periodicals, notably the *Christian Spectator* and the *New York Observer*, carried in their columns items pertaining to the reform.[35] Through the interest of Wil-

[33] *Ibid.*, 342.

[34] From January to August, 1828, William Lloyd Garrison edited the *National Philanthropist*. Noteworthy among these early papers was the *Genius of Temperance* edited by Phineas Crandall at Gardiner, Maine.

[35] The more important journals were: *Recorder*, Albany; *Herald*, Concord, New Hampshire; *Banner*, Northampton, Mass.; *Pledge*, Lowell, Mass.; *Recorder*, Philadelphia; *Herald*, Baltimore; *Advocate*, Columbus, Ohio; *Star*, Richmond, Va., *Cold Water Man*, Natchez Miss.; *Herald*, Augusta, Maine. See *Journal of American Temperance Union*, January, 1837.

liam A. Hallock, agent of the American Tract Society, funds of that organization were assigned to the publication and circulation of tracts containing the standard temperance arguments.

All this literature conveyed to its readers the impression that popular misconceptions, which had handicapped the workers in the early days of the movement, were slowly being corrected. The idea that ardent spirits prevented disease and relieved fatigue, so vigorously attacked by Dr. Rush, was being discredited by the investigations of physicians and the experiments of employers of labour. Scientific articles on the subject by Dr. Reuben Mussey of Dartmouth College, Dr. Walter Channing of Boston and Dr. Thomas Sewall of Washington, D. C., were changing the attitude of many in the medical profession. Seventy-five physicians in the state of New York, for example, had signed a statement to the effect that distilled spirits would no longer occupy a prominent place in their list of curatives.[36] The College of Physicians and Surgeons in Philadelphia had enlarged its curriculum by introducing a course in the pathology of intemperance.[37] State medical associations in Massachusetts and Vermont had taken the lead in officially denouncing the general use of spirituous liquors.[38]

Equally encouraging to the reformers were the reports from employers and labourers. In response to a questionnaire sent out by the New York State Temperance Society in 1832 to manufacturing establishments in New England and the middle Atlantic states, replies from forty employers indicated that they were unanimously opposed to the use of ardent spirits by their employees, because they believed that labour efficiency was thereby impaired.[39] The superintend-

[36] *Annual Report, New York State Temperance Society* (1833).
[37] *Journal of Humanity,* Feb. 17, 1830, p. 153.
[38] *Ibid.,* p. 154.
[39] *Annual Report, N. Y. State Temperance Society* (1833).

ent of construction work in connection with the building of the Baltimore and Ohio Railroad had issued a statement in 1830:

> The destructive and demoralizing effects of the use of ardent spirits became so manifest in producing riot, and other flagrant disorders, that I determined, with the sanction of the president of the company, to prohibit the use of it in all future contracts. And accordingly no contract since then [July, 1829] has been made either for graduation or for masonry, in which a clause was not inserted to that effect. It is believed that the work may be executed without the use of this dreadful poison, more advantageously to the interests of the company, and certainly much more agreeably to its officers and contractors, as well as beneficially to the laborers themselves.[40]

City labour, at this time manifesting class consciousness in the organization of scores of trade unions and labour societies, became interested in the problem of intemperance. Workingmen's abstinence societies appeared in the cities of New York, Baltimore, Philadelphia and Boston between 1833 and 1837. In Philadelphia an interesting experiment was tried. Several hundred artisans and mechanics decided on February 3, 1835, to abstain from using ardent spirits for a period of six weeks and at the end of that time to consider the advantages and disadvantages of abstinence. The test proved so satisfactory to the participants that three hundred signed the pledge and organized the Mechanics and Workingmen's Temperance Society of Philadelphia. Their influence in the labour circles of the city was sufficiently well-known to inspire Daniel Webster to write a letter complimenting them on the character of their work.[41]

On the farm as well as in the city employer and employee

[40] *Journal of Humanity*, Feb. 17, 1830, pp. 153–154.
[41] *Pa. Temperance Recorder*, March, 1835, p. 2; April, pp. 10–11; August, p. 48; *N. Y. Observer*, July 3, 1830.

were adopting a new attitude toward the use of distilled liquors. Farmers were becoming convinced, so ran the reports from the rural communities, that haying and harvesting, barn-raising and fence-building, ploughing and planting could be done more quickly and more cheaply without the stimulus of whisky. Since he no longer believed that alcohol relieved fatigue, the labourer was less dependent upon ardent spirits to aid him in the heavy tasks of field and forest. As the notion that cold water was dangerous in hot weather slowly disappeared, farm hands were less averse to working for wages that did not include a daily ration of whisky or rum. In the frontier communities of Michigan, Illinois and Missouri forests were being cleared away and fields cultivated with comparatively slight recourse to alcoholic stimulants of any sort. That the drinking customs of former generations were fast becoming obsolete was the story told in the records of the temperance societies.[42]

As a fair criterion of the changing tone of public sentiment the reformers cited the restraint which was practised on·holidays and other special occasions. The gay round of social calls, which characterized New Year's Day in the eastern cities, had always been accompanied by a considerable consumption of intoxicants. In the decade following 1830, however, many families refused to serve their guests with distilled spirits, replacing the stronger beverages with hot coffee or mild wines.[43] The New York *Sun* and the *New York Evening Post* commented editorially in 1837 upon several news items indicative of a change in social usage apparently

[42] *Journal of Humanity*, March 10, 1830, p. 167; Sept. 9, 1830, p. 61; April 28, 1831, p. 194; *Am. Quart. Temp. Mag.*, May, 1833, p. 176; *Pa. Temp. Rec.*, Oct., 1835, p. 64; *Diary of Elisha Risdon* in C. E. Sanford, *Early History of Hopkinton, N. Y.*, p. 308; *Western Carolinian*, May 10, 1834; Silas Farmer, *History of Detroit and Wayne County*, pp. 838–839; H. H. Hurlbut, *Chicago Antiquities*, pp. 108–109; *The Making of a Township*, E. M. Baldwin, editor, p. 90; *N. Y. Observer*, Aug. 28, 1830.

[43] *Mass. Spy*, June 13, 1830.

traceable to temperance principles. One citizen of the metropolis stated that in eighty calls on the first two days of the year he had been offered no ardent spirits. Another had made over fifty visits and had seen no distilled liquor provided for the entertainment of guests. A third had been host to nearly three hundred during New Year's Day, but his decanters had not been emptied, though in former years he had been accustomed to replenish them several times.[44] A similar attitude was evident on other holidays. The Fourth of July, for half a century a day of festivity too often marred by drunken excesses, was becoming rather a day devoted to the struggle against intemperance. The gala crowds, assembled in holiday spirit and attire for a season of merry-making, less frequently degenerated into disorderly mobs because of an abundance of intoxicants. The customary toasts, so indispensable a part of the celebration of national independence, were more often drunk in small beer or pure water. In some localities the temperance societies took charge of the exercises for the day and combined with great effectiveness in speech and song the praise of patriotism and sobriety.[45]

Evidence that the liquor traffic was steadily losing the respectability of former days appeared in the reports of dismantled distilleries and deserted grog-shops. Manufacturers and vendors were abandoning a business which caused them to lose caste among their fellows. From a score of states came statistics of plants which had discontinued the manufacture, and stores which had stopped the sale of distilled liquors. The report of the New York society, for example, listed more than 130 distilleries which had ceased oper-

44 New York *Sun,* January 3, 1837; *Pa. Temp. Rec.,* February, 1837, p. 11.

45 *Star and North Carolina State Gazetteer,* July 8, 1830; *Frankfort Argus,* July 10, 1833; *North Carolina Standard,* July 12, 1837; *Alton Commercial Gazette,* July 9, 1839; *National Gazette,* July 6, 1840; *Mobile Commercial Register,* July 6, 1841; Larned, *op. cit.,* II, 483.

ation in the five years between 1829 and 1834. Some of
these probably had been sold and consolidated with other
plants, but the majority were considered *bona fide* examples of
the decline of the liquor trade.[46]   The Kentucky State Temperance Society attributed the closing of forty-six distilleries
to the aggressive work of its ninety auxiliaries.[47]   Temperance stores and temperance hotels were not uncommon in any
part of the country.   Twenty-two grocers of Poughkeepsie,
New York, in 1832 signed an agreement that they would sell
no more ardent spirits to be consumed in their stores.[48]   The
retailers of Ipswich, Massachusetts, decided to confine their
trade in intoxicants to wines and malt liquors.[49]   The English soldier-traveller, Coke, in 1832 observed many public-
houses at which distilled spirits were not obtainable.[50]   Since
abstinence from the use of ardent spirits was the accepted
temperance standard of the time, all such taverns and hotels
were known as temperance houses.   New York claimed to
have over a thousand of them in 1834, and Massachusetts
boasted that every town of importance within its limits offered a reputable lodging-house for the abstainer.[51]   Travellers returning from the Mississippi valley reported that
houses which sold only mild beverages were more numerous
in Ohio, Indiana and Illinois than in the eastern states.[52]
Some reformers regarded the multiplication of such taverns
with considerable misgiving, for the temperance cause was
often harmed in a community by the spectacle of inebriated

[46] *Annual Report, New York State Temperance Society* (1833);
Temperance Almanac (1834).
[47] *Am. Quart. Temp. Mag.*, February, 1833, p. 96.
[48] *Temperance Recorder*, Sept. 4, 1832, p. 55; *Mass. Spy*, April 7,
1830; *National Gazette*, April 7, 1840.
[49] *Temperance Recorder*, 1832, p. 56.
[50] E. T. Coke, *A Subaltern's Furlough*, I, 33.
[51] *Temperance Almanac* (1834); *Mass. Spy*, Dec. 11, 1833, June 11,
1834, Jan. 1, 1835.
[52] *Journal of the American Temperance Union*, January, 1839, p. 4.

patrons staggering out of establishments which conspicu-
ously displayed the sign "Temperance House."

Since no enduring reform of social customs could be effected without the support of the youth of the country, it
was inevitable that the temperance forces would attempt to
arouse the interest of the younger generation and enroll as
many as possible in the movement. Some states arranged
county conventions each year which expressed the ideas of
the young men and endeavoured to give them a larger place
in the councils of the reform.[53] In Massachusetts this phase
of the work received the active support of Horace Mann,
who served the cause of temperance with the same unselfish
devotion that characterized his efforts in behalf of a free
public school system. He was largely responsible for the
state convention held at Worcester in 1834 for the purpose
of launching a campaign to organize a young men's society
in every town in the state. In spite of the pressure of other
duties, he accepted a position of leadership and toured the
state that he might urge teachers to use their influence in
support of the temperance program.[54]

The work which Horace Mann championed in Massachusetts was well supported in the colleges and universities. Although undergraduates were not notoriously abstemious,
their attitude toward the use of ardent spirits seemed to be
changing, for almost every institution of higher learning
could point to an active temperance society as evidence that
the customs of former days were not in favour with all students. Commenting on the commencement exercises at Dartmouth College in 1833 the *New Hampshire Courier* said:
"The most striking feature of this annual college celebration,

[53] *Temperance Recorder*, June 5, 1832, p. 27; Dow, *Reminiscences*, pp.
212-213; Chase, *op. cit.*, p. 499; H. R. Frost, *Address to the Young
Men's Society of Charleston* (1832); *Documents and Records of the
Massachusetts Temperance Society*, pp. 61-62.
[54] *Mass. Spy*, July 2, 1834; Clark, *op. cit.*, p. 227.

and the one which appears most prominent to the eyes of a stranger, is the shocking extent to which vice and intoxication are carried on by the assembled crowd." [55]   Yet these boisterous excesses of good fellowship were probably no more representative of the attitude of the college community than the earnest efforts of the young men who had formed a temperance society on the Dartmouth campus in 1828.   Under the encouraging guidance of Dr. Reuben D. Mussey, professor of anatomy, whose temperance articles were nationally known, the organization became a real part of the institution's life.[56]   The question of abstinence and its effects furnished the subject for numerous debates and the material for literary compositions.   When speakers were in demand in the neighbouring towns, members of the college society were usually available to carry the message, with the result that their influence went far beyond the circle of their fellow students.[57]

Dartmouth was but one of many colleges enlisted in the fight against intemperance.   From the beginning of his presidency at Amherst, Herman Humphrey advocated temperance doctrines, which had seemed fundamental to him when he was assisting Lyman Beecher to launch the Connecticut Moral Society.[58]   He was ably supported by Edward Hitchcock, a member of the faculty, whose lectures and essays on hygiene were frequently pointed against the use of distilled spirits.   Together they interested John Tappan in the idea

[55] Cited in F. P. Wells, *History of Newbury, Vt.*, p. 256.

[56] Dr. Mussey had been a student under Dr. Rush at the University of Pennsylvania in 1809 and had helped to organize the Massachusetts Society for the Suppression of Intemperance in 1813.

[57] The Phi Beta Kappa society at Dartmouth voted in 1835 that "no individual ought to consider himself bound in the least degree by any practise heretofore existing, to furnish a treat of any kind upon his election as a member of this society."   See John K. Lord, *A History of Dartmouth College, 1815–1909*, pp. 267–269.

[58] J. B. Dunn, "History of the Temperance Movement," *Centennial Temperance Volume*, p. 430.

of forming an organization at the college to carry on a campaign which would line up the entire student body against the liquor traffic. Tappan advanced funds for prizes to encourage students to write essays on various phases of the question, and in 1830 an association was formed. In their enthusiasm the student leaders directed attention to the evil effect of the use of tobacco as well as liquor, calling the new organization the Anti-venenean Society and pledging its membership to abstinence from the use of anything poisonous to the human system. In spite of the inclusive character of the pledge, the members confined their efforts largely to the fight against ardent spirits, and the society for twenty years enrolled annually three-fourths of the student body.[59] At Brown, Francis Wayland, a member of the Massachusetts Temperance Society at the time he became president of the college, did not allow his administrative duties to turn him aside from a firm resolution to discredit the dealers in intoxicants. His influence became the greatest single factor in support of the reform in Providence.[60] Of the same spirit as Dr. Wayland were such college presidents as Joshua Bates of Middlebury, Jeremiah Day of Yale and Eliphalet Nott of Union. Dr. Nott was undoubtedly the most vigorous temperance advocate among the educators of his day. His lectures to the student body portrayed the evils of intemperance with terrific vividness, and his writings in numerous periodicals were regarded as authoritative expositions of the Biblical statements on the subject.[61]

Western as well as eastern schools figured prominently in the reform movement. In 1832 Kenyon College at Gambier, Ohio, the site of which five years before had been a deep wilderness, reported a society with more than 200 mem-

[59] Edward Hitchcock, *Reminiscences of Amherst College*, pp. 151–158.

[60] *Mass. Spy*, April 11, 1832.

[61] J. B. Dunn, *op. cit.*, p. 442; Cornelius Van Santvoord, *Memoirs of Eliphalet Nott*, pp. 181–182.

bers.   Though the leaders realized that many "deep-rooted prejudices" would have to be overcome, they felt confident of success because the "people generally in this region can read" and a campaign of education would not be wasted on them.[62] At the same time the work of this Episcopalian stronghold was matched by an earnest group of Congregationalists who were laying the foundation of Oberlin College in Lorain County of the Western Reserve.   Their covenant pledged them to abstain from all strong and unnecessary drinks, an obligation which made their settlement a model of sobriety and sent forth from the college young men and women eager to bear a hand in the conversion of the unreformed.[63]   The outstanding weakness in the work of these college societies was the lack of co-operation between different institutions. Each group, concerned with its own immediate neighbourhood, was but slightly informed of the character of the movement in other schools.   Great as was the potential power of the educated youth of the country, it was never fully utilized because of the failure to establish a bond of unity among the youthful workers.

The rôle of women in the reform had not been definitely settled at the time that Oberlin College, because of its co-educational policy, tended to emphasize the equal participation of men and women.   In 1826, when the American Temperance Society was formed, the leaders had been conscious of the value of feminine influence and had discussed its relation to the temperance organizations.   Justin Edwards had insisted that one of the conditions of success was the acceptance of the family group as the basic unit in the formation of new societies, and he had urged that the wife and mother

---

[62] *Temperance Recorder,* Oct. 2, 1832, p. 61.

[63] J. H. Fairchild, *Oberlin, The Colony and the College.*   Other colleges which possessed societies whose work was recognized were: Princeton, Williams, Dickinson, Jefferson (Pa.), Miami (Ohio), and the University of Georgia.

be permitted to become an active member.[64] Some there were who did not go so far as Edwards; admitting the need of woman's aid, they believed that her influence would generally be in favour of the cause and could best be exercised in the home. In this reform, as in the anti-slavery movement, her membership in societies seemed unnecessary and undesirable, since it might alienate men opposed to the entrance of women into new fields of activity. A few concealed their innate prejudices behind the assertion that by taking a pledge to abstain from the use of ardent spirits women would impair the "usual confidence" which all gentlemen had in their purity and firmness of character.[65] As a result of these differences of opinion, there was great diversity in the practice of the temperance forces. Although in some communities women were specifically excluded from membership, they were admitted on an equality with men in most societies. At times, however, they chose to form separate groups that they might better serve the interests of their sex.[66] A convention at Worcester, Massachusetts, in 1831, and another at Utica, New York, in 1833 pronounced definitely in favour of encouraging women to assume a more responsible rôle in temperance work.[67]

Women did not work entirely through the regular organizations. Associations to boycott stores which sold ardent spirits were an effective way for house-wives to fight the liquor traffic. An Ohio society in 1829 adopted the following resolution: "We will discountenance all addresses in any of the male sex with a view of matrimony, if they shall be known

[64] *P. T. D.*, I, 15.

[65] Emily C. Blackman, *op. cit.*, p. 568.

[66] For opposing views in regard to the activity of women see *Temperance Manual* (1836), pp. 11–12; Clark, *op. cit.*, pp. 229–230; John Boyd, *Annals of Winchester, Conn.*, p. 494; *N. Y. Observer*, Feb. 28, 1829, March 12, 1834.

[67] *Mass. Spy*, Nov. 2, 1831; *Am. Quart. Temp. Mag.*, February, 1834, p. 27.

to drink ardent spirits, either periodically or on any public occasion." Such earnestness would not be denied.[68] After 1835 societies, formed to alleviate the sufferings of the drunkard's family, gave women an opportunity to express their sympathy for the unfortunate in practical service.[69] Their success in dealing with the poverty and misery that followed in the wake of intemperance brought commendation and recognition from the temperance leaders, and a new door was opened to them in the form of Temperance Beneficial Associations, which admitted women on the same terms with men.[70] These groups secured large followings in the cities, where the protection in case of sickness, offered at slight cost, was attractive to the working woman. Though their sphere of activity was constantly expanding, prior to 1840 women did not make their influence felt in the larger councils of the reform movement. During the decade following, however, they used their position in the temperance work, as in the anti-slavery crusade, to further the cause of sex equality and women's rights.[71]

The tendency to make abstinence from strong drink a matter of family concern raised the question of the proper attitude to be adopted by the temperance societies toward children. Many leaders were opposed to allowing boys and girls to sign the pledge, on the ground that children were unable to understand the solemn character of the obligation and, therefore, could not be expected to abide by it in later life. Others feared that if the immature were enrolled the charge of coercion would be brought against the temperance forces. The opposition would be able to accuse them of imposing opinions upon minds not able to reach a rational

68 *Pa. Temp. Rec.*, April, 1835, p. 14; *N. Y. Observer*, Jan. 17, 1829.

69 Henry Hall, *History of Auburn*, pp. 255–256. This developed into the Martha Washington societies.

70 *Constitution of the Female Branch of the Temperance Beneficial Association* (Philadelphia, 1838).

71 *Infra* pp. 215–217.

decision. Still other leaders challenged the advisability of swelling the ranks with recruits who might desert as they grew older. Belief in the old adage of the bent twig, however, was strong enough to make a majority of the reformers eager to win the allegiance of children. Through the medium of Sunday Schools, many boys and girls above the age of twelve were enrolled in young people's temperance societies.[72] As these groups increased in number, the age limit of twelve was generally adopted, although some localities allowed none under fourteen to sign the pledge.[73] Not every community was sufficiently interested in the children to organize a young people's society; some preferred to have the youth become nominal members of the groups primarily designed to express the conviction of their parents. Where children's societies were in existence, special meetings were arranged at which programs of songs and recitations were presented by the youthful volunteers.[74] The rhymed version of the pledge, widely used during the thirties, took a position beyond that adopted by adults:

> This little band do with our hand
> The pledge now sign to drink no wine,
> Nor brandy red, to turn our head,
> Nor whisky hot that makes the sot,
> Nor fiery rum to turn our home
> Into a hell where none could dwell—
> Whence peace would fly, where hope would die,
> And love expire 'mid such a fire;
> So here we pledge perpetual hate
> To all that can intoxicate.[75]

[72] *Boston Recorder*, July 23, 1829; *N. Y. Evangelist*, Aug. 3, 1833.

[73] *Journal of Humanity*, June 3, 1830, p. 6; *Mass. Spy*, March 21, 1832; *Pa. Temp. Rec.*, February, 1836, p. 11.

[74] *Journal of the American Temperance Union*, July, 1837, p. 112.

[75] *Columbus Democrat*, Aug. 24, 1839; Clark, *op. cit.*, 44–45; E. T. Fairbanks, *The Town of St. Johnsbury, Vt.*, p. 292.

Although many in "this little band" enlisted in the temperance forces under the guidance of their parents, some had already experienced the poverty and misery which too often accompany intemperance. They embodied a powerful emotional appeal, which remained a potential force until used with telling effect in the decade of the forties.

As the year 1835 drew to a close, the reformers felt confident that victory was well within their grasp. A million men, women and children were actively engaged in promoting temperance principles. The tone of public opinion in regard to the use of ardent spirits, they believed, was becoming daily more favourable to their cause. The achievements of the five years just past loomed up before them in more impressive fashion than the obstacles which remained to be overcome. Enthusiasm ran high and found conspicuous outlet in a series of regularly recurring conventions. There were city, county and state conventions with their schedules of speeches, reports, resolutions and petitions. In every state the delegates from town and village societies assembled annually and portrayed in terms belonging only to the zealous the progress of the reform in their respective districts.[76] With few exceptions these reports served to increase the rejoicing at the signs of success apparent on all sides. But had the enthusiasts carefully analysed the situation, they would have seen, what some of the leaders already feared, that the advance of the temperance forces would be halted not so much by opposition or indifference as by dissension within the ranks.

[76] *Georgia Journal*, June 5, 1830, June 9, 1831; *Ohio Monitor*, Feb. 24, 1834; *North Carolina Standard*, Jan. 23, 1835; *Anniversary Report of the Pennsylvania Temperance Society* (1833); *P. T. D.*, I, 343-345.

CHAPTER VIII

DISSENSION WITHIN THE RANKS

THE United States Temperance Union, created by the Philadelphia convention in 1833, won no victories under the leadership of General Stephen Van Rensselaer. This was not entirely the leader's fault; his associates, earnest reformers in their respective states, seem to have been little interested in a national organization to unify the work of state and local societies. At any rate, the special committee on ways and means of effecting centralized control allowed three years to elapse before it took any action. Then, in May, 1836, it issued a call for a national convention of societies in the United States and Canada to be held on the fourth of the following August in Saratoga Springs, New York. The response indicated that a spirit of unity was not lacking. Three hundred and forty-eight delegates, representing nineteen states and Upper and Lower Canada, enjoyed the hospitality of the New York State Temperance Society during the sessions. Sentiment in the convention strongly favoured an enlargement of the old Union in order to include the Canadas and any other part of North America that desired to co-operate. Accordingly, a plan of re-organization was worked out, the name being changed from United States to American Temperance Union. Henceforth, any society in North America might become auxiliary to the Union. As a final step the official personnel was entirely altered, and John H. Cocke of Virginia was chosen president.[1]

[1] P. T. D., II, 13–14; *Journal*, January, 1837, pp. 1–2; Marsh, *op. cit.*, 44–45.

General Cocke was quite as philanthropic and earnest as his predecessor. His career had been one of constant ac-tivity in many of the religious and social movements of his day.[2] As a young man, he had promoted Bible and tract societies in Virginia, eventually becoming an influential and generous member of the American Board of Commissioners for Foreign Missions. Like many other Virginia slave-holders, he was interested in the work of the American Colonization Society and served as one of its vice-presidents. Having accepted membership in the American Temperance Society shortly after its formation, he devoted his time to promoting the reform in his own neighbourhood. That his efforts were not in vain is attested by the high rank in temperance work early attained by Fluvanna County, where his estate was located.[3] General Cocke was fortunate in his associates on the new Union's executive committee, for the convention had selected men who had distinguished them-selves for energy and ability in their respective states.[4] As chairman, Edward C. Delavan of Albany inspired con-fidence because of his seven successful years at the helm of the strongest state society in the country. He had for lieutenants Joshua W. Leavitt, editor of the *New York Evangelist;* [5] John Tappan, charter member of the Massa-chusetts Society for the Suppression of Intemperance;

[2] Like Van Rensselaer, John H. Cocke was a landed proprietor. He had served as general commanding the Virginia troops during the war of 1812. His extensive estate in Fluvanna County was known far and wide as "Bremo." *National Cyclopedia of American Biography,* IV, 181.

[3] *Journal of Humanity,* files, 1831.

[4] The honorary vice-presidents were Matthew Newkirk of Pennsyl-vania, Samuel Hubbard of Massachusetts, Bishop Stuart of Canada, Theodore Frelinghuysen of New Jersey, Reuben H. Walworth of New York, Governor Lucas of Ohio, and ex-Governor Dunlap of Maine. *P. T. D.,* II, 14.

[5] Leavitt, like many other temperance advocates, was also an anti-slavery enthusiast. He followed Birney rather than Garrison. Under his editorship the *Evangelist* constantly preached total abstinence from all that intoxicates.

Christian Keener, executive secretary in Maryland; John T. Norton, financier of the Connecticut society; Isaac Collins and Isaac S. Lloyd, efficient agents for the Pennsylvania state society.

Having settled without difficulty the organization and personnel of the American Temperance Union, the convention turned to a more troublesome problem, that of stating fundamental policies. Early in the sessions it became evident that those in favour of a more drastic wording of the pledge were sufficiently numerous to compel acceptance of their views. Justin Edwards and Lyman Beecher led this movement for an obligation that would bind all temperance advocates to "total abstinence from all that can intoxicate." Although their plan to place fermented liquors under the ban met with the approval of a majority, it was not accomplished without a struggle. Many were opposed to abstinence from the use of wine because they believed such action would result in a disavowal of Scriptural teachings on the subject. Some feared that the term *intoxicants* might be construed to include malt beverages, the use of which did not meet with their disapproval. There were others in the convention who sympathized with the more enthusiastic reformers, but believed that it was wise to proceed slowly.[6] Professor Alonzo Potter of Union College and Dr. Levi H. Reese of Baltimore were leaders of the group that counselled caution, lest the adoption of a radical pledge should drive the conservatives into open hostility.[7] As a result of this long, and sometimes heated, discussion came a resolution worded to placate the moderates:

[6] *P. T. D.,* II, 21, 26; Marsh, *op. cit.,* pp. 44–45.

[7] Professor Potter later became a bishop of the Protestant Episcopal Church. His support of the temperance cause was sincere, but he believed that extremists should be restrained, lest they injure the cause by their excessive enthusiasm. M. A. De Wolfe Howe, *Memoirs of the Life and Services of the Rt. Rev. Alonzo Potter,* pp. 74–75.

That as abstinence from the use, as a beverage, of intoxicating liquor, is the only course in which it can be rationally expected that intemperate persons can ever be permanently reformed, and as the example and kind moral influence of the temperate is the grand means of leading the intemperate to adopt and pursue a course so essential to their present and future good, the more extensively this course is adopted by the moral part of the community, the more useful, in our view, will be the influence of their example, and the more speedy and universal the triumph of the temperance cause.[8]

As a further concession to the minority, the conciliatory spirit of the assemblage was embodied in another resolution:

That, in maintaining the propriety and necessity of total abstinence *from all that can intoxicate,* this convention make no decision as to the grounds of our united action, because we believe that our harmony and efficiency in the great cause of temperance forbid us to conflict, unnecessarily, with those who differ from us in theory, while we are united in practice.[9]

Thus, in language marvellously obscure, was a bid made for the support of those who, finding no fault with the use of wine, were willing to abstain, if it was deemed expedient.

The action of the Saratoga convention was no great surprise to informed observers. Although a majority of societies, previous to 1836, carefully distinguished between distilled spirits and other beverages containing alcohol, there had been opposition in many quarters to such a distinction. While some insisted that wine and beer, since they were seldom used to excess, were important instruments in suppressing intemperance, others were convinced that the use of fermented beverages was but the mild beginning of a

8 *P. T. D.,* II, 25.
9 *Ibid.,* 26.

drunkard's career.[10]   The latter view was constantly presented to readers of the *Journal of Humanity* with the result
that many local societies, ignoring the attitude of their
state organization, adopted constitutions which enjoined
abstinence not only from ardent spirits, but also from wine,
cider and beer.   As early as 1829 this was done in Falls
Spring, Virginia, and within four years the new type of
society had a large following in many sections.[11]   Ohio
reported seventeen groups whose pledge forbade the use of
wine, except as medicine or for sacramental purposes.   At
the same time the most successful societies in Vermont were
those that directed their pledge against "all that can intoxicate."   Conventions in other states discussed the wine
question, but usually failed to take action because of a
pronounced difference of opinion.[12]

So long as the radical groups felt that they were out-
numbered, they tactfully refrained from any attempt to
force the issue.   A rapid increase in their ranks, however,
convinced them in the autumn of 1836 that they were no
longer a minority faction.   During 1835 and the first six
months of 1836 state conventions in New Hampshire, New

[10] *Documents and Records of the Massachusetts Temperance Society*,
November 5, 1827; *Journal of Humanity*, May 27, 1829; *Georgia Journal*,
May 22, 1830.   The editor of the *Georgia Journal* spoke one word in
support of temperance and two against the tariff, when he insisted that
heavy duties upon imported liquors were partially responsible for the
growth of intemperance.   The imposition of the "American System,"
he asserted, had placed comparatively harmless beverages of European
production beyond the reach of the poor, compelling them to use such
"villainous stuff" as Yankee rum and Kentucky "blue ruin."   Repeal
of the duties on madeira, sherry, port and other wines would greatly
strengthen the temperance cause, for it was well known that drunkenness was uncommon in wine-drinking countries.   See *Journal*, June 5,
July 3, 1830.

[11] *Mass. Spy*, July 7, 1830, May 11, 1831; *Boston Recorder*, July 30,
1829.

[12] *Am. Quart. Temp. Mag.*, May, 1833, p. 174; *Temp. Rec.*, August 6,
1833, p. 47, February 4, 1834, p. 97; *Mass. Spy*, July 3, 1833; *The Galenian* (Galena, Ill.), March 21, 1834.

Jersey and Pennsylvania had substituted *intoxicating liquors* for *ardent spirits* in the pledge and had urged all auxiliaries to do likewise.[13]   The *Temperance Recorder* in accordance with instructions from the New York State Temperance Society had come out definitely in favour of total abstinence from all alcoholic beverages.   In explaining the new policy the editor wrote:

> Our views with regard to pure wine are, that the Bible sanctions its moderate use—that there can be no immorality in such use, under certain circumstances; but in our present condition with the fact that pure wine is fatal to the recovery of the drunkard, because it intoxicates, often forms the appetite for stronger drinks in the temperate, and its use by the rich hinders the poor from uniting with temperance societies—that all, or nearly all the wine in this country, is a most vile compound; these are the reasons why we urge abstinence from all wine.[14]

Other temperance periodicals had followed the course of the *Recorder*, till only a few clung to the doctrine that the use of wine was not contrary to temperance principles.[15]   Then it was that the teetotalers, as they were called, launched their campaign at the Saratoga convention and won a vote of confidence from the national organization.[16]

The success at Saratoga was but a skirmish preliminary to a prolonged struggle in almost every city and hamlet throughout the country.   Whether the temperance forces would support the American Temperance Union in its new program depended not so much on the decision of a national convention as on the attitude of hundreds of local societies.

[13] *Temp. Rec.*, April, 1835, p. 20, March, 1836, p. 3; *Pa. Temp. Rec.*, February, 1836, p. 15, April, 1836, p. 28; *P. T. D.*, I, 455, 474.

[14] *P. T. D.*, I, 514; *Temp. Rec.*, March, 1835, p. 10; April, 1835, p. 17.

[15] *Pa. Temp. Rec.*, October, 1835, p. 60.

[16] The name, teetotaler, seems to have been used first in Scotland, where it designated those temperance advocates who objected to the use of wine. When they signed their names to the pledge they usually added the initials T. A., standing for total abstinence.

During the autumn of 1836 the Union's executive committee decided to carry on its campaign through the columns of a new periodical devoted exclusively to the interests of the national organization.[17]   Edward C. Delavan, as he had so often done when the treasury was low, provided the necessary funds, and the initial number of the *Journal of the American Temperance Union* appeared in Philadelphia in January, 1837, carrying at the head of its first column a revised pledge:

We, the undersigned, do agree that we will not use intoxicating liquors as a beverage, nor traffic in them; that we will not provide them as entertainment or for persons in our employment; and that, in all suitable ways, we will discountenance their use throughout the community.[18]

In its editorials the *Journal* assailed those reformers who found no sin in the moderate use of good wines.   Their example, so the editor reasoned, would in the long run betray the temperance cause in the camp of its friends.

There was now an opportunity to test sentiment on this point.   Every society which affiliated with the Union became *ipso facto* a supporter of the new pledge.   Conservative groups which refused to become auxiliaries were not considered as active temperance organizations by the societies

[17] Marsh, *op. cit.*, pp. 45–46.   The intention of the committee was that E. C. Delavan should become editor of the *Journal* and executive secretary of the Union, but he declined the honour and John Marsh was chosen in his stead.   Eight years before Marsh had resigned his pastorate in Connecticut to become an agent of the American Temperance Society, in which work he was signally successful.   From Boston he went to Philadelphia where he accepted a position as executive secretary of the Pennsylvania Temperance Society and made it one of the oustanding state organizations.   Through his temperance addresses and pamphlets he became widely known among those interested in the reform.

[18] *Journal of the American Temperance Union*, January, 1837, p. 1. (To be cited *Journal*.)

in the Union.   At first reports from the executive committee
were encouraging, as society after society placed wines and
cider, and occasionally beer, under the ban.[19]   The apparently widespread sentiment in favour of the new pledge,
however, was not a fair indication of the real state of affairs.
Although in most local groups a majority was willing to
push forward a campaign against the use of mild intoxicants,
it sometimes happened that only a determined minority was
so inclined.   Then, too, dissension within the ranks was not
so evident in the refusal of societies to join the Union, as
in individual secessions from societies which did become
auxiliaries.   In Maine, the conservatives controlled a state
convention in 1837, whereupon the radicals seceded and
formed an organization of their own known as the Maine
Temperance Union, thus dividing the temperance forces in
the state into two hostile camps.[20]   The serious character
of such divisions and the effect on the progress of reform
served to discourage many faithful leaders.   In September,
1836, Edward C. Delavan resigned as chairman of the New
York state society, because he believed that his former
associates were not ready to follow him in a vigorous attack
on vendors and users of wine.   In later years he confessed
that at the time he was depressed by the defection of his
friends, not more than one-third of whom agreed with his
views on the question.   He estimated that nearly 2,000
societies failed to adopt the new pledge, some abandoning the
cause entirely.[21]   Of the situation in Ohio Governor Trimble
wrote:

[19] *Annual Report of the New York Young Men's Total Abstinence
Society* (1837); *Constitution of the Providence County Temperance
Society* (1838); *P. T. D.*, II, 42–46; Clark, *op. cit.*, pp. 34–35, 29.   Ex-
act definition of *intoxicating* was not attempted by the Union.

[20] Dow, *Reminiscences*, pp. 231–235.   In Georgia the division termi-
nated the existence of the old state society.   Scomp, *King Alcohol in
the Realm of King Cotton*, p. 319.

[21] See letter of E. C. Delavan in P. T. Winskill, *The Temperance Movement and Its Workers*, II, 205–206.

The temperance cause is on the advance in this place since the adoption, by a small portion of the old society, of the pledge of total abstinence from all drinks, as a beverage, that will intoxicate. We began a few weeks since with 48 members, and increased to 100, and hope to double again at our next meeting. The wine, cider and beer drinkers contend zealously for the use of these articles, even should habitual drunkenness occasionally follow. The societies that have adopted the total abstinence pledge are active and increasing their numbers. Those societies that go upon the principle that distilled spirits alone should be excluded, are dragging heavily, and I think retrograding, rather than advancing.[22]

Conditions in Ohio were typical.[23]   Advocates of the new pledge were slowly winning ground, but their victories had been costly ones.   In New York, for example, the statistics for the years 1836 and 1839 told the story.   In 1836 the state society reported almost 1300 auxiliaries with a membership of 229,000, while three years later 1178 societies enrolled 131,000 members who had signed the comprehensive pledge.[24]   As serious as the loss of members was the fact that many generous contributors to temperance funds were not willing to give financial support to an organization that barred the use of wine.[25]   Handicapped by lack of resources,

[22] *Journal,* March, 1837, p. 39.

[23] As many of the active leaders in Ohio and elsewhere supported the new pledge, old societies frequently were left leaderless, a loss which hastened their dissolution. Scomp, *op. cit.,* 319–320.

[24] *P. T. D.,* II, 126.

[25] No state society before 1840 had any definite plan for the supply of its treasury. Voluntary subscriptions and collections taken at meetings furnished the bulk of the funds. Large donations were made to the cause at frequent intervals by such prominent business men as John and Arthur Tappan, Stephen Van Rensselaer, John Jacob Astor, Peter Remsen, Edward Delavan, John H. Cocke and Henry Dwight. As donations declined when the wine controversy reached its height, many societies resorted to the assessment of dues. *Mass. Spy,* June 14, 1835; *P. T. D.,* II, 29; Charles Jewett, *The Temperance Cause, Past, Present and Future,* pp. 15–28.

the radicals were further embarrassed by attacks from the moderates, who forgot the real enemy in their desire to hold the reform within reasonable limits. In many sections the moderates were so numerous that for a time they turned attention from intemperance and its remedy to a consideration of the merits of the juice of the grape.

A bitter pamphlet warfare ensued over the wine question, each faction claiming for its views the stamp of authority. In its early stages the controversy revolved about the question of whether the reformers had been basing their policy on a false premise. It had been generally assumed that Dr. Benjamin Rush was correct when he recommended the use of beer and light wines as a corrective of intemperance.   His theory, modified slightly by those who came after him, stressed the importance of breaking down mankind's fondness for distilled spirits by substituting milder beverages.   The result, he believed, would be abstinence from the use of the worst form of intoxicants and consequent escape from the physical and mental evils of excessive drinking.   The reformers of the first three decades of the nineteenth century interpreted this to mean entire abstinence from ardent spirits and temperate use of fermented and malt liquors.   Sceptics there were, however, who challenged the theory, pointing out that the "specific evil" in ardent spirits, alcohol, was also present in fermented wine.[26]   They insisted that, since intoxication resulted from the use of wines in the same fashion as from the use of distilled liquors, the effect on the human mind and body was as harmful in one case as in the other. No less sincere friends of temperance, however, cited the sobriety of European wine-producing countries as evidence

[26] L. M. Sargent, *Letter to Rev. Caleb Stetson,* p. 25. Stetson published an article in the *Christian Examiner,* March, 1836, in which he lamented the tendency of some reformers to break down the distinction between distilled and fermented liquors.   Sargent's answer denied that the temperance forces could consistently make a distinction which rested upon ignorance of the alcoholic content of wine.

that intemperance in the United States was traceable to the American's use of distilled rather than fermented beverages. This group maintained that any nation could be made sober, if its citizens would rely upon light wines and beer for their stimulants.   They saw nothing but disaster for the temperance cause in the attempt to place mild liquors under the ban.[27] Their fears were well expressed by a correspondent in the *American Quarterly Temperance Magazine:*

By admitting wine, beer and cider into the temperance pledge, we are endeavoring to make the use of them as disreputable as the use of ardent spirits.   We are endeavoring to make the sin of drinking cider as great as the sin of drinking whiskey. The intent is to elevate the offense of cider drinking, beer drinking and wine drinking up to the enormity of dram drinking. . . . This view is fallacious.   Instead of elevating the offense of cider drinking, it will depress the offense of dram drinking down to the level of cider drinking.   It dilutes the temperance pledge. The moment the sin of dram drinking shall be deemed no greater than the sin of cider drinking, the whole fabric will be in ruins.[28]

Of those who dissented from the foregoing opinion, none were more energetic in placing their conclusions before the public than Edward C. Delavan, Lucius M. Sargent and Dr. Eliphalet Nott.   Before he became interested in temperance work, Delavan had been a connoisseur of choice wines. Having sacrificed the contents of his well stocked cellar for conscience' sake, he began to investigate the wine situation with hope of securing information which would persuade his friends to follow his example.   From conversations with wine importers and vintners, from personal observation and from the reports of expert chemists he collected a mass of material pertaining to the adulteration of fermented liquors. He published this information periodically in the *Temperance*

[27] *Mass. Spy,* April 4, 25, 1832.
[28] *Am. Quart. Temp. Mag.,* August, 1834, p. 75.

Recorder and distributed some of it in pamphlet form.   The
evidence tended to show that most wines used in the United
States were either vile adulterations or else cheap imitations
of European vintages.   Hence, any argument that wines
were harmless, Delavan maintained, was inapplicable to the
American situation, since only the wealthy received pure
stocks.   Commercial brands were heavily freighted with distilled spirits and drugs before they were sold and were,
therefore, more to be shunned than unadulterated whisky.[29]
There could be no defence for traffic in such concoctions.
Sargent, as well as Delavan, was interested in the terrible
frauds perpetrated by wine-dealers, but he was primarily
anxious to refute the widely accepted idea that European
wine countries were singularly temperate.   Basing his argument on observations of American travellers, he sought to
convince his readers that fermented liquors caused as much
intemperance as rum, brandy or whisky.   He further insisted that not a single drunkard would ever be reformed by
substituting one form of alcohol for another.   His conclusion was that no great decrease in intemperance would be
effected so long as temperance societies tolerated wine-drinking among their members.   The distinction between alcohol
produced by fermentation and that produced by distillation
seemed to him absurd, for in both cases the poison had the
same effect.[30]

Dr. Nott's chief contribution to this controversy was
contained in his ten lectures delivered to students at Union
College in the winter of 1838–1839.   His central theme was
an exposition of Scriptural injunctions in regard to the use

[29] Mr. Delavan republished the bulk of this material in a pamphlet
in 1850.   See E. C. Delavan, *Adulterations of Liquors*.   One unusual
example of adulteration for which the author vouched must have tested
the credulity of his readers.   He stated that the famous "nutty flavor"
of madeira was produced by dissolving a bag of roaches in the liquor.

[30] L. M. Sargent, *op. cit.*, pp. 10–25.   For the same views see Gerrit
Smith's argument in *Correspondence on the Principles of Right Reasoning Applicable to Temperance*.

of fermented liquors.   In the light of careful scholarship he attempted to explain several points which had long bothered temperance workers.   Did the Old Testament specifically approve the use of wine?   Were the teachings of the New Testament in accord with those of the Old on this subject? Were temperance advocates who refused to give up the use of wine because of religious scruples justified? [31]   Dr. Nott believed that a study of the Scriptures would correct many popular misconceptions.   His own position could be briefly stated.[32]   Although the Bible authorized the use of certain wines in Palestine, there were other wines, even in Palestine, the use of which was forbidden.   Nine words in the Hebrew of the Old Testament had been translated into English by the single word, wine.   But their various meanings in the original text, Dr. Nott maintained, could not be adequately expressed by any such inaccurate translation.   His study of different usages enabled him to assure his readers that the use of intoxicating liquors seldom received Scriptural commendation.   The wine repeatedly approved by the sacred writers was the juice of the grape in its natural state. Any fermented fruit juice was denounced as a "mocker." It was armed with the serpent's bite and the adder's sting.[33]

[31] Many friends of temperance had insisted that the Bible expressly recommended the moderate use of wine. This they considered an injunction which it was not for them to question. See Gustavus F. Davis, *A Sermon delivered in the Baptist Meeting House, Hartford, May 25, 1831.*

[32] Dr. Nott was not the first commentator to make this point. See William Shelton, *An Address before the Citizens of Buffalo,* pp. 6–8; Edward Hitchcock, *An Essay on Alcoholic and Narcotic Substances.*

[33] Eliphalet Nott, *Lectures on Temperance,* 75–121. Nott maintained that some alcohol was present in the unfermented juice of the grape. He also believed that the Scriptures approved in a few instances the use of *slightly* fermented wine. These beverages according to his contention were not intoxicating. This fine distinction was challenged by Dr. R. D. Mussey, Moses Stuart of Andover and E. C. Delavan. The ensuing controversy was long but friendly, Dr. Nott finally capitulating to his friends and agreeing that the Scriptures placed all fermented beverages under the ban. Marsh, *op. cit.,* 166–170.

The wine served at the famous marriage feast in Cana of Galilee was unfermented, and it was a similar beverage that Paul recommended to Timothy for his "stomach's sake." Few Syrian wines were of a sort with the fermented mixtures commonly used by Europeans and Americans.[34]

The appeal to the Scriptures was not ended by Dr. Nott's exhaustive exposition. For ten years the controversy raged within the temperance ranks, fuel being added occasionally in the form of spirited arguments from outsiders. The radicals viewed such attacks on the reform as that of Bishop Hopkins with disdain. They explained it as an indication that "fashionable, wealthy, wine-drinking congregations" in the Episcopal Church were displeased with total abstinence and propaganda in its favour.[35] Conservatives, on the other hand, charged radical leaders with betraying the temperance movement to its foes. The whole discussion of the wine question had been injected by those who desired to engender strife and start a factional quarrel. It was a clever plot to wreck the reform upon the rocks of internal dissension. In order to quiet the fears of the conservatives and meet attacks from outsiders who were making capital out of the controversy, the radicals spent considerable time and money in explaining their views. The most damaging charge against them was that they were trying to interfere with the use of wine for sacramental purposes. This they denied, insisting that their espousal of total abstinence did not force them to make a decision in regard to sacramental wine, since that more properly belonged to the deliberation of ecclesiastical bodies. Although there was a case against the use of intoxicants, for evidence indicated that the early Christian Church used unfermented beverages in celebrating

[34] Nott, *Lectures on Temperance,* pp. 161–177.

[35] *Supra,* pp. 120–121; also see *Reply to Bishop Hopkins' Attack,* By An Episcopalian, p. 9.

the Lord's Supper, it was the intention of the reformers to avoid a controversy on this point.[36]

But such forbearance was not for long. Before 1840 aggressive leaders were convinced that they had made a mistake by side-stepping the "communion question." Their failure to take a definite stand seemed to indicate that they feared a majority of church members would oppose them. Seeking to rectify this tactical error, they began a campaign to persuade ecclesiastical governing bodies to modify their eucharistic regulations. In 1841 a quarterly journal, *The Enquirer*, was established at Albany for the purpose of keeping the question before the public.[37]   In its columns appeared opinions by leading clergymen in different denominations. While all agreed that every church should be urged to study the practice of the early Christian Church, at least half the correspondents were opposed to any propaganda which might give colour to the charge that temperance reformers were attempting to dictate the kind of wine to be used in the celebration of the Lord's Supper. Some deplored all discussion of the matter, because it would inevitably involve the disputants in a larger controversy over the right of private judgment in the interpretation of the Scriptures. Evidently supporters of the *Enquirer* thought their efforts were not sufficiently rewarded, for in 1843 they abandoned their original policy and devoted the columns of the journal to the pathology of intemperance.[38]   Other

---

[36] *Temp. Rec.*, August, 1835; *Enquirer, December*, 1841, p. 18.

[37] Funds for the *Enquirer* were supplied by E. C. Delavan and a few friends. The editorial work was under Delavan's supervision. *Enquirer*, December, 1841.

[38] It is impossible to determine just how much this controversy affected the practice of Protestant denominations. Some congregations adopted resolutions against the use of fermented wine at communion, but the majority seem to have continued to use whatever wine was available, regardless of its alcoholic content. *N. Y. Tribune*, August 11, 1841; *Enquirer*, December, 1842.

temperance publications failed to take up the work, no doubt fearing the consequences of forcing the issue.[39]

While these controversies were threatening the unity of the temperance forces, another problem was responsible for additional discord. The national convention at Philadelphia in 1833 had condemned the traffic in ardent spirits and pointed out iniquities in the system under which liquor dealers were prospering. Though public control of the liquor trade, definitely established during the colonial period, had been put into effect in every state, there were many objections to the manner in which the control was exercised. The licensing system seemed far from an ideal solution. Some counselled a more vigorous enforcement of existing statutes, while others demanded that no governmental sanction be given to an immoral business. During the decade of the thirties the statutes generally provided that spirituous and fermented liquors might be sold in two types of establishment, in inns and taverns furnishing accommodations for man and beast, or in groceries, apothecary shops and victualling houses. The latter were forbidden to permit tippling on the premises.[40] In practice these limitations were frequently ignored. Retailers who made no pretence to accommodate the travelling public secured licences as reputable inn-holders and tavern-keepers. Others got around the regulations by taking out grocery licences and then converting their establishments into grog-shops of a low order. Chi-

---

[39] Temperance publications, however, continued to present evidence to show that the Bible did not place the stamp of approval upon the use of the intoxicants in any form. See Moses Stuart, *Scriptural View of the Wine Question*, pp. 54–56.

[40] Convenient summaries of licence laws for various localities will be found in the following: *Essex Register* (Salem, Mass.), July 4, 1820; *Mass. Spy*, June 22, 1831; Caleb Ticknor, *Prize Address to the Honorable Corporation of the City of New York* (1834); J. H. Stinness, *Rhode Island Legislation against Strong Drink*, pp. 28–29; E. O. Randall and D. J. Ryan, *History of Ohio*, IV, 510–517.

canery in granting licences and violations of the laws were so frequent that in the cities grog-shops and tippling-houses, forerunners of the American saloon, were the rule rather than the exception.[41] Yet none of them could have kept their doors open a day had the laws been strictly enforced.

While this situation caused some reformers to demand its immediate remedy through legislation, many were inclined to ignore the liquor traffic entirely. Their concern was with the consumer not the purveyor of intoxicants. Alteration of existing statutes was far from the purpose of editors of the *Journal of Humanity* as is evident from the following statements:

The American Temperance Society, it seems to us, stands pledged to the public fully, and we trust irrevocably, never to make any appeal to legislators or officers of the law, for the aid of authority in changing the habits of any class of their fellow citizens.   Its appeal is to the people.[42]

In regard to methods to be followed in the work of reform they were equally explicit:

Nothing can be more injudicious than an appeal to the civil power by a temperance society. Where the doctrine of abstinence has obtained, by legitimate means,—such as the influence of example and appeals to the reason and conscience,—such power over a community as to command a spontaneous vote of banishment against ardent spirit, we are glad to hear of it, and publish it with pleasure, as an evidence of the progress of reform.

---

[41] The licensing authority was usually in the hands of county judges or town selectmen and city aldermen. *N. Y. Observer*, Dec. 20, 1828, Feb. 21, 1829, Sept. 26, 1829; *Journal of Humanity*, June 3, 1829; *Natchez* (Miss.) *Statesman and Gazette*, June 20, 1829; *Report of Committee of Massachusetts Society for Suppression of Intemperance* (1831), *Mass, Spy*, March 5, 1834; *Pa. Temp. Rec.*, May, 1835, pp. 17–19, February, 1836, p. 9; *Charleston Courier*, August 12, 1839.

[42] *Journal of Humanity*, October 14, 1830, p. 82.

Temperance societies should look to such things as likely to be among the happy results of their labors,—not as proper to be used as means of attaining their object. . . . We attribute the astonishing success of temperance efforts, in no small degree to the scrupulous care, with which agents and societies generally have avoided every measure that could lead to the association of their labors, even in the minds of the ignorant and prejudiced, with the operations of government and law.[43]

Those who shared these views talked much of the power of moral suasion and the correct application of Christian principles of light and love, the inference being that vice could be dispelled by the light of truth, if care was taken not to offend the sensibilities of the erring one. It was folly, they reasoned, to force upon man by legislative enactment that virtue which he could only possess by the dictates of his conscience and the energy of his will. Underlying this unwillingness to resort to legislation was the fear that the temperance movement would be torn asunder by political strife. Many leaders believed that as soon as an attempt was made to alter or abolish the licensing system, the enemies of temperance would have an opportunity to draw the reformers into politics. Such a turn of affairs would be nothing short of disastrous. It would mean political parties constantly angling for the temperance vote with the result that temperance objectives would be lost amid the storm and stress of local, state and national elections.[44] To escape these consequences most societies refrained from attacking the licensing system and refused, as societies, to endorse particular men and measures. A few groups, it is true, pledged their members not to vote for any man for public office

43 *Ibid.*, June 10, 1830, p. 10.
44 *Ibid.*, January 27, 1831, p. 142; *Pa. Temp. Rec.*, March, 1835, p. 1; *Am. Quart. Temp. Mag.*, February, 1833, pp. 61–62; *Temp. Rec.*, Nov. 5, 1833, p. 67; Walter Channing, *Thoughts on the Temperance Reform* (1834).

whose influence was hostile to temperance, but prior to 1836 even such a pledge was often regarded as a dangerous principle.[45]

To some influential leaders, however, the slow process of changing public opinion by precept and example no longer seemed adequate. For ten years their proud boast had been that the only weapon necessary in their fight was moral suasion, but their early faith in the perfectibility of man was being sadly shaken by constant experience with man's obstinate refusal to forsake the error of his ways. The demand for a change in methods was gathering force. Moral suasion had been weighed in the balance and found wanting. Periodicals, which had scrupulously avoided the subject, now began to attack the liquor laws, suggesting that the entire licensing system be abandoned.[46] Said the editor of the *Pennsylvania Temperance Recorder* in 1836:

For ourselves we have ever been of the opinion that this great moral reform is not to be accomplished by any one movement, but by a great variety of movements. If the legislation of by-gone days, days of darkness, sustains a false public sentiment, it is important that that legislation be changed. The direction of the attention of the community to that legislation, an examination of its correctness by every man and woman who is asked to sign a memorial, will help to change that public sentiment. Hitherto the broad shield of legislation has been cast over the traffic in ardent spirits. And, though the object of the statute has been to restrict the sale within certain bounds, it has virtually legalized it; and men have plead that what was legally right could not be morally wrong. And hence our legislation, de-

[45] *P. T. D.*, I, 240–241; *Ga. Journal*, May 22, 1830; *Annual Report of the Young Men's Temperance Society of New Haven* (1836); *Am. Quart. Temp. Mag.*, May, 1833, p. 134.

[46] *P. T. D.*, I, 270–278.

signed for good, has stood much in the way of the temperance reform.[47]

In January, 1837, the New York *Temperance Recorder* carried an argument in favour of legislation as the only means to curb the "mercenary recklessness" of those who opposed temperance principles. In the same month the initial issue of the *Journal*, edited by the American Temperance Union, denounced the licence system as governmental sanction of an immoral traffic.[48]

So legislation was urged as a last resort in a critical struggle. All the achievements of a decade would be lost, said certain alarmists, if legislative enactments were not invoked against manufacturers and vendors of intoxicating liquor. The victories won by intellectual appeals would have to be preserved in the statutes of state and nation. Those who advocated more stringent legal restrictions admitted that it was seldom politic to summon legislation to the aid of reform. They realized that laws strikingly in advance of public opinion were destitute of efficacy, but they firmly believed that the psychological moment had arrived to translate the opinion of a well organized minority into law. It was time to amend the licensing system. Unfortunately for this group of reformers there was little harmony of counsel within their ranks. While some insisted that the cause could be best served by strict enforcement of an almost prohibitory system of licences, many desired to repeal all licence laws and make the sale of ardent spirits a misdemeanour. Still others believed that each local administrative district should be given power to deal with the traffic as the authorities deemed best. On one point only was there substantial agreement among the "legal restriction-

---

[47] *Pa. Temp. Rec.*, Feb., 1836, pp. 12–13.
[48] *Temp. Rec.*, January, 1837, p. 85; *Journal*, January, 1837.

ists"; some sort of legislative attack was to be launched against the trade in spirituous liquors.

Petitions and memorials to state legislatures were so numerous during 1838 that it was known as the "petition year." Despite differences of opinion among the petitioners, there was a dominant note in their appeals. It was the plea that the state should withdraw its approval from a business which constantly preyed upon society, taking its toll in the form of paupers, maniacs and criminals.[49] Although these appeals seemed to represent an overwhelming majority of the temperance forces, they served to arouse widespread resentment on the part of a minority group. Through pamphlets, newspapers and temperance journals the moral suasionists, as they called themselves, ridiculed the attempt to legislate intemperance from the nation, characterizing it as a device to make the constable a substitute for the teacher and the preacher. They regretted the folly of their radical friends who were willing to base a great moral reform on that most uncertain of all elements in social regulation, legal enactment. To depend upon the strong arm of the law to enforce a reformation in manners and morals was to confess defeat. Furthermore, between voluntary abstinence associations and laws forbidding the sale and use of distilled spirits there was a wide gulf fixed, which could not be bridged by any plea of expediency. Men might be persuaded to change their habits; they could not be coerced. It was, therefore, inevitable that an appeal to the government's coercive power would alienate many devoted friends of temperance. They would regard the new policy as a flagrant infringement of their personal liberty and as an unwarranted interference of

[49] Societies in Maine, Vermont, Massachusetts, Connecticut, New York, Pennsylvania, Maryland, Ohio and Tennessee were particularly active in presenting petitions. *P. T. D.*, II, 51–66, 204–206; *Pa. Temp. Rec.*, May, 1837, p. 37; *Journal*, May, 1838, January, 1839. For the result of this movement see Chapter XI.

non-political associations in the realm of political affairs.[50]

The fears of the moral suasionists became a reality in Georgia. Josiah Flournoy, a prosperous planter of Eatonton and an exhorter in the Methodist Church, decided in 1838 to campaign for the repeal of the state licence law. During the early months of 1839 he organized the temperance forces in support of such action and sought to bring pressure on the general assembly. It soon became evident, however, that the old-line politicians at the behest of the liquor interests intended to take no action in the matter. Accordingly, Flournoy urged his followers to nominate candidates for the new assembly in their respective districts and work for the election of temperance men. This was done in many districts, but the "Flournoy" candidates, new to the intricacies of politics, discovered that the temperance issue speedily gave way to a bitter factional fight between Van Buren and anti-Van Buren, or Union and States' Rights parties. Out of the confusion came defeat for the temperance candidates and a pronounced feeling of resentment against Flournoy's followers for their injudicious meddling in matters purely political. As a result the temperance cause in Georgia, as the moral suasionists had prophesied, suffered a disastrous set-back.[51]

It was with mingled pride and apprehension, therefore, that temperance editors noted the unusual consideration which their cause was receiving from professional politicians. While it was pleasant to have evidence that their forces

[50] *Cf.* Edward B. Hall, *The Temperance Reform,* pp. 1–14; Leonard Withington, *A Review of the late Temperance Movement in Massachusetts,* pp. 22–23, 26; Arethusa Hall, *Life and Character of the Rev. Sylvester Judd* pp. 312, 315. Several newspapers normally friendly to temperance principles attacked the new tendency as a fatal mistake on the part of the reformers. For example, see *Charleston* (S. C.) *Courier,* Sept. 24, 26, 1839; *Mass. Spy,* May 8, 1838; *Manufacturers and Farmers Journal* (Providence), Feb. 24, 1840, May 6, 1841; *Delaware Gazette,* May 13, 1842.

[51] Scomp, *op. cit.,* pp. 328–336.

were no longer a negligible element in the body politic, it was also dangerous to have party leaders vying with each other for the "temperance vote." Yet the reformers could not well control the ramifications of partisanship. During state and federal campaigns there was much recrimination of intemperance, most of it thinly veiled attempts to influence thousands of abstainers throughout the country. Did the Van Buren newspapers refer with righteous scorn to "federal feasts and champagne," rival journals rejoined in pointed paragraphs about the sojourn of the President's entourage in Richmond and the plentiful refreshment with "punch and julep." [52] The presidential campaign of 1840 made it particularly difficult for temperance men to keep their cause free from political quarrels. Whig log-cabins in nearly every village dispensed hard cider and enthusiasm, while the Democrats referred to them as "groggeries" and urged the enemies of the liquor traffic to beware.[53] In rebuke they drank their toasts in pure cold water. Preachers, heartily applauded by Van Buren men, anathematized the Whigs for their noisy devotion to strong drink, and outraged correspondents demanded that the temperance journals denounce Harrison and Tyler.[54] The leading reformers, however, were too cautious to be drawn into an alliance with a particular party. They welcomed Democratic editors who had suddenly become convinced of the advisability of abstinence, but they were careful to point out that General Harrison's qualifications for office far transcended the kind of campaign his friends were waging for him.[55] They

[52] *Albany Argus,* August, 1838; *Springfield Republican,* July 11, 1838, July 20, 1839.

[53] *Rough Hewer,* May 26, Aug. 13, Sept. 10, 1840.

[54] *New Haven Palladium,* May 22, 27, 1840.

[55] *Journal,* June, 1840, p. 93, July, pp. 101, 104, August, p. 115. The editor of the *Columbus* (Miss.) *Democrat* believed that the Whig campaign had made many Democratic editors temperance advocates. July 18, 1840; also *Richmond Enquirer,* Dec. 1, 1840.

deplored Whig methods, but refused to admit that, in matters unrelated to the liquor problem, there could be any such thing as the "temperance vote." Of course, this attitude did not prevent politicians from continuing their appeals to the rank and file of the reformers.[56]

In the meantime the question of abolitionism had arisen to threaten sectional disruption of a movement already divided by quarrels between moral suasionists and legal suasionists, between supporters of the old pledge and of the new. After William Lloyd Garrison established the *Liberator* in 1831, many southerners began to distrust the temperance journals which came out of New England. They recalled that for several months in 1828 Garrison had been editor of the *National Philanthropist*, allied with the American Temperance Society, and they interpreted this editorial relationship as an indication that a strong bond of sympathy existed between temperance and abolition periodicals. In South Carolina the state society recommended in December, 1832, that its auxiliaries subscribe for the *Temperance Recorder*, published by the New York state society. This selection was made because the executive committee found that the *Recorder* was "exclusively confined to the subject of temperance, and has manifested no disposition to meddle with the local institutions of the South."[57] The same recommendation could have been given to most northern journals of this period, for temperance editors were usually careful not to offend their southern associates in the reform. It was true, however, that northern temperance societies were filled with determined anti-slavery men and women, who were

[56] In New York Governor Seward paid tribute to the temperance cause at the New Year's Day reception in 1842, when he ordered that nothing but lemonade and cold water should be served. *Autobiography of William H. Seward*, p. 589.

[57] *Permanent Temperance Documents of South Carolina*, p. 108. Cited in Scomp, *op. cit.*, p. 300.

not averse to stating their position.[58]   In 1833 the state
society of Pennsylvania took cognizance of this fact in its
annual report.   A carefully worded statement explained
that, while many members were personally hostile to slavery
in the abstract, no society had so far forgotten the design
of its formation as to attempt to aid the anti-slavery cause.
An appeal was made to the "southern brethren" not to allow fancied grievances to interfere with a national campaign
against intemperance.   The Pennsylvania leaders were sure
that the temperance movement would never be used to discredit southern institutions.[59]   Such assurance from the
North did not remove all causes of irritation.   In Georgia
the fact that subscribers to the *Temperance Recorder* were
deluged with abolition literature gave colour to the charge
that the abolitionists and the temperance leaders were working together.   This the editor of the *Recorder* indignantly
denied, but in 1835 the Georgia state society instructed its
members to discontinue the New York journal.   At the same
time the executive committee took action to sever its tenuous
connection with the American Temperance Society, declaring that the Georgia society had never been an auxiliary of
the Boston organization.[60]   Although none of the other
southern states followed the example of Georgia, the relations between northern and southern groups were not entirely
cordial after 1836.   When the American Temperance Union
took up the work of the national organization, it experienced
great difficulty in securing information concerning the progress of reform in the lower South.

With numerous factions working at cross purposes it was

[58] The prominent position in temperance councils of such enemies of
slavery as William Jay, Theodore Frelinghuysen, Arthur and Lewis
Tappan and Gerrit Smith did not tend to reassure the southern
societies.

[59] *Anniversary Report of the Pennsylvania State Temperance Society*
(1833), p. 7.

[60] Scomp, *op. cit.*, pp. 301–302.

not strange that the temperance movement fell upon lean
years.   The reformers, however, managed to put on a bold
front.   When achievements at home were few, they proudly
proclaimed triumphs abroad, which testified to the ever
widening sphere of their missionary activity.   During the
last half of the decade of the thirties thousands of copies of
a *Circular to Emigrants* were sent to London for distribution
in Great Britain and continental countries, that persons in-
tending to migrate to the United States might learn of the
temperance reform before entering the country.[61]   In
France, Robert Baird had constituted himself an advance
agent for the spread of propaganda.   His *History of the
Temperance Societies of the United States* was translated
into French, Dutch, German, Swedish, Russian and Hun-
garian and distributed through his efforts in the countries
mentioned.   As a result of Baird's energetic work the Crown
Prince of Prussia became a patron of a total abstinence
society, and King Frederick William III ordered that a society be organized in every province.[62]   In Stockholm a temperance periodical, approved by Charles XIV, enjoyed a
considerable circulation among the Swedish and Norwegian
peoples.   The far-flung borders of the reform already included points in Asia, Africa and the islands of the Pacific.
In Odessa, on the Bosphorus, in Madras and Bombay the
Journal of the American Temperance Union was read with
interest.[63]

No developments in Europe were quite as encouraging to
Americans as those in the British Isles.   English and Scotch

[61] The circular was first published by the New York State Temperance
Society.   See *Temp. Rec.*, July 2, 1833; *Journal*, September, 1839, p. 132.

[62] Baird represented the French Evangelical Association, a missionary
union supported by Protestant denominations in the United States
and France.   H. M. Baird, *Life of the Rev. Robert Baird*, pp. 105–143;
P. T. D., II, 100–101.

[63] *P. T. D.*, II, 101–105; J. S. Buckingham, *History and Progress of
the Temperance Reformation in Great Britain*, pp. 97–98.

leaders in temperance work had paid the American societies the sincere compliment of imitation, in many instances making public profession of the fact that their inspiration came from the United States.[64] Some of the first temperance pamphlets distributed in Great Britain were of American origin, and editors of later publications drew upon American experience to give point to their arguments.[65] The two movements learned to co-operate with each other so effectively that methods adopted by one were speedily taken up by the other. Harmonious relations were further insured by a happy exchange of visits between distinguished reformers in the two fields. From 1837 to 1839 James Silk Buckingham, famous for his exhaustive reports to Parliament on intemperance and its remedy, brought encouraging messages from Great Britain to hundreds of audiences in all parts of the United States. At the same time Edward C. Delavan received an enthusiastic reception in England and Scotland, an eloquent testimonial of unity of spirit that knew no geographical barriers.[66]

During the years which Buckingham spent in America and Delavan in Europe the most signal victory of the temperance forces was won in Ireland. Early in April, 1838, Theobald Mathew, a Catholic priest of the Capuchin order, announced his intention to devote a large share of his time to the promotion of temperance among his parishioners. For many years he had been a member of the Board of Governors of the city work-house in Cork, where his duties had brought him into close contact with the baneful effects of intem-

[64] Buckingham, *op. cit.*, pp. 11–12; Dorchester, *op. cit.*, pp. 320–321; Samuel Couling, *History of the Temperance Movement in Great Britain and Ireland*, p. 28.

[65] John Dunlop, one of the pioneer reformers in Scotland, drew largely upon the American situation for material in writing his treatise *On the Extent and Remedy of National Intemperance*. Henry Forbes, who organized the first abstinence society in England, used Beecher's *Six Sermons* as his first tract. Couling, *op. cit.*, p. 42.

[66] *P. T. D.*, II, 135–136; Buckingham, *op. cit.*, 95, 98.

perance. At the earnest solicitation of William Martin, a
Quaker and one of his associates on the Board, Father
Mathew agreed to organize a total abstinence society in his
congregation. At the initial meeting he and fifty-nine of his
parishioners signed the following pledge: "I promise while
I belong to the teetotal abstinence society to abstain from
all kinds of intoxicating drink, unless used medically, and
that I will discountenance by advice and example the causes
of intemperance in others." For a few weeks the popular
priest addressed audiences twice a week in the largest hall
in Cork, where more than 4000 crowded in to hear him. So
immediate was the response to his appeals that within eight
months 156,000 names had been entered on the books of the
society. Delegations came from the neighbouring counties
of Waterford, Limerick, Clare, Tipperary and even remote
Galway, listened in a spirit of veneration to the lectures and
took the obligation as if they were performing a religious
rite. When Father Mathew visited Limerick in December,
1839, the crowds that assembled to see and hear him were
larger than the city could accommodate. At one ceremony
it was estimated that more than 15,000, kneeling in the
streets through which he walked, received the pledge. Wherever he journeyed in his native land the people flocked to
him, as if they were making a sacred pilgrimage.[67]

This "glorious news from Ireland" was fully reported
in American temperance journals and called forth numerous
speculations concerning its effect on Irish Catholics in the
United States. Most leaders hoped there would be a per-
ceptible quickening of interest, for the time seemed right to

[67] The best description of Father Mathew's work in Ireland is to be
found in J. F. Maguire's *Father Mathew*, pp. 8–149. See also *Illustrated
Memoir of Father Mathew* (1847); *Journal*, files for 1840. Many
attributed his phenomenal success to the fact that the medals which
he gave to all pledge-signers were prized by their recipients for their
power to heal the sick. J. G. Adams and E. H. Chapin, *The Fountain*,
pp. 18–22.

enlist Catholic congregations in the reform.[68]   The hopes of the leaders were realized.   During 1839 and 1840 accounts of the movement in Ireland and the arrival of immigrants who had signed Father Mathew's pledge encouraged priests and bishops in this country to press more vigorously the fight against intemperance among their people.   As a result Catholic abstinence societies were formed in many of the larger cities.   The Boston Catholic Confraternity was organized in 1840 on the basis of total abstinence from all intoxicants.   In Philadelphia Bishop Kenrick presided over a meeting in the cathedral which established a society on the principles advocated by Father Mathew, while in New York the congregation of the Church of the Transfiguration took the lead in espousing the cause.[69]   Father Curry in Providence and Father Schneller in Albany were hailed as worthy disciples of the Irish priest.[70]   These manifestations of the influence exercised by a humble priest hundreds of miles across the sea convinced friends of temperance that an effort should be made to bring Father Mathew to the United States.   Although the invitation was extended by both Catholics and Protestants, and was accepted, the visit had to be indefinitely postponed because of Father Mathew's pastoral duties.   Not until 1849 was the Irish reformer able to test his power in a strange land.

[68] *Manufacturers and Farmers Journal*, June 22, 1840, March 1, 22, 1841; *Delaware Gazette*, July 15, 1842; *Journal*, February, 1840, p. 28, March, pp. 44–46; May, pp. 77–79.

[69] *Journal*, March, 1840, p. 48, April, p. 57, May, p. 80, July, p. 105, Marsh, *op. cit.*, pp. 73–75.

[70] *Manufacturers and Farmers Journal*, Oct. 8, 1840; *Baltimore Patriot*, March 21, 1842.

CHAPTER IX

THE WASHINGTONIAN REVIVAL

THE dissensions which marred the temperance movement just prior to 1840—the quarrels between conservatives and supporters of a total abstinence pledge, the controversy over the advisability of invoking the aid of legislation, the complication of the abolition question—all were overshadowed or forgotten during the opening years of the Washingtonian revival. Signs of hesitancy and discouragement, apparent in many of the older societies, seemed gradually to disappear before the force of an intense emotional appeal that swept the country. It was an appeal voiced largely by reformed drunkards, a class which hitherto had played an inconspicuous rôle in the drama of temperance reform. Believing that the confirmed inebriate was hopelessly beyond regeneration, most reformers had given scant consideration to his plight. They had rather devoted their time to the task of saving the moderate drinker from becoming a drunkard. But now they were confronted by the spectacle of the drunkard trying to save himself.[1]

The Washingtonian revival originated, so far as any complex movement may be said to have a single origin, among a group of tipplers in Chase's Tavern, Baltimore, Maryland. On the evening of April 2, 1840, six convivial friends, long accustomed to while away their evenings in gaming and drink-

[1] Justin Edwards, at the time of the formation of the American Temperance Society, had scouted the idea that the drunkard could be reformed. Not all reformers agreed with him, but few directed their efforts toward saving the degenerate.

182

ing, met at the tavern with no thought of changing the usual program. In a spirit of fun, however, one of their number suggested that they send a committee to hear a temperance lecturer who was announced to speak in a nearby church. The committee returned from the lecture with an enthusiastic report of what they had heard, which started a spirited discussion of the total abstinence principle and its power to change men's habits. This interchange of views resulted in a decision to form a society which would commit them to abstinence from the use of all intoxicants. William K. Mitchell, who was delegated to put their resolution into writing, presented the following pledge for their approval: "We, whose names are annexed, desirous of forming a society for our mutual benefit, and to safeguard against a pernicious practice which is injurious to our health, standing and families, do pledge ourselves as gentlemen, that we will not drink any spirituous or malt liquors, wine or cider." Having signed this comprehensive pledge, the six charter members turned their attention to the election of officers, the method of obtaining revenue and the problem of securing new members. It was agreed that each member should bring a friend to the first regular meeting, that an initiation fee of twenty-five cents should be charged, and that the monthly dues should be twelve and one-half cents. A suggestion that the new association be named in honour of Thomas Jefferson having been rejected, the group decided that the society should be called the "Washington Temperance Society." In choosing the Father of his Country as their patron they were guided by an admiration of his character, rather than by a desire to imitate his practice regarding the use of intoxicants.[2]

2 These facts are contained in the *Annual Report of the Maryland State Temperance Society* (1842). See also *Journal,* January, 1841, pp. 6–7; *P. T. D.,* II, 289–290. The charter members were William K. Mitchell, David Anderson, Archibald Campbell, John F. Hoss, James McCurley and George Steers.

Labelling themselves as reformed drunkards, the founders of the new movement were immediately successful in persuading others to join them. Within a few weeks it was necessary for them to seek more extensive accommodations in a hall of their own. As the society grew, the problem of making the meetings interesting demanded solution. President Mitchell, quick to sense that which would be popular, suggested that the programs of stated meetings be limited to a narration of personal experiences by members who had felt the saving influence of the pledge. In conformity with this suggestion the Baltimore society admitted no outside speakers, unless they desired to relate their experiences as reformed men. Thus, the standard for other Washingtonian societies was set, and the chief characteristic of the movement became the reformation of drunkards by reformed drunkards. "Experience meetings" attracted the attention and held the interest of hundreds who had not been reached by educational propaganda issued by the older societies. Shocking stories of degeneracy mingled with joyous testimony of redemption, now and then relieved by humorous anecdotes, proved so effective in winning converts that by Christmas of 1840 more than 1000 in the city called themselves "Washingtonians."

From the beginning the missionary impulse was strong in the Baltimore society, but the first promising opportunity to extend the influence of the movement beyond the confines of its native city came in the spring of 1841,[3] when an invitation was accepted to carry the message to New York City. A delegation of five under the leadership of William K. Mitchell and John H. W. Hawkins conducted a series of eighteen meetings during the latter part of March, which were attended by thousands whose curiosity had been aroused through reading the reports from Baltimore. Churches of various Protestant denominations threw open their doors to

[3] *Journal*, July, 1840, p. 102.

the speakers, but no auditorium was large enought to accommodate the crowds. The initial session gave promise of the success that was to follow, for Hawkins' dramatic recital of the sordid incidents in his life deeply moved his audience. Several interrupted with the plea that they desired to sign the pledge at once and be saved. At the conclusion of his address scores pressed forward to grasp his hand and receive his words of encouragement. Others crowded up to the platform, eager to take the obligation of total abstinence. The revival in New York had begun. Each successive meeting was the scene of an enthusiastic response to the emotional appeals of the Washingtonians. As the audiences grew ever larger, it seemed wise to arrange an open air meeting. At a gathering in City Hall Park more than 4000 had an opportunity to hear the novel manner in which the reformers presented their message. To the crowd's delight the speakers mounted upturned rum-kegs from which vantage point they related their numerous experiences with the demon, rum. While the meeting was in progress, agents were busy in the throng securing members for the first Washington Temperance Society in New York City. Many of the curious must have been convinced, for at the close of the campaign almost 1800 had signed the total abstinence pledge and enlisted under the new banner.[4]

Following their triumphs in New York the Washingtonions returned to Baltimore in order to participate in the first anniversary celebration of their society. Elaborate preparations had been made for a procession which would represent every temperance organization in the city, whatever its origin or principles. The efforts of the committee on arrangements were well rewarded on April 5 by the presence in the line of march of more than 6000, each society with its own standard and every member wearing an appro-

[4] *N. Y. Commercial Advertiser*, March 22, 1841; *Journal*, April, 1841, pp. 49–53.

priate badge.   The place of honour was given to the reformed drunkards who had joined the Washingtonian ranks
during the year, but the section most observed by spectators
who lined the streets was that containing nearly one thousand boys and girls, volunteers in the "Cold Water Army."
These youthful soldiers, parading in their white and blue
uniforms, waving their inscribed banners, and singing temperance songs, gave more promise for the future than the
hundreds whose lives had been reformed.[5]

News of the successful work in Baltimore and New York
was not slow in reaching other parts of the country, with the
result that Washingtonian speakers and organizers were
much in demand.   On April 13 Hawkins and his friend, William E. Wright, arrived in Boston to conduct a series of
meetings in the churches.   Their arrival having been well
heralded in the press, crowds larger than those in New York

[5] In 1836 Thomas P. Hunt, one of the leading Presbyterian ministers
of his day, began to interest boys and girls in societies which he called
units in his Cold Water Army.   During his travels over the country
he tried to organize such a society in every Sunday School which
he visited.   Though hundreds of units were formed there was no attempt to effect a central control of the movement.   Rev. Hunt
stressed the participation of his "volunteers" in all temperance
processions and pageants.   He wrote the following pledge for the
army:

> We do not think we'll ever drink,
> Whisky or gin, brandy or rum,
> Or anything that'll make drunk come.

The work among the children was carried forward with great success
and the army became a colourful part of the temperance celebrations.
Thomas P. Hunt, *The Cold Water Army;* W. P. White, "A Historic
Nineteenth Century Character," *Journal of Presbyterian Historical
Society,* X, 164; *Journal,* May, 1841, p. 76; Marsh, *op. cit.,* p. 98;
Manufacturers and Farmers Journal, March 2, 1840; *State Banner*
(Bennington, Vt.), July 12, 1842; *Baltimore Patriot,* Jan. 4, 1842;
Daily Evening Transcript, May 28, 1844; *Boston Daily Journal,* May
18, 1846.

welcomed them.[6] Of one of the first meetings the *Daily Mail* said:

The Odeon was filled to its utmost capacity, last evening, by a promiscuous audience of temperance men, distillers, wholesalers and retail dealers in ardent spirits, confirmed inebriates, moderate drinkers, lovers of the social glass, teetotalers, etc., to listen to the speeches of the famous "Reformed Drunkards," delegates from the Washington Temperance Society of Baltimore, who have excited such a deep interest in the cause of temperance in other places. . . . Mr. Hawkins, of Baltimore, was the second of the "Reformed Drunkards" introduced to the meeting. He was a man forty-four years of age—of fine manly form—and said he had been more than twenty years a confirmed inebriate. He spoke with rather more fluency, force and effect, than his predecessor, but in the same vein of free and easy, off-hand, direct, bang-up style; at times in a simple conversational manner, then earnest and vehement, then pathetic, then humorous—but always manly and reasonable. Mr. Hawkins succeeded in "working up" his audience finely. Now the house was as quiet and still as a deserted church, and anon the high dome rang with violent bursts of laughter and applause. Now he assumed the melting mood, and pictured the scenes of a drunkard's home, and that home his own, and fountains of generous feeling, in many hearts, gushed forth in tears—and again, in a moment, as he related some ludicrous story, these tearful eyes glistened with delight, sighs changed to hearty shouts, and long faces were convulsed with broad grins and glorious smiles.[7]

The skill with which Hawkins played upon the emotions of his hearers was signally demonstrated a few days later when he addressed an audience that filled even the standing room in Faneuil Hall. The historic building, draped in mourning for the services in memory of President Harrison,

[6] Extracts from Hawkins' diary in W. G. Hawkins' *Life of John H. W. Hawkins*, pp. 81–82.

[7] *Boston Daily Mail*, April 16, 1841.

was a fitting setting, the speaker said, for the obsequies of
old King Alcohol.   With his usual repertoire of humorous
and pathetic stories Hawkins carried his audience from
smiles to tears and back again, crowning his efforts with a
recital of the wickedness of his unregenerate days and the
joy that followed his "moral resurrection."   As he concluded
his remarks, men in the audience asked permission to relate
their experiences, and the meeting closed with several hundred
moving forward to sign the pledge.   Some were none too
steady of step as their friends urged them to follow Hawkins' example.   It was truly a reformation of the intemperate.   Those who had doubted whether the reformers would
be able to repeat their triumphs in Boston were now convinced that the Washingtonian appeal was as effective in
Massachusetts as in Maryland.[8]   So encouraging were the
results of the meetings that the Boston Temperance Society
employed Hawkins to devote several months to a tour of the
New England states.[9]

The Washingtonians were regarded by many of the older
organizations as valuable allies in the temperance battle.
They were highly honoured at the anniversary meeting of the
American Temperance Union in New York City, May 11,
1841, and two months later at Saratoga Springs they
received the commendation of the national convention.
Shortly after the Saratoga convention a delegation of the
reformed men went out, two by two, to carry their message
into the West and South.[10]   Some of these temperance teams
achieved a fame only to be exceeded later by the evangelists,
Moody and Sankey.   Pollard and Wright [11] began their circuit in central and western New York, where results were

[8] *Boston Mercantile Journal,* April 22, 1841; *Journal,* May, 1842,
p. 73.

[9] W. G. Hawkins, *op. cit.,* pp. 109–110.

[10] *Journal,* September, 1841, p. 138.

[11] J. F. Pollard and W. E. Wright of Baltimore.

far from encouraging. They persevered, however, and soon were cordially welcomed wherever they went. During the summer and autumn they toured New York, New Jersey and Pennsylvania, securing more than 23,000 signatures to the pledge. Their meetings normally followed the type which had become so well known in Washingtonian circles. One of their converts has left us this description:

Some of the meetings took the air of deep religious solemnity, eyes that never wept before were suffused, and hearts from which all feelings seemed to have departed, were suddenly converted into flesh. The simple tale of the ruined inebriate, interrupted by a silence that told of emotions too big for utterance, would awaken general sympathy, and dissolve a large portion of the audience in tears. The spell which had bound so many seemed to dissolve under the magic eloquence of those unlettered men. They spoke from the heart to the heart. The drunkard found himself unexpectedly an object of interest. He was no longer an outcast. There were some who still looked upon him as a man. A chord was reached which had long since ceased to respond to other influences less kind in their nature. . . . A few leaders in the ranks of intemperance having signed the pledge, it appeared to be the signal for the mass to follow: and on they came, like a torrent sweeping everything before it. It was for weeks the all-absorbing topic. Men and women went hand in hand to the work; and day after day the evening sun set upon the crowd standing in the open places of our city to listen to the arguments and appeals of the temperance advocate.[12]

Leaving behind them hundreds of enthusiastic supporters, Pollard and Wright journeyed south through Maryland and Delaware into Virginia. The spring of 1842 found them conducting meetings in Charlottesville, Richmond and Petersburg, where considerable work was done among the

[12] *P. T. D.*, II, 306–307. The account was given by a correspondent living in Hudson, N. Y.

Negroes.[13]   At Charlottesville students of the University of Virginia organized one of the largest and most aggressive societies in the state.[14]

In the meantime Vickers and Small,[15] having started into the West, selected Pittsburgh as their first important objective.   They found that intemperance was general among the labouring population of the rapidly developing industrial centre, but they were able to win several thousand for the cause of total abstinence.[16]   From their success in Pittsburgh Vickers and Small proceeded to Wheeling and then to Cincinnati, where they received the hearty co-operation of Lyman Beecher, then president of Lane Theological Seminary.   Due to the excellent preliminary work which had been done, the Washingtonians addressed large crowds during the entire stay in the city and secured a number of disciples who were willing to carry the message into neighbouring states.   Several months, therefore, were spent in organizing delegations and planning itineraries for future work in Ohio, Kentucky, Tennessee, Indiana and Illinois.   The actual execution of the plans was left to the discretion of the Cincinnati societies which had adopted Washingtonian principles.[17]

Of all the self-appointed orators and lecturers who rose up during this phase of the reform John H. W. Hawkins was easily the most widely known and the most successful.   He was an unusual representative of many hundreds of drunkards who were reformed by the ministrations of Washingtonians.   Born of English parents in the city of Baltimore, September 28, 1797, Hawkins was early deprived of the home

[13] *Richmond Whig,* Jan. 28, Feb. 8, Feb. 13, 1842; *Journal,* March, 1842, p. 44. The Washingtonians were not the first to organize societies among the Negroes. In 1831 the Georgians had already established several groups under the guidance of other societies. *Georgia Journal,* June, 1831.

[14] *Journal,* March, 1842, p. 44.

[15] Jesse Vickers and Jesse W. Small of Baltimore.

[16] *N. Y. Tribune,* June 25, 1841.

[17] *Journal,* October, 1841, p. 157.

influence by being bound out as an apprentice to a hat-maker. His master's establishment was "as perfect a grog-shop as ever existed." Here the boy learned to drink, developing a fondness for intoxicants which was not corrected by his religious conversion in 1815. At the conclusion of his apprenticeship, three years in the frontier communities of the Ohio valley only served to send him far along the path of the prodigal son. Conquering his bad habits for a time, he returned to Baltimore to follow his trade, but the next twenty years were a losing battle against intemperance. His "relapses" became more frequent and of longer duration as the years passed, while his family endured the miseries of poverty. The failure of his employer during the financial and industrial depression of 1837 was disastrous for Hawkins. Unemployment added to intemperance forced him to seek public aid. For almost three years he was unable to provide a decent home for his family, a fact which so preyed upon his mind, when he was sober, that he more often sought the comfort of intoxication. Such was Hawkins' condition when the vigilant workers of the Washington Temperance Society in Baltimore persuaded him to sign the total abstinence pledge.[18] It did not take his associates long to discover that he had the qualities of a leader. A splendid physique and commanding presence, combined with a gift for extemporaneous speaking, made him an ideal lecturer. During his first week as a Washingtonian he began a missionary campaign among his old companions. He was not so successful, however, in his personal visits to the unregenerate as in his appeals from the platform. His ability to tell a story well, his judicious mingling of anecdote and argument and his understanding of the psychology of a crowd gave him an unusual mastery over large audiences.

A less robust body could not have endured the exacting labours which John Hawkins undertook after 1840. Al-

18 W. G. Hawkins, *op. cit.,* pp. 3–65.

though New England was his special field for a few years, within a decade he had been called into every section of the country.   In 1842 he visited Washington in a successful attempt to revive the Congressional Temperance Society and reorganize it on a total abstinence basis.   The following year he left Massachusetts long enough to tour the western and northern counties of New York, as well as parts of Vermont, New Hampshire and Maine.   In November he arranged an itinerary through the South, which took him to the principal cities in the Carolinas and Georgia.   Forced to return to Boston before his swing around the circle was complete, he undertook a western trip in the autumn of 1845.   Having visited towns in Ohio, Indiana and Illinois, he started down the Mississippi in the spring of 1846, concluding his campaign with remarkable revivals in New Orleans and Mobile.   Hawkins' journal indicates that for eight consecutive months he spoke at least once each day, besides supervising the work of his numerous assistants.   Wherever he lectured, he endeavoured to effect an organization which would carry on the work after he had departed for another district.   It is estimated that in his first ten years as a reformer Hawkins travelled more than 100,000 miles and delivered as many as 2500 addresses, a record scarcely equalled by the most peripatetic Chautauqua lecturer of to-day.[10]

Hawkins' greatest rival as a temperance orator was John Bartholomew Gough.   Like Hawkins he was a reformed drunkard, but he did not attribute his reformation to the work of the Washingtonians.   He was, however, in sympathy with the new movement.   At the age of twelve Gough was sent by his parents, then living at Sandgate, Kent, England, to learn a trade in the United States.   The family in whose

[19] W. G. Hawkins, op. cit., pp. 156–326.   In his biography of his father W. G. Hawkins quotes frequently from letters and journals written during the course of these lecture trips. See also N. Y. Tribune, June 2, 1841; Delaware Gazette, February 18, 1842.

care he was entrusted settled on a farm near Utica, New York, where the boy was forced to perform the ordinary farm chores.   Dissatisfied, because he was allowed neither to learn a trade nor to attend school, he finally secured his father's permission to leave the farm and seek work in New York City.[20]   There he entered upon an apprenticeship in a cheap book-bindery in the winter of 1831.   His mother came from England to be with her fourteen year old son, but she died shortly after her arrival, leaving the boy disheartened and disconsolate.   He sought relief from his loneliness in the sociability of the grog-shops and tippling-houses, where he met a number of young people whose reckless pastimes interested him.   During the next few years dissolute habits grew upon him, though he managed to work regularly at his trade.   In the meantime he was married.   When the panic of 1837, by wrecking the financial fortunes of his employer, threw him out of work, he tried to make a living in the theatre.   For a time he played low comedy parts along the Bowery, and later his ability as a mimic earned him a chance with a company of strolling minstrels.   His theatrical career ended abruptly when the minstrel company left him in Worcester, Massachusetts, to recover from an attack of delirium tremens.   His wife, who was ill at the time, came to Worcester to nurse him, but did not live to see her husband's

[20] The references to his boyhood, which Gough later incorporated in some of his speeches, were distorted so as to make it appear that he had been ungrateful to the family that brought him to the United States. The matter aroused the resentment of the Mannering family, and in 1845 a pamphlet appeared in New York entitled *The Echo of Truth, or John B. Gough's Early History*, By His Foster-Father. It was written by Jesse Pound, pastor of St. Matthew's Church and a close friend of the Mannerings. Pound insisted that Gough was guilty of slander and was lightening the pockets of the public by falsely playing upon its sympathy. In answer to this charge Gough denied that he had been correctly quoted in the press. He branded the rumour that he had been made a drunkard by the Mannerings as untrue, but he refused to withdraw his statement that he had not received proper treatment while working on the Mannering farm. The question was one of veracity, and the public could draw its own conclusions.

recovery. After his wife's death Gough found his chief
solace in the lowest grog-shops, where he amused the loafers
with his songs and stories, taking his pay in the form of
treats. Occasionally he worked at his old trade in a local
book-bindery.[21]

In October, 1842, Joel Stratton, an employee of the temperance hotel in Worcester, persuaded John B. Gough to
sign the pledge. It was not at first apparent that the young
temperance recruit would develop into one of the most popular lecturers of his day. Gough's notoriety as a drunkard,
however, made his reformation the more interesting, and the
societies in Worcester desired his services. For a few
months he confined his efforts to an occasional relation of his
experiences, usually speaking to a small audience in some
neighbouring town. As the demands upon his time increased
he quit his job in the publishing house in order to enter seriously on the work of a reformer. During this probationary
period, five months after he had signed the pledge, Gough
suffered his first relapse, a weakness which was destined to
interfere with his work at a later date. On this particular
occasion he confessed to the Worcester society that he had
violated the pledge, expressed his sorrow and penitence and
was forgiven. In the summer of 1843 he made his début in
Boston, where he was so cordially received that he decided to
undertake an extensive tour of the New England states. On
this tour he made 383 public addresses and received through
voluntary contributions $1059, out of which he paid all ex-
penses. In four years his travels amounted to 6840 miles,
and he counted his reward in 15,218 signatures to the pledge.
It was evident to the young reformer and his associates
that he had found his life work.[22]

In September, 1845, while on a visit to New York City,

[21] *Autobiography and Personal Recollections of John B. Gough*, pp.
20–127. See also Carlos Martyn, *John B. Gough, The Apostle of Cold
Water.*

[22] Gough, *Autobiography*, pp. 160–161.

Gough suddenly disappeared. His friends, fearing foul play, conducted a diligent search and finally located him in a house of ill-repute in Walker Street. He was evidently recovering from a drunken debauch which had lasted the greater part of a week. As soon as he was able, he issued a public statement explaining his actions. According to his version of the affair, he had been accosted on the street by a chance acquaintance, whose name he could not remember, who had invited him to have a glass of soda at a nearby drug store. After drinking the soda, so the statement read, he became dazed, lost his way and wandered aimlessly through streets that he had never seen before. How he reached the house in Walker Street he could not explain. He did not remember whether he had taken any liquor after the first glass of soda or not. He would plead guilty to violation of the pledge and throw himself on the mercy of his friends. He believed that his misfortune was traceable to intoxicants or drugs in what he thought was a harmless social glass.[23] The incident was the subject of much discussion and newspaper comment.[24] Gough's enemies were jubilant, believing that his reputation had been ruined. They charged him with drunkenness and disorderly conduct and with publishing a false explanation of that conduct.[25] The temperance press generally accepted Gough's statement and found in his experience only one more proof of the evil power of the liquor dealers. Some of the Washingtonian journals, however, doubting Gough's sincerity, were severe in their condemnation of a man who could be so easily led

[23] *Ibid.*, pp. 195–209.

[24] In New York the *Herald,* ever opposed to temperance, was in an ecstasy of joy; the *Tribune* was unconvinced by Gough's statement, but was charitably inclined toward him; the *Commercial Advertiser* openly defended Gough. *The Massachusetts Spy,* a strong supporter of temperance, was non-committal. See *Anti-Slavery Bugle,* Sept. 26, 1845.

[25] For specimens of the attacks on Gough's veracity see *Goffiana: A Review of the Life and Writings of John B. Gough* (1846).

astray.[26]   In spite of the publicity given to this indiscretion, Gough's popularity did not wane. His services were so greatly in demand that for the next five years towns in every section of the country were on his waiting list.

The secret of Gough's power as a public speaker is not revealed in his printed addresses, for it was more his manner of delivery than the substance of his discourse that won his audience.[27]   His arguments, when read to-day, sound rather forced, and many of his anecdotes are surprisingly pointless. Contemporary reporters of his speeches seem to have realized that the printed page was an inadequate record of his eloquence, for they frequently lament their inability to reproduce his vigour of utterance.[28]   Enthusiastic admirers described his voice as a "noble instrument of many keys" upon which he played melodies that charmed his hearers.   Few who heard him, even if they did not agree with his message, failed to pay tribute to his intense earnestness, his impassioned delivery and his sure sense of the dramatic.   Describing him at the beginning of his public career, a correspondent to the *New York Observer* wrote:

Mr. Gough now rose, a youth of a pale countenance, bordering even on pensiveness, personally a stranger to us all, and burdened with a reputation for eloquence, which it seemed difficult for him much longer to carry.   But oh, that conciliatory exordium! Was it the power of nature, or was it the perfection of art? There was art in it, but it was learned, not in the school of the

[26] *Journal,* October, 1845, p. 162. The *Journal* for December, 1845, contains the report of a special committee from the Mount Vernon Church in Boston, of which Mr. Gough was a member, completely exonerating him. See also a pamphlet in his defence, *A Minute and Authentic Narrative of the Conduct and Conversation of John B. Gough during each day of his late absence* (1845).

[27] See J. B. Gough, *Platform Echoes, or Leaves from My Notebook of Forty Years.*

[28] *Journal,* February, 1845, p. 17, April, p. 51.

Rhetorician, but of Nature. It was indeed an ingenuous disavowal of all claim to the character of an instructor, or to the gifts of a well-furnished public speaker. As to education, his audience had doubtless enjoyed advantages superior to himself, he said, since he had never been at school. This deference to his audience, composed of the flower of an intelligent city, combined with the unaffected modesty of his demeanor in all things touching himself, opened a clear way for the march of his oratory. We were now prepared to go with him into any field he might select. The wand of the magician began to exert its influence, the magician himself the while seeming to be unconscious of the waxing power of his enchantment. . . . All were under the spell of this young charmer, who charmed so wisely; alternately elevated by the grand, thrilled with the horrible, dissolved with the tender, enchanted with the beautiful, and all this without a plan or a purpose on the part of the speaker, except to try to rescue the fallen from the pit and the mire of intemperance, and invigorate the principles of those who stand on firm ground.[29]

The pale, pensive youth lost none of his power as his years of platform experience increased. Though he generally used the vernacular of the uneducated, he never shocked the sensibilities of his hearers with vulgarities nor sought to arouse passion by bitter denunciation. A gift of mimicry, first cultivated while he was playing low comedy parts on the Bowery, won many a critical audience and made him a great favourite with the children, whose praise was the great guarantee of his future fame.

In the meantime a host of orators and organizers, inglorious in comparison with Hawkins and Gough, but charged with something of their energy, were reaping a bountiful harvest for the Washingtonian societies. Reports from every field of activity emphasized the unusual success

[29] Letter of Rev. J. N. Danforth to the *New York Observer.* Copied in *Journal,* April, 1845, pp. 51–52.

of the new phase of the reform. In 1843, if we may credit the figures recorded in the enthusiasm of the moment, a half million intemperate drinkers and one hundred thousand habitual drunkards had been persuaded to sign the pledge.[30] The changes wrought in some communities, said the reports, surpassed "all the marvelous tales of fiction." Of all temperance statistics, however, these were the most unreliable, for few of the "mushroom" societies kept permanent records. Still, the lack of an accurate enumeration does not alter the fact that Washingtonianism was sweeping the country. From every state came word that in a few years the "reformed drunkards" had done as much good as the older societies in their fifteen years of organized effort. Not only were inebriates being reformed, but moderate drinkers were abandoning moderation and accepting total abstinence as the correct principle of conduct. The press was devoting a greater amount of news space to temperance, while editorials on the subject were couched in more laudatory terms.[31] Certainly, if publicity was any criterion, the revival that came out of Baltimore was arousing the public to action.

The Washingtonians, possibly taking their cue from the methods of the political parties in the election of 1840, used mass demonstrations frequently and effectively to keep up the morale of the movement. Washington's Birthday, the Fourth of July, and the anniversary of the formation of the first society were occasions for parades, open air meetings, picnics, fairs and bazaars. Several times each year in the larger cities the total strength of the temperance societies

---

30 These figures included the results of three years' work, 1841–1843.

31 For press notices concerning the success of Washingtonianism see *Providence Daily Journal,* Oct. 20, 1842; *Manufacturers and Farmers Journal,* July 12, 1841; *Delaware Gazette,* Jan. 21, 1842, Feb. 3, 1843; *Baltimore Patriot,* Feb. 10, Sept. 16, 1842, March 8, 1843; *Richmond Enquirer,* May 21, 1841; *N. Y. Tribune,* July 5, 1841; *Maysville* (Ky.) *Eagle,* Feb. 26, 1842; *Indiana State Sentinel,* April 17, 1845; *Alton* (Ill.) *Telegraph,* May 14, 1842.

was marshalled for an impressive procession.[32] A typical demonstration of this character was the celebration held in Boston on May 30, 1844. Committees from the various Washingtonian societies, responsible for the arrangements, made every effort to secure the co-operation of all temperance organizations in Massachusetts and neighbouring states. As a result of this effective preliminary work many county societies sent large delegations to the city, where they joined similar delegations from societies in Connecticut, Rhode Island and New Hampshire. The city was in gala attire for the occasion. Banks were closed, and most business houses arranged for a half-holiday. Before noon thousands of visitors had found vantage points from which to view the parade. Promptly at twelve the procession moved from the State House down Beacon street to Park. It was formed in twenty-three sections, each headed by a brass band. The Washington Light Infantry, composed entirely of total abstainers, served as an honorary escort. The various societies marched under their distinctive banners, and the individual members wore badges or ribbons indicating the group with which they were affiliated. As the line moved forward, it was apparent that one of the Catholic societies in Boston, St. Mary's Mutual Benevolent Total Abstinence Society, was represented by the largest delegation. Here and there among the marchers appeared interesting floats which attested the ingenuity of several enthusiastic organizations. The South Boston Washington Society presented a moss-covered well with two men drawing buckets of cool water

[32] For interesting items regarding these temperance celebrations see the following: *Providence Daily Journal,* Jan. 21, Feb. 23, 25, 1842; *Delaware Gazette,* April 8, 15, 1842; *Baltimore Patriot,* Jan. 3, 1842, April 3, 1843; *N. Y. Tribune,* Feb. 23, 1842; *Richmond Whig,* July 4, 6, 1842; *Cleveland Plain Dealer,* Feb. 22, 1849; *Diary of Philip Hone,* II, 80; A. D. P. Van Buren, "That Glorious Fourth," *Pioneer Society of Michigan, Collections,* V, 422–426. Fairs and bazaars, similar to the anti-slavery fairs, were designed to raise money for the cause.

from its depths.   The Naval Washington Society came with a full-rigged ship, while the New Bedford society members manned a sturdy whale-boat to the plaudits of the spectators.

As the procession passed down the Mall, boys and girls of the Cold Water Army took their places on either side of the line of march, making a pretty sight in their blue and white uniforms.   Whenever possible, they sang temperance songs to the tunes played by the bands as they marched by.   The procession's destination was Boston Common where the members of the ladies' societies awaited its arrival.   As soon as the first marchers came into view, the women joined in the chorus of "The Teetotalers Are Coming," which was taken up by the entire multitude that had assembled for the speeches.   The oration of the afternoon, lauding the work of the Washingtonians, was delivered by Governor George N. Briggs who had long been active, as a member of the House, in the Congressional Temperance Society at Washington.   After the exercises on the Common were finished, picnic suppers were served in several parts of the city, and many delegates remained for an evening meeting at Tremont Temple which was addressed by Governor Briggs, William K. Mitchell and John B. Gough.   For at least one day Boston had been in the hands of the temperance forces.[33]

An account of the Boston celebration published in the *Journal of the American Temperance Union* concluded with this sentence: "We regretted that the old Massachusetts Temperance Society, and the Massachusetts Temperance Union, were not seen as such in the procession."   Unimportant as the statement may seem at first glance, it is a significant indication of a serious problem that confronted the reformers.   Under the compulsion of popular demand many of the old societies had employed Washingtonian

[33] Gough, *Autobiography*, pp. 177–182; *Journal*, June, 1844, p. 96, July, pp. 105–107.

speakers to revive a waning interest, but they had been disappointed that the new pledge-signers could seldom be persuaded to join existing organizations. Wherever Washingtonian workers conducted campaigns, it was necessary either
to form a new society officered by reformed men, or to convert the old group into a Washington abstinence society.
To some who had laboured long in temperance work, it seemed
unwise to abandon organizations which had been in existence
ten or fifteen years in favour of a new and untried principle.
It appeared to them that the Washingtonians had no interest in the triumphs of the struggle prior to 1840. The
younger movement seemed to be unwilling to learn anything
from the older. Its membership scoffed at the methods and
principles formerly held in esteem. A movement was on foot,
said some conservatives, to substitute noisy and sensational
demonstrations for systematic, educational propaganda.
Emotion was supplanting reason. The old leaders were being set aside. Any Tom, Dick or Harry could direct the
course of the reform.[34] Washingtonian "Heralds," "Standards" and "Advocates" were springing up everywhere, living
just long enough to cripple the recognized journals, and
then expiring from lack of funds. Their existence was too
often marked by unpleasant controversies with other temperance periodicals. The Washingtonians, on the other
hand, charged that the older societies refused to co-operate
with them, criticized their methods and ridiculed their principles.[35]

Although this mutual resentment was not universal, it

[34] For evidences of this distrust of the Washingtonian movement see:
Journal, October, 1841, p. 156, November, pp. 171–172, January, 1842,
p. 6, July, p. 104; *Cleveland Herald,* March 9, 1842. *Cf.* Marsh, *op. cit.,*
pp. 174–175; Jewett, *op. cit.,* pp. 29–30; Dorchester, *op. cit.,* pp. 271–272.

[35] Washingtonian scorn for the efforts of the older societies is revealed by sarcastic statements in the New York *Organ* and the *New
England Washingtonian.* See extracts copied in *Journal,* August, 1844,
p. 124.

developed into a distinction between "old" and "new" societies which seriously interfered with harmonious action.
One heresy charged against the Washingtonians was that
they repudiated all connection with organized religion and
denied that their reform was based on Christian principles.
Those who pressed the charge asserted that no Washingtonian meeting was ever opened with prayer, that ministers were
seldom invited to speak and that some members openly proclaimed their atheism. These accusations were greatly over-
drawn. It was true that many reformed drunkards and
others, who had signed the same pledge, were neither devout
nor deeply interested in the relation between religion and
reform. They were indifferent to the idea that their reformation was due to the "hand of God in human affairs."
They spent no time speculating whether they would be able
to keep their pledge without relying on the Almighty for
strength and guidance. But they were not atheists. The
religious aspect of the situation simply did not interest them.
Only a few of the extremists among them denounced the introduction of religious principles into a secular reform as
a dangerous manifestation of sectarianism.[36]

These extremists, however, were so vociferous that many
Christians came to regard atheism as a characteristic feature
of the Washingtonian movement.[37] Fearful that the whole
temperance program would lose the support of devout church

[36] The distinction between "old" and "new" societies was by no
means sharply defined. Many Washingtonians, anxious to work in
harmony with the older groups, found the existing organizations of
great value to them. The files of the *Columbia Washingtonian*, published at Hudson, N. Y., for 1842 and 1843 indicate that signers of the
new pledge were of many minds as to the proper way to promote
temperance. See *Columbia Washingtonian*, March 16, 1843.

[37] Writing of the situation in later years, John B. Gough complained
that he was the object of bitter invective in certain Washingtonian
journals because he insisted that temperance was based on piety and
urged his hearers to seek divine guidance before signing the pledge.
Autobiography, pp. 246–247; Martyn, *op. cit.*, pp. 115–117.

members, the editor of the *Journal of the American Temperance Union* undertook to champion the cause of religion. After the autumn of 1842 the *Journal's* columns contained frequent attacks on "men of infidel and wicked minds" who were using the temperance reform to arouse opposition to Christian principles.[38]   A statement of the editor of the *Essex Washingtonian* to the effect that if Washingtonianism prevailed the religious sects would "be blown to the moon" called forth this comment:

In the late extraordinary reformation of drunkards, a subject of thankfulness, however transient, but more especially when resulting, as it has in thousands of cases, in permanent sobriety; a deep sympathy was felt for this unfortunate class—prejudiced against religion and religious men by long absence from the Sabbath's influence and by subjection to the vile and debasing principles of the bar-room and dram-shop. To induce them to sign the pledge, these prejudices, it was supposed, must be consulted. The wharf, the market-house, the public hall, rather than a church, must be the place of meeting. Under the influence of a glee song, an animated speech, a loud huzza, not deterred or thrown back by any gloomy forms of religion or any presentation of moral obligation, they must be induced as gentlemen to come up and sign the pledge. . . . That the exclusion of all religious forms and the entire abstraction of religion from temperance, was necessary for the reclamation of the drunkard, we have never believed. There can be no necessity for atheism anywhere in this world. The drunkard may have felt hostile to religion while in the bar-room and amid the fumes of liquor, and he may feel so after he has reformed and been taught to believe that he is better than a Christian, but never did a poor drunkard go up in sincerity to sign the pledge, without feeling himself a prodigal, commencing a work of return to his Heavenly Father, and needing that Father's help; and who would not have gratefully knelt and listened to a prayer

[38] *Journal*, September, 1842, p. 137, October, p. 152, December, pp. 179, 182, February, 1843, pp. 17, 27.

for that help on his new endeavors. And we believe that if the hundreds of thousands of signatures in our country had been accompanied with prayer and some religious enforcement, their power and efficiency would have been incomparably stronger. . . . We trust our Washingtonian friends will not view us their enemies for this exposure of the arts of infidelity. We believe there is not one in a thousand but would abhor them, if they understood them. We say to them, cut loose from them all, or they will prove the ruin of your enterprise. In the prevalence of pure Washingtonianism, the reformation of drunkards and the relief of the miserable, every philanthropist, every patriot and Christian ought to rejoice, but when the unprincipled improve a temperance meeting to revile the Clergy, the Churches or the Magistracy, they should receive the withering rebuke of every virtuous citizen.[39]

Thus did John Marsh warn his associates to be on their guard. Thirty years before Lyman Beecher had extolled the temperance reformers as strong supporters of "the Clergy, the Churches and the Magistracy," but the developments of a generation had carried the movement far from the principles of the pioneers.

Controversies over the religious opinions of the Washingtonians were soon overshadowed by the more important question of their attitude toward legislation. We have seen that prior to 1840 a considerable portion of the temperance forces had become convinced of the impossibility of driving intemperance from the land without the aid of legal restrictions on the liquor traffic. This group was keenly disappointed that within the Washingtonian movement there was developing a determined opposition to the enforcement of temperance by statute. With an unusual consideration for the feelings of the liquor dealer many reformed men refused to countenance any action against the men interested in the

[39] *Journal*, April, 1844, pp. 56–57.

traffic.[40]   William K. Mitchell, for example, championed the cause of the retailer so consistently that he permitted liquor dealers to sign the pledge and join societies which he organized.[41]   Thomas F. Marshall, Congressman from the Ashland district in Kentucky, was particularly vehement in his opposition to any legislative interference.[42]   In a speech at the Broadway Tabernacle, New York, on May 4, 1842, he sounded a warning to his fellow Washingtonians:

Let not the cause of Temperance—ye who are members of its societies—ye who are the priests of Temperance principles—let it not mingle itself with any other cause whatever.   Above all things on earth, eschew all political alliance.   The cause is too high for law.   Make no statutes, nor attempt to make any, on the subject.   It began in weakness—leave it, unaided by human enactments, to the mighty instruments which God himself, the author of this great revolution, has selected in the first instance as the means of its support.   Let politicians, as politicians, and legislators, *alone.*   If they join you—as some have done—O! in God's name open your arms wide to receive them! but don't go to them.   Let them wage their factious warfare.   Let them vex the walls of the national Legislature, and weary the very atmosphere with the din of their party contests.   Keep the Temperance ear sealed up against them!   Persecute nobody. Look, rather, with compassion and sympathy on the unfortunate wretches who yet have not power to break their chains; but O! don't make laws against them!   God knows they are under a law hard enough already!   This cause is too high for law.[43]

The fact that Marshall was in politics in Kentucky may

[40] *P. T. D.,* II, *Eighth Report,* pp. 27–30; Arethusa Hall, *op. cit.,* p. 313.

[41] *Journal,* November, 1842, p. 172.

[42] Marshall was one of the most gifted of the Washingtonian orators of the period.   His decision to sign the pledge in the spring of 1842 seems to have been the occasion for the rejuvenation of the Congressional Temperance Society, which was reorganized with George N. Briggs as president.   *P. T. D.,* II, 331–332.

[43] *Speeches of Thomas F. Marshall on Alcohol and Intemperance,* p. 4.

have determined his personal opinion, but he expressed the view of many who had no political future at stake. While it is impossible to discover what proportion of the Washingtonians agreed with him, there is abundant evidence that the legal suasionists, as the supporters of restrictive statutes were called, received little support from the "reformed drunkards." [44]   A writer in the *Columbia Washingtonian* pointed out the fallacy of attempting to reconcile two such antagonistic principles as persuasion and coercion. If the former had ever been the proper method of temperance work, and he believed it had, it should not be supplanted by the latter at a time when it was proving highly successful.[45] Another correspondent to the same journal argued that the liquor dealers were anxious for the temperance supporters to commit the error of legislating against the traffic in intoxicants.

The rum-sellers [he wrote] at this moment are trembling at the inroads made into the ranks of their customers, and that portion of them who are determined to hold out to the last, are already aware of the certain destruction which awaits their craft. . . . They dread nothing so much as the use of the Washingtonian weapons of light and truth, and court nothing at our hands so much as a resort to legal suasion, relying on the proneness of the community to frown upon persecution and to sympathize with its victims. Many, too, who now in their hearts wish well to the temperance cause would easily avail themselves of the reason furnished by the Washingtonians in resorting to coercive means with the rum-seller, to halt in their present standing, turn their backs upon our cause, and content themselves

[44] The *Augusta* (Ga.) *Washingtonian* for several years argued for moral suasion, but finally adopted the view of those who believed that the aid of law should be invoked. Scomp, *op. cit.,* pp. 400–401. The *Columbia Washingtonian* was likewise in favor of legislative action, but published much material on the other side of the question. See issue of Dec. 29, 1842.

[45] *Columbia Washingtonian,* Feb. 2, 1843.

with having been almost persuaded to take upon them the total
abstinence vows.   Many, too, there is reason to fear, who are
now determined and able advocates of temperance would revolt
at the manifestation of a desire to persecute, and go back and
walk no more with us.[46]

The officers of the American Temperance Union had little
faith in arguments of this character, but it seemed expedient
to them to recognize the numerical strength of the moral
suasionist faction.   The columns of the *Journal*, therefore,
were apportioned with even-handed justice to the controver-
sialists, who proceeded to confuse the issue with a bewilder-
ing array of conflicting opinions.   In the midst of the verbal
warfare the enemies of the liquor dealers marshalled their
forces, scarce knowing whether to regard the Washingtonians as friends or foes.   Fortunately, for their particular interest they were not long embarrassed by this apparent opposition within the temperance ranks, for Washingtonianism
collapsed almost as suddenly as it had risen.

In the early days of the movement shrewd observers had
pointed out two fundamental weaknesses which might prove
its undoing.   In the first place, there was no connection between the various societies that carried forward the work of
spreading Washingtonian principles.   Each group was allowed to follow its own course, centralized control being considered too great an infringement on the rights of the individual society.   As a result systematic organization was
impossible; uniformity in methods was never attained; and
chance largely determined the formulation of principles.   A
second weakness lay in the character of the Washingtonian
membership.   Many were reformed inebriates who had signed
the pledge during a period of emotional exaltation and were
liable to suffer a corresponding relapse.   As a matter of
fact, such relapses were not infrequent and tended to impair public confidence in the movement.   Though some were

[46] *Ibid.,* Feb. 23, 1843.

reclaimed after they had fallen, they were a liability rather than an asset to the temperance cause. Within ten years after that famous meeting in Chase's Tavern, Baltimore, Washingtonianism, as a distinct phase of temperance work, had virtually disappeared. That portion of its membership which remained faithful to the total abstinence pledge either found a place in the renewed activity of the older societies, or joined one of the rapidly growing fraternal orders.[47]

As early as the autumn of 1842, it was apparent to several earnest members of the Washington Temperance Society in New York City that the new movement was not properly organized to retain the fruits of its victories. They believed that something would have to be done to prevent the reformed drunkard from violating his pledge and returning to his former habits. Desertions were so numerous, it seemed to them, that the Washingtonian forces were in imminent danger of disintegration. Their problem, therefore, was to devise an organization which would hold the interest of its members after the first enthusiasm had spent itself. The first steps to solve the problem were taken in Teetotalers' Hall, 71 Division street, on the evening of September 29, 1842. As announced on the invitation card, the purpose of the meeting was to organize a "beneficial society based on total abstinence," to be known as the New York Division, No. 1, of the Sons of Temperance. Such a plan met with the approval of the sixteen Washingtonians who attended the initial meeting, and a committee was appointed to draw up a constitution.[48]

[47] *P. T. D.,* II, *Eighth Report,* p. 17; Jewett, *op. cit.,* pp. 29–30; Clark, *op. cit.,* pp. 53–54; Scomp, *op. cit.,* 386–387; W. M. Thayer, *Charles Jewett, Life and Recollections,* pp. 165–166; *Temperance in the City of New York* (1844).

[48] *Journal of the Proceedings of the Grand Division of the Sons of Temperance of New York* (1845), pp. 47, vii–xlvii. The leading spirits in the formation of the Order were Daniel H. Sands, John W. Oliver and Isaac J. Oliver.

Having worked for several months to perfect various details of the proposed Order, the charter members of New
York Division were ready in January, 1843, to announce the
result of their deliberations. In a circular "to the friends
of temperance in the United States" they stated that the
Sons of Temperance had three distinct objects in view: "To
shield us from the evils of intemperance; afford mutual assistance in case of sickness; and elevate our characters as
men." The first object was to be effected through the instrumentality of the pledge which read: "No brother shall
make, buy, sell, or use as a beverage, any spirituous or malt
liquors, wine or cider." The protective feature was to be
taken care of through the payment of a nominal initiation
fee and weekly dues. Permanent organizations of the Order consisted of three classes, namely, subordinate divisions,
grand divisions, and a national division. The subordinate
division was the local lodge which selected its membership by
the usual process from men over eighteen years of age, who
had signed the total abstinence pledge. The grand division
consisted of all past and acting Worthy Patriarchs of local
lodges within a state, while the national division was composed of the past and acting Grand Worthy Patriarchs of
the state divisions. Thus, control in the Order was vested in
a hierarchy which was presided over by the officers of the
national division.[49]

The highly centralized form of organization enabled officers to supervise carefully the conduct of the members.
Furthermore, the fraternal bond encouraged the brethren
to guard each other against violations of the pledge. Every
member was urged to report any infractions of the rules
that came to his notice, in order that the division might
take proper action. From the number of suspensions and
expulsions recorded in the journals of the several grand

[49] *Ibid.*, xxxiii–xxxv.

divisions it is evident that a strict discipline was maintained within the Order.[50]

Neither centralized control nor excellent discipline, however, could secure uniformity of opinion. The Sons seem to have been as hopelessly divided over the advisability of legislating against the liquor traffic as were the temperance folk outside their ranks. The editor of the *Organ*, official journal for the fraternity in New York, was openly favourable to the cause of the legal suasionists, devoting a portion of nearly every issue to a discussion of the question.[51] But his view was not acceptable everywhere in the Order. In 1847, for instance, a subordinate division in Philadelphia appealed to the quarterly session of the Pennsylvania Grand Division, charging that certain members were trying to commit the fraternity to the support of legislative restrictions on the liquor traffic. After an extensive investigation a special committee reported that the charges were well founded and recommended that the members be censured for their interference in a matter of general policy. The Grand Division at its regular meeting in 1848 heard the committee's report and ordered it laid on the table, evidently unwilling to risk a record vote on the question.[52]

Differences of opinion did not seriously affect the harmonious relation between divisions, nor interfere with the rapid growth of the Order. In 1844 grand divisions were established in New Jersey, Maryland, Pennsylvania, Connecticut and the District of Columbia. The following year there were enough subordinate divisions in Maine, Delaware,

[50] *Journal of the Proceedings of the Grand Division of Pennsylvania* (1848), pp. 136–149; *Journal . . . of . . . New York* (1846), pp. 143–145. In Pennsylvania, for example, during 1848 approximately 1500 were suspended and 3200 expelled for violating the pledge.

[51] *Organ,* Oct. 26, Nov. 23, 30, Dec. 14, 28, 1844, Jan. 4, 11, 1845.

[52] *Minutes of the Quarterly Session of the Grand Division of Pennsylvania,* Jan. 26, 1848, pp. 100–119. See also B. A. Clark, *Oration Delivered before Niagara Division, No. 109, of the Sons of Temperance* (1846).

Virginia, North Carolina, Missouri, and Ohio to justify the creation of state jurisdictions. The 180 lodges then in existence enrolled nearly 10,000 members. Within the next five years the growth of the fraternity was so rapid that in 1850 the National Division reported 36 grand divisions, 5894 subordinate divisions and 245,233 paying members.[53]

These years of expansion were also years of conflict. Although the hostility to secret societies and fraternal orders, which was manifested in the anti-Masonic agitation of the twenties and thirties, had gradually subsided, there were many who remembered the prejudices of former days. Their presence in the temperance movement furnished a spirited opposition to the Sons of Temperance. They regarded the Order as a secret society, organized to perpetuate principles similar to those of the Masonic fraternity or the Independent Order of Odd Fellows. Therefore, the organization was objectionable as an agency in the work of moral reform. The attack on it was led by John Marsh for the American Temperance Union. In the columns of the *Journal* he rebuked the temperance papers which had hailed the secret fraternities as the *summum bonum* of the temperance reform. His objections to the Sons of Temperance and similar orders were based, he said, not upon prejudice but upon knowledge.[54] None of the organizations were "beneficial societies" in the true sense of the word. They gave no aid to the poor, miserable inebriate, unless he was able to pay an initiation fee and monthly dues. The Independent Order of Rechabites refused to elect anyone to membership

[53] *Journal . . . of . . . New York* (1845), pp. viii–ix; P. S. White and E. S. Ely, *Vindication of the Order of the Sons of Temperance,* pp. 26–30; Dorchester, *op. cit.,* p. 278.

[54] The Independent Order of Rechabites, taking its name from that religious order among the Israelites which abstained from wine and dwelt in tents, was securing a following in the United States at the time the Sons of Temperance was organized. It was of English origin, the first "tent" having been formed in 1835. In 1848 there were 253 primary tents with 14,253 members in the United States and Canada.

who was not free from "all bodily disease or infirmity that would render him burdensome to the tent," while the Sons of Temperance rejected anyone who was incapacitated from earning a livelihood, or had no visible means of support. These regulations prevented both Orders from serving the men most in need of their benevolence.

Furthermore, any attempt to carry on temperance work behind the veil of secrecy, Marsh insisted, would inevitably arouse distrust and fear in the minds of many friends of reform. It mattered not that the Order of the Sons of Temperance had announced to the public its object, its laws, its numbers and its officers. It remained a secret society because its meetings were closed to all except the few who had been carefully selected for membership. The absence of elaborate regalia and extensive ritual did not free it from the taint of aristocratic intrigue. Finally, the organization of the fraternity was such as to constitute a menace to all who took its obligation. Control was so centralized in a small hierarchy that the principle of democracy was replaced by that of oligarchy; and it would not be difficult for the oligarchy to become despotic.[55]

The editor of the *Organ*, answering this attack, laughed at Marsh's lack of humour in applying the same standards to the Sons of Temperance as he would apply to a Bible society, a tract society or a missionary auxiliary. As for the charge of secrecy, he considered it ridiculous that a few pass-words, which were the only secrets that members of the Order enjoyed, should be made into a bogey to frighten people. He reminded the *Journal* that his fraternity was not designed to do the work of ordinary temperance societies. Its function was to take care of "follow up" work after the propaganda of the regular organizations had been successful.[56]

[55] *Journal*, May, 1844, pp. 65–66, September, pp. 137–138, October, pp. 145–146.
[56] *Organ*, Oct. 26, 1844.

So numerous became the attacks on the Order from Christian congregations, ministerial associations and ecclesiastical assemblies that it seemed necessary to publish an elaborate defence.   Philip S. White, Most Worthy Patriarch of the National Division, and Dr. Ezra S. Ely, Chaplain of the Grand Division of Pennsylvania, wrote an able "Vindication," which was circulated in 1848.   Their chief concern was to quiet the insistent charge that membership in the Sons of Temperance was regarded by the Order as a substitute for membership in a Christian church.   The "Vindication" categorically denied that any of the divisions was attempting to control the religious beliefs of its members and cited as proof the large number of Protestant ministers of different denominations, who occupied official positions in the grand divisions of their respective states.[57]   The most significant statement, however, defined the relation of the Order to the wider scope of the temperance movement:

> We seek to reclaim inebriates; to confirm men in total abstinence from all that can intoxicate them; to encourage and animate in every good work all reclaimed drunkards; to retain none any longer than they continue faithful to their solemn promise; and to afford assistance, in case of sickness or death of a brother, or the decease of his wife, to such persons as are by our constitution entitled to the same.   Our halls are also intended to be pleasant places of resort and social intercourse, in which young men especially may acquire habits of public speaking, and of transacting the business of a popular assembly; and by which many who have leisure, may be lured from the bar-room and other scenes of dissipation.[58]

Here, at last, was a group which offered a substitute for the social attractions of the grog-shop and tippling-house. Dr. Rush had recognized the value of the compensating substitute in his recommendation that drinkers of ardent spirits

[57] P. S. White and E. S. Ely, *op. cit.,* p. 39.
[58] *Ibid.,* p. 33.

try the milder stimulation of wine and malt liquors. The advocates of total abstinence, however, did not include in their scheme of things any provision for softening the hardships of self-denial. In their plan virtue was its own reward. The problem of the abstainer's leisure time received scant attention, though occasionally the suggestion was made that hours formerly spent in convivial tippling or drunken carousal might well be devoted to furthering the work of some moral or religious society. It remained for the Sons of Temperance to make the first feeble gesture toward an idea which later became tremendously important in meeting the challenge of the saloon.

The period of the Washingtonian revival was marked by the increased interest and more active participation of women in the reform. As the drunkard's reformation directed attention to social and economic conditions in his family, it became apparent that some form of organized charity was needed to assist in the establishment of a proper home life. In this work the women of the country quickly took the lead. Under the name of Martha Washington societies and Ladies' Benevolent societies they not only cared for the poor and unfortunate victims of intemperance by providing food and clothing, but they also attacked the vice of drunkenness among their own sex and secured signatures to the total abstinence pledge.[59] But their task was chiefly a work of charity, for American women had earned a reputation for abstemiousness long before the temperance reform enlisted their aid. Wherever the Washingtonian movement spread, then, it was apt to be supplemented by auxiliary organizations of women whose benevolent efforts were often the means of holding ground that had been won. Not only were their services invaluable, but their financial

59 *Journal*, November, 1841, p. 171, January, 1842, p. 7, July 1, 1843, pp. 99–100; *N. Y. Tribune*, Jan. 13, 1842; J. G. Woolley and W. E. Johnson, *Temperance Progress in the Century*, p. 90.

contributions to the reform were far from negligible, for they swelled the treasury of many a society by the proceeds from temperance fairs and bazaars.

The activity of women in temperance work seems to have called forth less opposition than it did in the case of the anti-slavery movement. After 1840 many temperance publications urged women not to confine their influence to the home, but to affiliate with some active society. In October, 1843, two of the charter members of the Sons of Temperance, Daniel Sands and John W. Oliver, assisted in the formation of a similar organization among the members of the Martha Washington societies in New York City. The new Order, known as the Daughters of Temperance, was a mutual benefit association which elected to membership women above the age of fifteen who had signed the total abstinence pledge. Weekly benefits were paid during the illness of a member, and in the event of death a definite sum was applied to the payment of funeral expenses. This protective feature was stressed in an energetic campaign to increase the strength of the Order, but the popular response was discouraging. Few locals were established outside of New York, Pennsylvania and the New England states. The influence of the existing local unions was weakened by dissension within the Order which finally resulted in the formation of a rival sorority.[60]

It was in a local union of the Daughters of Temperance at Canajoharie, New York, in 1849 that Susan B. Anthony made her first speech in favour of temperance, an opportunity which she used to secure a hearing for the cause of

[60] *Organ*, June 21, 1845, November 9, 1844; Clark, *op. cit.*, 67–72. In 1846 certain members of the Sons of Temperance were responsible for the formation of the Cadets of Temperance, which enrolled boys between the ages of twelve and eighteen. Each section of the Cadets was under the guardianship of three responsible Sons of Temperance. In 1849 the Cadets claimed between eight and nine thousand members, a majority of them in Pennsylvania. Marcus E. Cross, *The Mirror of Intemperance*, pp. 157–159.

women's rights. Frequently in her subsequent career she presented the two reforms as complementary to each other.[61] Miss Anthony, however, was not the first woman to attack the vice of intemperance from a public platform. In 1840 Lucretia Mott, one of the American women denied admission to the World's Anti-slavery Convention in London, had lectured several times in England and Ireland on the anti-slavery movement, the social condition of women and the temperance reform. Elizabeth Cady Stanton, who heard her in London, was so impressed that she decided to seek an opportunity to present her views in public. Two years later, while living in Johnstown, New York, she made her début in a temperance plea before an audience that contained more than a hundred men. During these years Abby Kelly, who was winning fame and not a little notoriety as an unusually vigorous opponent of slavery, began to champion total abstinence with considerable success. After 1847 her achievements were rivalled by those of Lucy Stone, who found that audiences interested in temperance were sometimes willing to listen to arguments in favour of women's rights.[62]

The efforts of these pioneer women were not heralded in the columns of the *Journal of the American Temperance Union,* possibly because no information reached the editor. It is more probable, however, that the *Journal's* silence was dictated by a desire to avoid embarrassment. Any mention of the service rendered to temperance by these women enthusiasts would be apt to precipitate a controversy over the propriety of their conduct and the safeness of their anti-slavery views. Either question, revealing important differences of opinion among the reformers, would tend to destroy harmony, a situation which the officers of the Union greatly desired to avoid.

[61] Ida H. Harper, *The Life and Work of Susan B. Anthony,* I, 53–55.
[62] *Ibid.,* I, 62–63, 67–68; *James and Lucretia Mott,* Anna D. Hallowell, editor, pp. 187, 191, 228; *Reminiscences of Elizabeth Cady Stanton,* p. 111; Erasmus Wilson, *op. cit.,* p. 906.

Indeed, at this time the temperance leaders were learning that any reform is apt to attract the support of advocates who hinder rather than help the cause. The zeal of the anti-slavery element threatened to cause serious trouble, as several incidents between 1846 and 1850 gave evidence of hidden feeling over the question. At the first session of the World's Temperance Convention, which met on August 4, 1846, in the hall of the London Literary Institution, a remark by Rev. E. N. Kirk of Albany to the effect that many slave-holders were good men aroused the anger of those who held abolitionist views. William Lloyd Garrison, although not a regularly elected delegate, secured the floor for the purpose of denouncing Kirk's statement. Much to his disgust, however, he was not permitted to finish, for a majority of the Convention desired to prevent an acrimonious debate on the subject. But it was some time before the meeting was quieted sufficiently for the transaction of business.[63] The alacrity and unanimity with which the American delegation silenced Garrison did not reveal personal hostility so much as a desire to refrain from giving offence to the friends of the institution of slavery. At the closing session of the conference in Covent Garden bitter feeling was again aroused, this time by the Negro orator, Frederick Douglass. He attacked the temperance movement in the United States for its failure both to make provision for the Negro in its ranks and to concern itself with his bondage. The speech was apparently cut short by the presiding officer, whereupon Rev. E. N. Kirk arose and answered it to the extent of denying that American temperance reformers were supporters of slavery. As a result of this episode Rev. Samuel H. Cox of Brooklyn wrote a vigorous letter to the editor of the *New York Evangelist*, charging Douglass with being in the pay of interested parties and accusing the abolitionists of a plot

[63] *Journal*, October, 1846, p. 145; *William Lloyd Garrison, The Story of his Life*, III, 157.

to injure the temperance movement, since they could not control it.[64]

Although the accusations against Douglass were not based on any evidence, subsequent events made some temperance advocates believe that the Garrisonian abolitionists were determined to make trouble for them.   On July 2, 1849, Father Mathew arrived in New York City for an extensive tour of the country, which had been long awaited by those who had followed his work in Ireland.   A formal welcome by Mayor Woodhull expressed the hope that the "apostle of temperance" might be as successful in the United States as he had been in his native land.   After spending three weeks in the vicinity of New York, during which time he administered his pledge to thousands of Catholics, he departed for Boston where he experienced an embarrassing encounter with the abolitionists.   The Board of Managers of the Massachusetts Anti-slavery Society extended its welcome to him in the form of an invitation to speak at a mass-meeting in Worcester, arranged to celebrate the anniversary of the abolition of slavery in the British West Indies.   In its communication the committee reminded Father Mathew that he had signed an "Address," drawn up by Daniel O'Connell in 1841, urging the Irish in America to support the cause of abolition. When the communication was presented, Father Mathew informed William Lloyd Garrison that his position as a Catholic priest and as an advocate of temperance, who intended to visit the slave-holding states, made it necessary for him to decline to attend the Worcester meeting.   So irritated was Garrison by the incident that he spread several accounts of it in the columns of the *Liberator*, portraying Father Mathew as a man without honour who sacrificed his principles for the sake of expediency.[65]   The newspapers

---

[64] *Journal*, October, 1846, p. 159; *Life and Times of Frederick Douglass*, Written by Himself, pp. 305–309; *N. Y. Evangelist*, Sept. 5, 1846.

immediately took up the story, commenting on its various aspects. Generally sentiment was favourable to the priest, editorials either praised his conduct, or defended his course as the best way out of a trying situation. The *South Carolina Temperance Advocate* was convinced that the Irish leader was not a fanatic on the slavery question, and Judge John B. O'Neall, president of the state society, invited him to visit the home of Calhoun.

Not all Southerners, however, viewed Father Mathew's attitude in the same light. Reports of the Boston interview published in Georgia emphasized the importance of the Irish "Address" which had been read at the great anti-slavery meeting in Faneuil Hall on January 28, 1842. Since Father Mathew had signed this abolition document, it was evident that he was an enemy of slavery. Accordingly, the president of the Georgia State Temperance Society, Judge Joseph H. Lumpkin, wrote to the distinguished reformer expressing regret that the Society was forced to withdraw its previous invitation to visit the state. In subsequent correspondence, however, Father Mathew assured Judge Lumpkin of his "single-mindedness in the advocacy of the all-absorbing cause of temperance" and his resolution "not to interfere in the slightest degree with the institutions of this mighty Republic." These assurances placated the Georgians and they welcomed the "apostle of temperance" to Augusta in January, 1850, with a torchlight procession.[66]

While the difficulties arising out of the interview with Garrison were still unsettled, Father Mathew reached Washington on his trip southward. He was enthusiastically received by the Catholics of the city, many of whom accepted

[65] Garrison attributed Father Mathew's attitude to the admonition of the "slaveite," Bishop Hughes of the New York diocese. *William Lloyd Garrison*, III, 248; *Liberator*, XVIII, 126.

[66] For Father Mathew's letter to Judge Lumpkin see Scomp, *op. cit.*, pp. 447–450,

the total abstinence pledge.   He was entertained by President Taylor at the White House, and was honoured by an invitation to occupy a seat in the House of Representatives. A resolution, presented by Senator Walker of Wisconsin, that he be requested to pay a visit to the Senate met with unexpected opposition.   Senator Clemens of Alabama declared that he was willing to honour a famous champion of temperance, but he objected to Father Mathew because he was an abolitionist.   In the debate that followed a score of Senators attacked and defended the resolution, their comments dealing chiefly with the attitude of the Irish priest toward slavery.   Clay, Cass and Seward, not often united in support of any measure, agreed that the whole discussion was much ado about nothing, since Father Mathew had given adequate assurance that he was interested only in carrying forward the fight against intemperance.   Jefferson Davis, however, was not convinced.   He demanded that all abolitionists, whatever their mission, be excluded from the Senate Chamber.   John P. Hale of New Hampshire stated his intention of voting for the resolution, but he did not want his vote to be interpreted as a sanction of the artful manner in which Father Mathew had dodged the slavery issue.   When the vote was finally taken, the resolution passed in spite of the opposition of eighteen Senators from slave-holding states. The result was in the nature of a calamity, however, for the temperance champion must now carry his cause among people whose representatives in Congress had publicly condemned his slavery views.[67]

Father Mathew's tour of the South, though in no sense a failure, was disappointing to his intimate friends.   They attributed his moderate success to the unfavourable reports

[67] *Congressional Globe*, 31st Cong., first session, pp. 51–59; *Annual Report of the Massachusetts Anti-slavery Society* (1850); *Journal*, February, 1850, p. 21; *Liberator*, XIX, 190, 194, XX, 15, 24; *William Lloyd Garrison*, III, pp. 247–261; Maguire, *op. cit.*, 479–486.

which had preceded his visit, but there were other factors which were at least equally responsible. Many Catholics were displeased because he appeared in public too frequently at meetings which were manifestly under Protestant auspices. The Protestants, on the other hand, accepted his ministrations with little enthusiasm. As might be expected, in view of the increasing nativist sentiment in the country, the charge of "Romanism" was often used against him. Some there were who criticized his custom of requesting persons to kneel and receive the sign of the cross as they took the pledge. Despite religious prejudice, however, Father Mathew's work was not limited to persons of his own faith. Although his first concern was to encourage the existing Catholic Total Abstinence societies and to organize others, he administered the pledge to all who presented themselves. His journal refers constantly to the number of "dissenters" who attended services at the churches where he celebrated mass. Many of them, he thought, came out of curiosity, but some remained to hear his temperance plea at the close of the service.[68]

In comparison with the emotional response which he had aroused in Ireland, Father Mathew made little impression on American Catholics. But it is manifestly unfair to judge his work in the United States on the basis of his extraordinary success in his native land. In Ireland, he had virgin soil; in America he gleaned after many who had reaped harvests. Still, in New York, Boston, Philadelphia and Baltimore thousands were induced to adopt the principle of total abstinence and temperance sentiment among the Catholics was signally strengthened. Reasonably successful meetings in Richmond, Charleston, Augusta and Mobile reached their climax in New Orleans, where more than 12,000 were

[68] *Journal*, August, 1849, p. 123, April, 1850, p. 61; Maguire, *op. cit.*, pp. 488–500; J. G. Shea, *A History of the Catholic Church within the limits of the United States*, pp. 186–187; Woolley and Johnson, *op. cit.*, 95–97.

reported to have signed the pledge during the days that Father Mathew preached at the old St. Louis' Cathedral. As he journeyed northward along the Mississippi, he was handicapped by ill health, but by the time he reached St. Louis his strength had returned.   At the urgent request of Bishop Rapp of the Cleveland diocese he visited northern Ohio and western Pennsylvania in the autumn of 1850.   Returning South for the winter he was pleased to find "Father Mathew" societies flourishing in the states which he had previously visited.   When the time came for his return to Ireland in November, 1851, the *New York Herald* estimated that he had travelled 37,000 miles through twenty-five states and had administered the pledge to almost half a million.[69]   If this be correct, the Irish priest had reached almost one-third of the Catholics in the United States.[70]

In the opinion of many temperance workers there was one important defect in Father Mathew's theory and practice.   Failing to stress sufficiently the moral culpability of the liquor dealer, he did not reach the conclusion that legal restriction was necessary to combat the evil of intemperance. Like so many reformers before him, he relied upon the power of a symbol to keep men sober.   He voiced no plea for legislation to prevent the rum-seller from undoing the work of reform.   It was true that he condemned the distiller and retailer, but he did not urge his hearers to use their political power to break up the trade in intoxicants.   This significant omission, many reformers believed, made it necessary to discount greatly his value to the cause.   The accessions to the ranks of total abstainers were important.   But how much more important, if they had been taught to work and vote for the legal destruction of the liquor traffic.

[69] *N. Y. Tribune*, July 4, 6, 20, 27, 31, 1849; *N. Y. Herald*, Nov. 8, 1851; *Journal*, May, 1850, p. 74, July, p. 103, November, p. 161; Maguire, *op. cit.*, pp. 500–551; G. F. Houck, *The Church in Northern Ohio and in the Diocese of Cleveland*, pp. 23, 26.

[70] The Roman Catholics in the United States in 1850 were enumerated as 1,500,000. Channing, *History of the United States*, V, 220.

CHAPTER X

THE LITERATURE OF PROTEST

FEW special interest groups in the history of the American people have surpassed the temperance reformers in the distribution of literary propaganda. Periodicals, pamphlets and broadsides fell from the press with a rapidity that belied the slender resources of the organizations financing their publication. It seemed to be the aim of the societies to present to the reading public every conceivable appeal and argument that could be made through the medium of the printed page. Factional quarrels and doctrinal disputes, which threatened to disrupt the unity of the movement, tended to increase the normal output of literature because of the unusual interest aroused by the controversies. Hundreds of thousands of pages were annually reported by printing committees of the state societies, until the very bulk of the publications seemed to augur success for the cause.

Despite this activity, the financial resources of the reformers were not only slight, but also uncertain. The problem of securing funds was always with them. Prior to 1840 no state society had incorporated in its constitution a provision for the permanent supply of its treasury. All relied upon donations, special collections and receipts from publications to provide revenue sufficient for their needs. The American Temperance Society encouraged contributions by offering honorary memberships for thirty dollars and by conferring on every donor of two hundred and fifty dollars the title of honorary vice-president. The executive com-

mittee of the American Temperance Union did not apportion
its expenses among the various auxiliaries, but depended
upon the gifts of generous friends and the proceeds from the
sale of periodicals and tracts.   In many societies, both
state and local, the financial burden was borne by the officers
with little assistance from the rank and file.   In New York,
for example, the state society was kept solvent for seven
years through the generosity of Edward C. Delavan, who
used personal funds to pay deficits that exceeded three
thousand dollars annually.[1]

As the societies multiplied, requests for lecturers and organizers increased, but there was little money available with
which to meet the demand.   Some of the older organizations
supported agents who eked out their salaries by taking up
special collections in the communities they visited.   Their
number never was large, however, and their time was often
spent in trying to secure sufficient funds to meet their travelling expenses.   As a result the missionary activities of the
societies came to depend more and more upon gratuitous
labour, and it was generally understood that whoever worked
for the temperance cause accepted a sort of financial martyr-
dom.   In 1840 Dr. Charles Jewett, secretary of the Massachusetts Temperance Union, persuaded his organization to
revise its constitution in order to place its finances on a
sound basis.   A plan was adopted which resulted in the
enrollment of several thousand members, each pledged to
pay one dollar annually, so long as he was able.   In consideration of the regular support thus given the Union,
every member received a subscription to the official organ,
The Temperance Journal.   Unfortunately few societies

[1] *Mass. Spy*, Aug. 24, 1836; *Sixth Annual Report of the American
Temperance Society* (1833); *P. T. D.*, II, 303.   The Massachusetts
Society for the Suppression of Intemperance was an exception to the
rule.   Its members paid a two dollar membership fee.

followed the lead of Massachusetts in formulating a new system, and haphazard methods continued to hinder effective work. Even the enthusiasts who were responsible for the Washingtonian revival received little support from the treasuries of established organizations. They secured their expense money and salaries from the people among whom they laboured, and there is little evidence that they found the venture highly profitable.[2] Such popular lecturers as Hawkins and Gough, of course, were able to demand more than a living wage for their services, but Gough tells us in his autobiography that he lectured for two years without earning enough to pay his expenses.[3]

If the temperance organizations often felt the pinch of poverty, it was not because of extravagant expenditures. One is impressed in reading the records by the amount of work accomplished with funds so limited. During the first ten years of its existence the New York State Temperance Society, the most active of the state associations, printed and distributed more than 12,000,000 copies of tracts and periodicals at a cost of less than one cent a copy. From the proceeds of the sale of these publications it defrayed two-thirds of its total expenses during the period.[4] Prior to 1836 the American Temperance Society prepared annually a report of approximately one hundred pages, which contained a survey of temperance activity in all parts of the world. The bulk of the society's funds was devoted to the

[2] Charles Jewett, *The Temperance Cause; Past, Present and Future*, pp. 27–28.

[3] *Ibid.*, 23–26; Gough, *Autobiography*, pp. 247–248. After 1853 Gough's work was exceedingly profitable.

[4] *P. T. D.*, II, 29, 126. It is interesting to note that the publications of the American Tract Society for its first ten years did not bulk much larger than those of the New York State Temperance Society during a similar period of time. *Tenth Annual Report of the American Tract Society* (1835).

gratuitous distribution of these reports, sending out between twenty and twenty-five thousand a year.[5]   When the
American Temperance Union was formed in 1836, its executive committee took over the task of collecting data in
regard to the progress of reform, but the reports were not
so widely circulated as formerly.   The Union, attempting
to evolve order out of the confusion which characterized publicity work, centred its efforts on the publication of periodicals, leaving the printing of tracts to state and local societies.   Its resources, never more than $10,000 in any one
year, enabled it not only to support a central office in New
York City with Rev. John Marsh in charge, but also to
distribute monthly 5000 copies of the *Journal* and 20,000
of the *Youth's Temperance Advocate*, in addition to an
annual sale of 50,000 temperance almanacs.[6]

In the dissemination of information and opinion state and
local societies received valuable assistance from the American
Tract Society.   Almost one-tenth of the tracts issued by
the Society prior to 1833 were standard temperance publications, such as Benjamin Rush's *Inquiry into the Effects
of Ardent Spirits* and Justin Edwards' *The Well Conducted
Farm*.   For the convenience of those who desired a more
permanent record of this pamphlet literature a small volume

---

[5] *Sixth Annual Report of the American Temperance Society* (1833).
The society seldom received more than $5000 in any one year.

[6] *P. T. D.*, II, 271, 303, *Eighth Report*, p. 3.   Between 1840 and 1850
there were never fewer than thirty weekly and monthly temperance
journals in circulation.   Of these the more important monthlies were:
Temperance Journal and Total Abstinence Gazette, Boston; *Journal*,
New York; *Youth's Temperance Advocate*, New York; *Pennsylvania
Temperance Recorder*, Philadelphia; *Star*, Richmond; *Advocate*, St.
Louis; *Ohio Temperance Advocate*, Columbus; *South Carolina Temperance Advocate*, Columbia; *Banner*, Penfield, Ga.   The well known
weeklies were: *New England Washingtonian*, Boston; *Essex Washingtonian*, Lynn, Mass.; *Columbia Washingtonian*, Hudson, N. Y.; *Organ*,
New York; *Maryland Temperance Herald*, Baltimore.   See Clark,
op. cit., pp. 201–224, for an excellent bibliography of temperance
papers in Massachusetts.

of twenty of the best essays was published in 1839, but its sale was not large. Much more in demand were the single tracts, five million of which had been sold by the Tract Society between 1825 and 1856.[7] In the latter year this feature of publicity work received additional support from the Order of the Sons of Temperance, which decided to set aside a portion of its reserve funds to be used in the distribution of a new series of pamphlets.[8]

In this propagandist literature the appeal of the reformers was fully developed. Although to the present-day reader it may seem to be a parading of the obvious in the garb of hyperbole, a century ago it represented the earnest desire of many devoted people to arouse public opinion against a great social evil. Taking their cue from the writings of Dr. Benjamin Rush, the temperance publicists were determined that their fellows should at least be enlightened as to the physiological effects of intemperance. With little thought of scientific investigation they generalized from unusual incidents which came to their attention, often accepting as evidence that which they wished to believe. They endeavoured, whenever possible, to bolster up their own conclusions with impressive citations from the writings of European and American medical authorities. Indeed, their so-called expository treatises were not so much an analysis of the effects of intoxicating liquors on the human mind and body, as a dogmatic statement that ardent spirits caused a large proportion of the physical and mental ailments to which mankind was heir.

Not only the drunkard, who might be expected to pay for

[7] *The Temperance Volume of the American Tract Society* (1839); *Twenty-fifth Annual Report of the American Tract Society* (1850); *Eighth Annual Report of the American Tract Society* (1833). An anonymous tract with the intriguing title, *One Glass More,* proved most popular, 800,000 copies being sold in twenty years.

[8] The first tract in the Sons of Temperance series was written by Horace Greeley.

his excesses, but also the moderate drinker was subject to the baneful reaction of the poison, alcohol. Of course, he did not suffer so much as his less abstemious fellows, but there was no escaping the consequences of his indulgence. Though the day of reckoning might be long postponed, it would bring the greater toll of misery. Present appearance of health did not signify permanent immunity. As to the nature of these ills to which even the temperate drinker was a prey, the reformers were exceedingly explicit. One explanation was given by Edward Hitchcock, professor of chemistry and natural science in Amherst College, in his essay addressed to students:

God has given to the animal constitution, a capacity to exert an amount of physical power, much superior to what is necessary for ordinary occasions. The key to this store house of strength is, in the excitability of the system; and this is put into requisition by the action of alcohol. Alcohol does not create any new physical power; it merely rouses into action that which already exists in the constitution. . . . That secret energy, which nature has in reserve for seasons of great bodily and mental effort, is thus prodigally and irretrievably wasted. The friends of temperance are very frequently urged to point out any bad effects, resulting to a man's constitution, from a very moderate and prudent use of ardent spirit or wine. In the statement just made, we have the answer. The premature exhaustion which is thus infallibly produced, in a greater or less degree, renders the individual peculiarly liable to the attacks of violent and dangerous disorders. He is seized with fever, or dropsy, or apoplexy; but never suspects that his prudent use of ardent spirit or wine is the cause.[9]

Less restrained, but more specific, was the statement of Dr. Thomas Sewall, professor of anatomy and physiology in

[9] Edward Hitchcock, *An Essay on Alcoholic and Narcotic Substances,* pp. 20–21.

Columbian College, Washington, D. C.   Of the fate in store for the habitual drinker, he wrote:

Dyspepsia, jaundice, emaciation, corpulence, dropsy, ulcers, rheumatism, gout, tremors, palpitation, hysteria, epilepsy, palsy, lethargy, apoplexy, melancholy, madness, delirium-tremens, and premature old age, compose but a small part of the catalogue of diseases produced by ardent spirit.   Indeed, there is scarcely a morbid affection to which the human body is liable, that has not, in one way or another, been produced by it; there is not a disease but it has aggravated, nor a predisposition to disease which it has not called into action; and although its effects are in some degree modified by age and temperament, by habit and occupation, by climate and season of the year, and even by the intoxicating agent itself; yet, the general and ultimate consequences are the same.[10]

In describing the effects of excessive use of distilled liquors the reformers threw all qualifying phrases aside. No laws of nature operated with greater regularity and precision than the laws of intemperance. The career of the habitual drunkard was everywhere the same. Its succession of horrible excesses constituted a form of suicide, the more terrible because death was preceded by excruciating mental and physical torture. Fortunate was the victim who sank into an untimely grave before he had been bereft of reason, or deprived of his physical powers. But, in spite of these awful warnings, temperate drinkers were constantly furnishing recruits for the ranks of the intemperate. Benjamin Rush's estimate at the opening of the century that the toll of in-

[10] Thomas Sewall, *Effects of Intemperance on the Intellectual, Moral and Physical Powers*, pp. 11–12. For similar opinions see Mark Tucker, *A Plea for Entire Abstinence*, pp. 12–13; R. D. Mussey, *An Address on Ardent Spirit*, pp. 5–6; John Marsh, *Putnam and the Wolf*, pp. 15–16. The pathology of intemperance was also set forth in elaborate drawings prepared by Dr. Sewall, which showed the effect of alcohol on the vital organs. These drawings reproduced in coloured plates were widely used by temperance speakers. See *P. T. D., Seventh Report*, p. 4, *Eighth Report*, p. 4.

temperance in the United States was four thousand lives annually no longer represented the real situation. In 1825, according to the statistics of the temperance propagandists, between ten and fifteen thousand died prematurely from the effects of using ardent spirits. Ten times as many habitual drunkards were well started toward the same fate, and more than a million, who called themselves temperate drinkers, had taken the first step. These figures were appalling. Ten thousand deaths! The late war between the United States and Great Britain, said the reformers, had taken an annual toll of less than five hundred lives. The scourge of yellow fever, so devastating in 1793, had claimed less than four thousand victims. Yet here was a malady that killed its ten thousand and more every year without apparently arousing the anxiety of the nation. Was it not time for united action against the ravages of the destroyer? [11]

Preserved in this literature dealing with the pathology of intemperance is a curious and amusing evidence of the credulity of enthusiasm. The "spontaneous combustion" theory, which Charles Dickens used so ingeniously in *Bleak House* to explain the mysterious disappearance of the notorious Mr. Krook, seems to have been accepted by the temperance reformers after 1827. In that year Jonathan Kittredge, a reformed drunkard, delivered an address before a public meeting in Lyme, New Hampshire, in which he discussed fatalities caused by intemperance.

This death [said he] happens in various ways. Some are killed instantly; some die a lingering, gradual death; some

[11] John G. Palfrey, *Discourses on Intemperance*, pp. 5–7; David Pickering, *The Effects of Intemperance*, pp. 8–9; Jonathan Kittredge, *An Address upon the Effects of Ardent Spirits*, pp. 7–9; Albert Barnes, *Essays on Intemperance*, pp. 4–5; Joel Parker, *An Address delivered before the Association in Keene*, pp. 12–13; Francis Wayland, *An Address before the Temperance Association*, pp. 4–5; Daniel Dow, *A Discourse before the Gloucester Temperance Society*, pp. 5–6.

commit suicide in fits of intoxication, and some are actually burnt up. I read of an intemperate man a few years since, whose breath caught fire by coming in contact with a lighted candle, and he was consumed. At the time, I disbelieved the story, but my reading has since furnished me with well authenticated cases of a combustion of the human body from the use of ardent spirits. Trotter mentions ten such cases, and relates them at length. They are attended with all the proof we require to believe any event. They are attested by living witnesses, examined by learned men, and published in the journals of the day without contradiction.[12]

Within the next few years this version of death from intemperance, based on reported cases which the medical journals considered extraordinary, was widely accepted as an effective argument against the use of ardent spirits.[13]   The *Journal of the American Temperance Union* in 1837 published several articles, presenting instances of spontaneous combustion listed in the *Dictionaire de Médecine* as having occurred between 1692 and 1829.[14]   Perhaps the most impressive statement of the theory, however, appeared in the lectures delivered by President Eliphalet Nott to the student body of Union College during the winter term of 1838.

When a few years since [said Dr. Nott] a case of spontaneous combustion, occurring in the person of an habitual drunkard, was

[12] In his essay on drunkenness the eminent English physician, Thomas Trotter, inserted without comment an article by Pierre Aime Lair, which appeared in the *Journal de Physique* in 1799. See Thomas Trotter, *An Essay on Drunkenness*, pp. 69–94; Jonathan Kittredge, *op. cit.*, p. 9.

[13] Instances of spontaneous combustion were cited in the *Georgia Journal*, May 15, 1830. The *Massachusetts Spy* for May 12, 1830, noted that Dr. Peter Scofield of Johnstown, Upper Canada, had reported the case of a man roasted from head to foot because of the combustion of ardent spirits. See also Thomas Sewall, *op. cit.*, p. 8; R. D. Mussey, *op. cit.*, p. 8.

[14] *Journal*, March, 1837, p. 40, October, 1837, p. 145.

referred to in a temperance address by a distinguished layman, it was generally regretted. Few of the friends of temperance were prepared to endorse what then seemed to them so improbable a statement, while the manufacturers and vendors and drinkers of this fiery element took occasion to proclaim more loudly than ever the folly and fanaticism of men who could be so weak themselves as to believe, and so impertinent as to attempt to impose on others the belief of such ridiculous occurrences. But these cases of the death of drunkards by internal fires, kindled often spontaneously in the fumes of alcohol, that escape through the pores of the skin—have become so numerous and so incontrovertible, that I presume no person of information will now be found to call the reality of their existence in question.[15]

In support of this statement Dr. Nott cited a score of cases reported by reputable journals in Europe and America. In every instance the victim, usually an aged woman, had been long addicted to the use of ardent spirits and wine. Ignition of the alcoholic fumes was traceable in most of the cases to a lamp, pipe or stove, but several exceptions proved that combustion might take place without the presence of an external agent. Their will to believe so far transcended the reasonable objections to this theory that the temperance forces presented it in pamphlet and periodical as the extreme penalty which the intemperate might be called upon to pay. What mattered it that none of them had ever witnessed a case in point? At any moment the dread destroyer might take its victim from their very midst.[16]

In the cholera epidemic of 1832 the reformers found further proof of the deadly effect of intemperance. From

[15] Eliphalet Nott, *Lectures on Temperance,* pp. 197–201.

[16] *Enquirer,* August, 1846, p. 170. The *Pennsylvania Temperance Recorder* for February, 1836, appeared with scare headlines, Fire! Fire! Blood on Fire!, as the caption of an article which stated that Dr. J. C. Hanson of South Berwick, Maine, on bleeding a common drunkard had applied a match to the blood with the result that it burned for thirty seconds with a blue flame.

Albany the *Temperance Recorder* sent out extras and broadsides urging abstinence from the use of all intoxicants as
the only safeguard against the prevailing disease. Every
case in the city, which resulted fatally, was investigated by
temperance workers. Their report showed that of the three
hundred and thirty-six who died during the summer months,
only two were members of temperance societies, while but
five others practised abstinence from distilled liquors. In
New York City conditions were similar. Records of Park
Hospital indicated that six out of two hundred and four
cholera patients were abstainers. Taking these figures as
a text, the *Commercial Advertiser* charged that the ravages
of the epidemic in the city could be explained on no other
basis than the presence of four thousand grog-shops. In
Washington, D. C., the board of health forbade the sale of
ardent spirits for a period of ninety days as a precaution
against the spread of the disease. Reports from Montreal,
after 1200 had suffered from the malady, stated that not a
drunkard who had been attacked had recovered, and that
almost all the victims had been at least moderate drinkers.
It seemed to the temperance propagandists as if the cholera
was a scourge of Providence to aid the cause of temperance.
Its deadly effect in the case of the drunkard became a striking warning to the moderate drinkers, urging them to accept
the principle of abstinence.[17]

Though arguments based on considerations of health
bulked large in the temperance propaganda, the various
appeals to economic interest received an even wider circulation at the hands of the reformers.[18] Periodicals were filled
with articles, similar to those of Jeremiah Evarts in the

[17] N. Y. *Commercial Advertiser* cited in *Mass. Spy,* June 27, 1832;
Temp. Recorder, June 5, 1832, p. 30, November 5, p. 8; *P. T. D.,* I,
96–97, 280–281. See also Nathan S. S. Beman, *The Influence of Ardent
Spirits in the Production of the Cholera.*
[18] The religious phase of the temperance propaganda has been discussed in Chapter VI.

Panoplist during 1810, which stressed the cost of intemperance to the community. Spokesmen for the reform, basing their calculations on conditions in their respective districts, estimated the total liquor bill for the nation and described the grave consequences of such an expenditure.[19] In their opinion the waste of money involved in purchasing a commodity so harmful to the consumer was less deplorable than the burden thereby imposed on the tax-payer. Since the responsibility of the liquor traffic for poverty and crime could be easily demonstrated, the tax-payer's assessments for the maintenance of work-houses and jails, of poor-houses and asylums, were in large part chargeable to intemperance. Statistics from charitable and penal institutions were a rich mine of information in support of this point. The records in general, said the propagandists, revealed that seventy-five per cent of those whose lives had been wrecked could trace their misfortune directly or indirectly to alcoholic beverages.[20] A significant confirmation of this contention was contained in a voluminous report published by the New York State Temperance Society in 1834. Through the generosity of a wealthy member of the Society, Samuel Chipman had been employed to investigate county poor-houses and jails, and the state institutions of a similar character. His task was not to record his impressions, but to secure facts from whatever records were available. The care with which he collected his data and compiled the

[19] *Cf.* J. G. Palfrey, *op. cit.,* 32–33, 38; Jonathan Kittredge, *op. cit.,* pp. 7–8; *Journal of Humanity,* Feb. 10, 1831; W. Cranch, *An Address delivered at the annual meeting of the Washington City Society,* pp. 4–8. In 1831 Judge Cranch, of the District of Columbia, published his famous estimate of the financial loss suffered by the nation through the traffic in ardent spirits. He estimated the nation's annual liquor bill at $48,000,000.

[20] *Plain Facts Addressed to the Inhabitants of Boston* (1834); *Mass. Spy,* Feb. 16, 1831; *P. T. D.,* I, 45; L. M. Sargent, *Address delivered at the Beneficent Congregational Meeting House, July 4, 1838,* p. 11; *Delaware Gazette,* Jan. 20, 1843.

results made his report a valuable contribution to temperance literature.

From the superintendent of each institution he visited Mr. Chipman secured a signed statement which contained a summary of the information possessed by the authorities relative to the proportion of crime and poverty caused by intemperance. An analysis of these returns indicated that in every county at least sixty per cent of the men and women held on criminal charges were habitually intemperate, while in some sections the percentage was even higher. With few exceptions at least fifty per cent of the inmates of each county poor-house testified that the use of spirituous liquors was the cause of their poverty. Furthermore, a general average of governmental expenditures throughout the state showed that more than two-thirds of the county taxes were appropriated annually to defray the cost of criminal justice and poor relief.[21] So important were Mr. Chipman's conclusions, and so well documented, that his report was used by organizations in all parts of the country as an effective exposition of the costliness of the liquor traffic.[22]

Besides such appeals to tax-payers a great many economic arguments were levelled at employers of labour. Circulars addressed to proprietors and superintendents of manufacturing establishments emphasized particularly the relation between total abstinence and labour efficiency. Wherever the temperance principle had been applied in an industrial enterprise, said the reformers, it had tended to increase the profits of the business. This fact had been demonstrated by a constantly increasing group of employers who enforced restrictions against the use of intoxicants during working hours. The reasons for it were obvious. Temperate workmen were capable of more productive labour in a day's time

---

[21] *Report of an examination of poor-houses, jails, etc., in the State of New York,* By Samuel Chipman.

[22] *P. T. D.,* I, 397–402; *Journal,* February, 1840, p. 21.

than intemperate workmen.   The loss of property owing to
negligence of employees was greatly reduced, and the inter-
ruption of operations because of incapacitated help was
practically eliminated.   The problem of labour turnover was
less serious, since fewer men were discharged as a result of
intemperate habits.   Furthermore, sober employees were
willing to co-operate with the management to make the business a success, for they realized that their own prosperity
depended upon the profits of their employer.[23]   So ran the
arguments designed to win the support of the rising "captains of industry."

The reformers believed that the most powerful factor
in the promotion of temperance among the wage-earning
class was the self-interest of the employer.   Their records,
so they said, indicated that business men were being converted
to the principle of abstinence because of its important bearing on labour efficiency.   With increasing frequency employers of labour were demanding that their employees refrain from the use of spirituous liquors.   These hopeful
signs, however, were not used as an excuse for failure to
bring the temperance cause directly to the attention of the
wage-earner.   Mechanics and artisans, clerks and shop-
workers were confronted with the spectre of unemployment.
They were reminded that in times of industrial depression it
was the intemperate man who first lost his job.   When
business was prospering, it was the sober man who accumu-
lated a surplus against the inevitable hard times.   Since
total abstinence meant increased profits for the employer,
it brought to the worker higher wages, promotion and,

[23] *P. T. D.*, II, 18–24; *Am. Quart. Temp. Mag.*, August, 1833,
pp. 220–224. A publication from the press of the American Temperance Union maintained that if all manufacturing establishments
in the United States adopted the principle of total abstinence, no
protective tariff would be necessary. The cost of production would
be sufficiently reduced to permit competition with all parts of the
world.

finally, financial independence.   Its blessings fell upon rich and poor alike.[24]

The fact that the nation was still predominantly agricultural was reflected in the bulk of literature devoted to the interests of the farmer.   Almanacs were published by the American Temperance Union and several state societies for sale and free distribution in the rural districts.   Of the numerous tracts designed to carry a special appeal to the farming classes Justin Edwards' *The Well Conducted Farm* long retained its popularity.   Written in 1825, this brief essay contained the arguments so frequently repeated in various forms during the next generation.   It related the experience of a Massachusetts landowner who decided to operate his six hundred acre farm without the use of spirituous liquors.   Though his neighbours assured him that he would be unable to secure help on such terms, he found that by paying his men a dollar more each month he was able to hire as many as he needed.   All the hands were pledged to abstain from the use of ardent spirits.   At the end of a year the proprietor had tangible evidence of the value of his experiment.   The benefit to the men was noticeable in an increased vigour and activity, in the performance of the same labour without the usual fatigue, and in the greater amount of money which they were able to save from their wages.   The employer profited because more work had been accomplished than in any preceding year.   His barns and other improvements were in splendid condition, and his land had never before been so productive.[25]

[24] For a specimen of these appeals see *Letter to the Mechanics of Boston* (1831); *Circular to Immigrants* (1833). A scheme similar to modern advertising methods was used in 1833. A wholesaler in New York City who marketed 250,000 sheets of sandpaper each year offered to print a temperance argument on the back of each sheet if the state society would provide the copy. *Temp. Recorder*, March 5, 1833.

[25] Justin Edwards, *The Well Conducted Farm* (Andover, 1825).

This simple narrative and many similar tracts were widely circulated, but the reformers realized that one important aspect of the farmer's relation to the liquor problem had not been sufficiently stressed. This deficiency they attempted to correct through temperance periodicals. Frequent appeals were sent out to the growers of grain, urging them to cease furnishing rye and corn to the distilleries. One journal presented the matter in this light:

Farmers, every bushel of grain you sell to the distilleries is to you in the end a dead loss. You may try the experiment ten years, growing each year 400 bushels of rye and corn, and selling it to the distillery, and at the end of the ten years you will be poorer than when you commenced. But cease to furnish rye and corn to the distiller, feed them out to your cattle and hogs, and three things will be the result. 1. The market will be supplied with beef and pork of good quality, instead of that which is inferior and diseased. This will increase the value of these articles in the market. 2. If there is any profit, the farmer will receive it, and thus receive a fair compensation for his labor. 3. A death blow will be struck to the business of manufacturing ardent spirit, a business ultimately injurious to individuals, to society and to the world.[26]

Farmers who read this appeal must have been impressed more by the zeal of the writer than by the economic validity of his suggestions. It is doubtful whether such arguments persuaded many that it was good business to refuse a cash price for their grain in order to gamble for higher profits in the live-stock market. Still, the temperance journals continued their campaign without much variation in their attack. The scarcity of foodstuffs following the bad harvests of 1836, however, gave an added significance to their articles on the wasteful consumption of grain. The *Pennsyl-*

[26] *Temp. Recorder,* Oct. 2, 1832, p. 59. See also *Pa. Temp. Rec.,* April, 1835, p. 12, September, 1836, p. 77.

vania Temperance Recorder ran a cartoon of a distillery under the caption "The Bread Eater." The distilleries of the United States, so the explanatory paragraphs stated, used 11,000,000 bushels of grain each month, enough to make 20,000 barrels of flour. This was going on at a time when the cry for bread was heard in all parts of the land.[27] The *New York Journal of Commerce* was responsible for the charge that importations of foreign breadstuffs were being diverted to distillers and brewers, who paid a high price in order to obtain what they required.[28] According to estimates in the *Boston Recorder* the grain consumed in one year by the manufacture of spirituous liquors was sufficient to provide the American people with food for four months. It seemed contrary to the public welfare to permit such a condition of affairs when flour was selling for $12 a barrel and bread cost six cents a pound.[29] The editor of the *Pennsylvania Temperance Recorder* was positive that the liquor problem was responsible for all the country's ills. The high price of foodstuffs, the industrial depression and the financial stringency were forms of punishment visited upon the people because of their intemperance. "A nation," said he, "which has rioted as we have upon the bounties of Providence, which has so wickedly converted the grains and the fruits of heaven into the drink of the drunkard, and squandered one hundred million annually to the most debased appetite;—must expect to be scourged for its sins." [30]

Not all of the temperance propaganda was cast in the form of exposition or argument. As the novelty of the reform wore off, it became necessary to make the usual appeals more attractive. Temperance journals came to depend largely on imaginative writing to hold the interest of

[27] *Pa. Temp. Rec.*, January, 1837, p. 1.
[28] Cited in *Pa. Temp. Rec.*, January, 1837, p. 8.
[29] *Ibid.*, May, 1837, p. 40; *Journal*, March, 1837, pp. 35–37.
[30] *Pa. Temp. Rec.*, June, 1837, p. 44.

their readers. Poetry and fiction crowded out the material
of an earlier day. Stories dealing with unrequited love,
poverty, disease and death, fashioned after the same model
as other early attempts at the American short story, were
nothing more than thinly disguised presentations of temperance platitudes. Verses of little merit recounted in
rhymed metre the blessings of sobriety. As a special feature
for the ladies several periodicals ran serial stories, tales of
such saccharine morality that they merited, and sometimes
achieved, a place in the columns of *Godey's Lady's Book*.[31]
Although this fiction was generally the work of mediocre
writers, occasionally a short sketch appeared by some author
destined to win fame. The *Temperance Almanac* for 1843
contained "A Rill from the Town Pump" by Nathaniel
Hawthorne, which no doubt seemed appropriate to "the
cold water men." A narrative by John G. Whittier setting
forth the effects of intemperance was featured in the *Organ*
for November 30, 1844.

During the decade of the forties a few publishers, as much
interested in reform as in profits, presented propaganda in
the form of temperance gift books, that particular product
of the publisher's art being at the height of its vogue. In
1847 William Sloanaker of Philadelphia announced *The
Fountain*, a temperance annual edited by Hastings Weld,
"in Turkey morocco binding with gilt edges and back."
The volume contained eight mezzotint embellishments en-
graved especially for it by the elder Sartain.[32] There were
poems by John G. Whittier and Lydia Huntley Sigourney;
short articles by Horace Greeley and Bayard Taylor; and
stories by Fanny Forrester and Timothy S. Arthur. The
Philadelphia Enquirer said of it: "The volume is indeed
chaste, choice and elegant—and fully equals in literary

[31] For example see *Godey's Lady's Book,* files 1842–3.

[32] The reference is to John Sartain, the English artist, one of the first
to introduce the mezzotint style of engraving in the United States.

treasures as well as appropriate illustrations any annual that we have met with for a long time. Temperance, morality and elegance are here combined, and in a form at once tempting, attractive and unexceptionable." [33] Less pretentious was the gift book published the same year by George W. Briggs of Boston. The compilers, J. G. Adams and E. H. Chapin, designed their little work as a pocket manual, "a home friend, or travelling companion to the lover of temperance." Several poems by Oliver Wendell Holmes and Nathaniel P. Willis somewhat compensated for the mediocrity of the remainder of its literary offering. [34]

In the selection of material for publication the interests of the boys and girls in the "cold water armies" were not neglected. Periodicals intended primarily for adults found space for children's stories whenever suitable copy was at hand. The American Sunday School Union included in its series for Sunday School libraries several collections of juvenile temperance tales. [35] In 1840 Charles Jewett, executive secretary of the Massachusetts Temperance Union, edited two volumes which he hoped would supply a "deficiency in the Sabbath school library, as well as in private libraries of parents and such as are entrusted with the education of youth." [36] Realizing that there was quite enough unmeaning trash on the market in the form of books for children, he had attempted to prepare works, he said, which would exert a salutary influence on youthful minds. His *Temperance Toy* was a series of rather clever parodies of well-known nursery rhymes and jingles. The *Youth's Temperance Lecturer*

[33] *The Fountain* (Philadelphia, 1847), pp. 4–5.

[34] *The Fountain*, edited by J. G. Adams and E. H. Chapin, pp. 44–45, 247–248. There is no record to indicate how profitable such ventures were for the publishers.

[35] For example see John Hall, *The Harvey Boys* (Philadelphia, 1834); Cyrus Mann, *The Clinton Family* (Boston, 1833); *My Native Village* (New York, 1844).

[36] Charles Jewett, *The Temperance Toy;* also *Youth's Temperance Lecturer*, p. 3.

was intended for older children. It contained fifteen cheap engravings portraying the causes and effects of drunkenness, each picture being fully explained in prose and verse. Among the exhibits, which no doubt appealed to the boys, were the still, the wine-press, the grog-shop and the tavern bar. Mr. Jewett may have believed that children can govern the habits of their parents. At any rate he was careful to impress his youthful readers with the disadvantages of having a drunken father. Of the boys and girls who were so unfortunate he wrote:

> He drives them off, to toil all day
> And a part of the weary night,
> And takes their hard-earned pennies away,
> And at the bar will he daily stay
> To drink, and curse and fight.

> Shoeless, over the frozen ground
> His wretched children go;
> And away he staggers to where the sound
> Of drunken revel is ringing around,
> To taste the cup of woe.[37]

A similar attempt to provide literature for the young temperance advocate was responsible for *The Boy's Temperance Book*, edited in 1848 by John Marsh. Marsh's work, however, was not so successful as that of Jewett, for he apparently lacked an understanding of what the child mind could appreciate. The *Boy's Book* with the exception of a few dialogues was composed of extracts from speeches and magazine articles prepared for mature readers. One can scarcely imagine anything more uninteresting to the

---

[37] *Youth's Temperance Lecturer*, p. 25. Matthew D. Finn's *Moral and Temperance Table Book* instructed its young readers in the elementary principles of arithmetic and penmanship and at the same time warned them against the dangerous influence of intoxicants.

normal boy.[38] This same fault was evident in the first periodical designed "to gain the hearts and guide the habits and practices of the young." [39]   In 1839 the executive committee of the American Temperance Union had decided that the *Youth's Temperance Advocate* should be issued monthly, under the editorship of John Marsh. The little journal fell far short of gaining the hearts of the boys and girls. The idea of the editor and his associates seems to have been that by inserting the phrase, "now dear children," any commonplace material clipped from other temperance publications could be made attractive to the juvenile reader. Although the paper was circulated extensively through the agency of the Sunday School unions, one doubts whether the children who received it took the trouble to carry it home.[40]

One of the most interesting specimens of early temperance fiction is a novel published by the artist and playwright, William Dunlap, in 1836. The author had never been a total abstainer, but at the age of seventy he became an ardent temperance advocate. In *Thirty Years Ago; or, The Memoirs of a Water Drinker* he combines a great deal of material drawn from his own experience and observation with some of the standard temperance arguments of his day. The novel is in part autobiographical, but many of the more exciting incidents are taken from the life of Dunlap's friend, the English actor, George Frederick Cooke, whose career was so pitifully marred by intemperate drinking. Several of the scenes are laid in the vicinity of the Old Park Theatre in New York City, which Dunlap knew so well. Undoubtedly, the author's association with the theatre and,

[38] John Marsh, *The Boy's Temperance Book*, pp. 63–104.
[39] *Youth's Temperance Advocate*, I, 1.
[40] *Ibid.*, files for 1839–1841. The *Cold Water Army*, a weekly established by Isaac F. Shepard in Boston, September, 1841, was an admirable children's periodical. The *Temperance Offering*, published at Salem, Massachusetts, for a few years after 1845 contained an excellent youth's department.

particularly, his friendship with Cooke were important factors in convincing him of the manifold evils of intemperance.

Zebediah Spiffard, the hero of *Thirty Years Ago*, is an under-sized, red-haired comedian, who at the opening of the story is about to wed the lady of his choice. Though he knows it not, both his fiancée and her mother are addicted to the use of liquor in immoderate quantities. As a result Spiffard's marital career progresses none too happily for him, for his pet aversion is the use of alcoholic beverages. This, of course, gives the hero opportunity for frequent moralizing, which not only interrupts the action, but also dulls the reader's interest. Episode follows episode in a rather disconnected fashion, each one serving to present some new horror connected with the drink evil. Some of the descriptions are exaggerated to the point of absurdity, yet none are intended to be caricatures. The novel is probably the least praise-worthy of Dunlap's numerous literary efforts. One critic has even characterized it as an "inferior specimen of Sunday school fiction." [41] This may be a fair appraisal of its worth from the standpoint of the literary craftsman, but it does not take into account the book's propaganda value. By the public it was well received, the newspapers carrying uniformly favourable criticisms. In fact, so rapidly did the first edition sell that the author found it necessary to bring out a second edition in 1837. [42]

More influential than William Dunlap, however, in the development of temperance fiction between 1830 and 1850 was Lucius Manlius Sargent. With him in the first rank also belong Lydia Huntley Sigourney and Timothy Shay Arthur. While none of their works will stand the severe tests of the critic, they are excellent examples of effective attempts to further moral reform among the American people.

[41] Oral S. Coad, *William Dunlap*, pp. 274–279.
[42] William Dunlap, *Memoirs of a Water Drinker* (New York, 1837).

Sargent's contribution is perhaps the most impressive because of its bulk and its influence. Lucius Manlius Sargent was the youngest son of Daniel Sargent, a prosperous Boston merchant. In 1801 at the age of fifteen he entered Phillips-Exeter Academy to prepare for college, having previously enjoyed several years of study under the tutelage of Rev. Jesse Appleton, later president of Bowdoin. This kindly preceptor of his youth had opened to him the treasures of the classics and quickened his interest in good literature. At Harvard Sargent gave good account of his early training. During two years in residence he distinguished himself as a classicist, but he did not remain to finish his course. In 1806 he began the study of law in the office of Samuel Dexter. Like Appleton, Dexter was concerned over the prevalence of intemperance in the country, and the young student in his office heard considerable discussion of methods to curb the evil. Perhaps, it was during these years that Sargent decided to devote his literary talent, which he was constantly improving, to the cause of temperance. At any rate, when he inherited a competence from his father's estate, he abandoned the practice of law and turned his entire attention to philanthropic enterprises. For more than thirty years he wrote and spoke in favour of total abstinence, always advocating any method, coercive or persuasive, that would break the power of the liquor traffic.[43]

Although Sargent's lectures were frequently printed and widely distributed, his most effective appeals were made through the medium of fiction. In 1835 the Massachusetts Temperance Society published a small volume containing three of his stories, "My Mother's Gold Ring," "The Stage-Coach" and "Groggy Harbor." The warm reception ac-

[43] John H. Sheppard, *Reminiscences of Lucius Manlius Sargent*, pp. 7–16.

corded this initial offering convinced the author that he had discovered the way to reach a large reading public, and he continued to write in the same vein. Within the next fifteen years he prepared eighteen more stories, but even this number was insufficient to meet the demands made upon him. The original three went through more than one hundred editions and were translated into several foreign languages. While the stories usually appeared first in some temperance periodical, they were collected from time to time and reprinted by numerous societies. A large edition of six volumes was printed for the American Temperance Union in 1848 to supply the demand in the United States and Great Britain.[44]

The popularity of these *Temperance Tales* seems to prove that there was a widespread interest in the subject of temperance, for they were not of such literary merit as to attract unusual notice. Sargent drew the tone of his stories from the conventional English fiction of the period. With few exceptions his plots, if a series of incidents may be called a plot, were uninteresting and unconvincing. They served as a pretext for much shallow moralizing with its normal accompaniment of over-wrought sentimentality. Occasional use of the mysterious and horrible suggested the novels of Charles Brockden Brown, while a few characterizations in some of the later tales might have been crude imitations of Dickens' art.[45] In spite of their imperfections, however, the *Temperance Tales* were a distinct success, for they reached readers who found in them inspiration to labour more diligently for the cause. Their author, though not a literary genius, possessed certain qualities essential to the production

[44] Sheppard, *op. cit.*, pp. 17–22; *Documents and Records of the Massachusetts Temperance Society*, pp. 99–100.

[45] The characters in "The Temperance Meeting in the Village of Tattertown" remind one of Mr. Pickwick's select circle. *Temperance Tales*, VI, 173–293.

of great literature: sincerity, forthright directness of purpose, and the desire to move men to action.[46]

Scarcely less noteworthy than Sargent's stories was the contribution of Lydia Huntley Sigourney. Both as a writer and an editor she made herself an energetic champion of all movements for moral reform. Born in Norwich, Connecticut, September 1, 1791, Lydia Huntley was heir to the ennobling influences that pervaded the finer type of New England home. In the life of her immediate family she saw exemplified those domestic virtues, which in later years were so often the subject of her thought and writing. A schooling, made possible by the kindness of a wealthy friend, enabled her to become proficient in Latin literature and the English classics. Having decided in her nineteenth year that teaching was to be her life work, she opened a select school for girls in Chelsea. So successful was this venture that in 1814 several residents of Hartford persuaded her to establish a similar school in that city. During the next five years she became a leader in the educational and social life of Hartford, but her career as a teacher was interrupted by her marriage in 1819 to Charles Sigourney, a wealthy merchant who was also a student of literature and art.

After her marriage Mrs. Sigourney devoted what time she could spare from domestic duties to the development of her literary talents. She was less interested, however, in achieving perfection in her art than in using her ability for the advancement of philanthropic enterprises. The calls made upon her by friends, by charitable organizations and by patriotic societies were answered so far as her physical

[46] Besides the stories already mentioned the following had a wide circulation as single pamphlets: *Margaret's Bridal, The Life Preserver, Fritz Hazell* and *Kitty Grafton. The Life Preserver* portrayed the dangers of granting spirit rations, while the other three attacked the use of wine and cider.

powers permitted.   Her published writings numbered fifty-seven volumes, and contributions to newspapers and magazines must have bulked almost as large.   The result, as she herself stated, was that she wrote too much to achieve distinction either in invention or in style.   But the popularity of her works, both in this country and in Great Britain, is sufficient evidence that her offering was not considered mediocre by her readers.[47]

Mrs. Sigourney's support of temperance principles was closely associated with her concern for the preservation of the American home.   Since she was opposed to any custom or practice that tended to destroy the harmony and happiness of family life, the use of intoxicants never met with her approval.   Regarding intemperance as one of the chief causes of marital unhappiness, she denounced the vice in prose and poetry.   During the two decades prior to 1850 her lyrics and stories frequently appeared in the regular temperance publications, while occasionally the editorship of a gift volume gave her an opportunity to introduce selections of temperance fiction.[48]   In 1847, at the suggestion of the Scottish Temperance League in Edinburgh, she collected the best of her writings on the subject and published them under the title of *Water-Drops*.   The volume was intended particularly for women, "to propitiate their influence in the structure of domestic life, against a foe that lays waste their dearest hopes, and to quicken them in impressing upon the tender minds committed to their charge the subjugation of

[47] Mrs. L. H. Sigourney, *Letters of Life*, pp. 5–49; E. B. Huntington, "Lydia H. Sigourney," in *Eminent Women of the Age*, James Parton, editor, pp. 85–101; Grace L. Collin, "Lydia Huntley Sigourney," in *New England Magazine*, XXVII, 15–30.

[48] *Journal*, files 1839–1841. The following gift books which she edited contain temperance material: *The Religious Souvenir* (1840) and *The Young Ladies' Offering* (1848). For her own contributions see *Poems* (1834), *Boy's Reading Book in Prose and Poetry* (1839), and "The Widow and Her Son," in *The National Temperance Offering* (1851), pp. 241–264.

the appetites, and the wisdom and beauty of self-control." [49]

Like most of her other prose, Mrs. Sigourney's temperance stories are exceedingly sentimental. While the plots are uniformly more ingenious than those used by Sargent, the style seems unnatural and stilted. The affected conversation of the characters often clashes unpleasantly with the scene in which the action is set, usually some simple American home. Modern critics have either found much to condemn in this fiction or have ignored it entirely. We must remember, however, that the extent of Mrs. Sigourney's influence is not to be gauged by the fleeting character of her fame. Any study of manners and morals in the United States during the mid-nineteenth century must chronicle the unusual power which she wielded as an author and editor.[50]

In 1836, while Mrs. Sigourney was serving as associate editor of *Godey's Lady's Book*, the stories of Timothy Shay Arthur began to appear in the columns of that popular monthly. At the time Mr. Arthur was trying out his ability in order to decide whether he should make writing his vocation. The background of his early life seemed to be all against such a decision. His schooling in Baltimore, which became his home after his parents left Newburg, New York, in 1817, had not been satisfactory to himself or his parents. Teachers in the private school which he attended pronounced him an unusually stupid boy and advised his father to apprentice him to some trade. In 1822, therefore, his education, so far as school was concerned, came to an end. But Arthur believed that he had not received proper instruction and determined to continue his studies. At the age of thirteen he sacrificed pleasure and recreation in order to spend his leisure time reading. By his own efforts he managed to master the elements of grammar and make some progress

[49] *Letters of Life,* p. 354.

[50] Mrs. Sigourney was an associate editor of *Godey's Lady's Book* from 1836 to 1849.

with arithmetic, but steady application injured his sight. Forced to give up his trade, he secured a position in a mercantile establishment where his duties were so light that he had a great deal of time to himself. During the three years that he remained with the firm he wrote several stories which were published in local journals. In 1833 he accepted a position as western agent for a Baltimore banking company, but the institution failed within a few months and he returned to the city out of employment.[51]

Fortunately, Arthur soon received an offer to undertake the editorial work for a literary magazine, the *Baltimore Athenæum*, which he accepted. As the salary was small, he sought to increase his income by writing fiction. The encouragement which he received from Mrs. Sigourney and the possibility of selling his stories to *Godey's Lady's Book* seem to have affected his style at this period. A marked tendency toward sensationalism disappeared, and in its place came a fondness for sentimental situations. Each story was designed to enforce some moral truth. Since the subject matter usually dealt with the obligations and rewards of family life, the themes were by no means easy to develop without the intrusion of a false note. The superficial fashion in which the relation of husband and wife, of mother and child, was treated leads one to suspect the author of insincerity. But the tales must have rung true to Arthur's contemporaries, for they were of a sort with the fiction published by periodicals which enjoyed a wide circulation.[52]

His career as a writer was well begun when the Washingtonian revival in Baltimore aroused Arthur's interest in temperance reform. Although he had been a member of the first temperance society in the city, he had never taken any part in its activity. A few visits to the testimony meet-

[51] T. S. Arthur, *Illustrated Temperance Tales* (1850), pp. 3–7.

[52] *T. S. Arthur, His Life and Works*, By One Who Knows Him; pp. 11–17. For Arthur's style see *Advice to Young Ladies on their duties and conduct in life;* also *Godey's Lady's Book*, files for 1839–1842.

ings of the Washingtonians inspired him to write a story, *Six Nights with the Washingtonians*, which favourably advertised the new movement. After 1841, when he moved to Philadelphia in order to establish closer connections with journals and publishers in that city, Arthur continued to write for temperance papers and other periodicals interested in the reform. His serial story, "The Temperance Pledge," was featured in several issues of the *Delaware Gazette* in 1842, while the *Organ* for 1845 contained a number of his contributions. During this period he edited .several gift books in which he included extracts from his previous writings.[53] In 1850 a number of these pieces were published in Philadelphia as *Illustrated Temperance Tales*, a souvenir volume for the friends of the cause. Though Arthur is remembered to-day for his *Ten Nights in a Bar-Room*, which appeared in 1853, one suspects that his fame has endured more because of the story's title than because of its merit. More widely sold than any of the other tales, it represents neither the author's best style, nor his most convincing arguments.[54]

A story in the *National Temperance Offering*, edited by Timothy S. Arthur in 1850, is typical of the sentimental, moralizing fiction of the period. In "Love's Eclipse" by Clara Lee the pathetic ending of a delightful romance is the mainspring of the plot. Marian Linvale, one of the gentlest, sweetest girls in the pleasant little village of Alderton, had promised her heart and hand to handsome, high-spirited Mark Wilford, son of the venerable Judge Wilford. In accordance with his family's position in the community it was necessary for Mark to go to Boston for his college

---

[53] *Delaware Gazette*, April 8, 15, 22, 1842; T. S. Arthur, *A Christmas Box for the Sons and Daughters of Temperance; Gift of Friendship* (1849), pp. 13–20; *Sons of Temperance Offering* (1850), pp. 47–61, 184–196.

[54] T. S. Arthur, *Illustrated Temperance Tales; Ten Nights in a Bar-Room.*

education.   Being a gay-hearted youth, he entered with zest
into the free life of his college chums, earning among them
an enviable reputation as a jolly good fellow.   During his
first vacation he returned to Alderton and called to see
Marian, inviting her to accompany him on a drive through
the country.   Not far from the village was a quaint way-
side inn, at which the lovers stopped for refreshment.   Despite Marian's protests, Mark insisted that a bottle of the
best pale sherry be served them in a rustic arbour nearby.
There, over his wineglass he sang her one of Tom Moore's
songs.   Though Mark realized it not, Marian's spirit was
crushed that her lover should care as much for his wine as
he did for her.   She reproved him gently, and they parted,
never to see each other again.   One year later Mark Wilford, once more home from Boston, stood above a grassy
hillock beneath which his former sweetheart slept.   Thus,
by a few glasses of pale sherry, love had been eclipsed.[55]

In song as well as story temperance appeals were given
full expression.   The practice of singing hymns at meetings, early adopted by some societies, caused a demand for
verses which might be set to sacred tunes.   John Pierpont,
pastor of the Hollis Street Church in Boston, composed a
number of temperance odes as part of his contribution to the
reform.   Others followed his lead, till in 1842 it was possible for the American Temperance Union to announce a
volume of hymns and songs suitable for "temperance meetings and cold water celebrations." [56]   As the gala days observed by the reformers grew in number, the output of musi-
cal propaganda increased.   Selections appropriate for anni-
versaries, Fourth of July celebrations, picnics and parades
sold rapidly.   The Washingtonians were particularly insistent that their gatherings should be enlivened by song.
In 1845 appeared the *Washingtonian Teetotalers' Minstrel*

---

[55] *National Temperance Offering*, T. S. Arthur, editor.
[56] *Journal*, July, 1837; *Providence Daily Journal*, April 16, 1842.

with such touching lyrics as "The Rumseller's Lament," "Dear Father, Drink No More," "Mother Dry that Flowing Tear" and "The Drunkard's Wife's Lament." The latter was fittingly set to the tune of "Oft in the Stilly Night." [57] A patriotic song, known as "Jonathan's Declaration of Independence," which must have echoed at many a Fourth of July picnic, was scarcely a fair sample of Rev. John Pierpont's ability as a poet. It was sung to the stirring strains of "Yankee Doodle."

> Says Jonathan, says he, today
> I will be independent,
> And so my grog I'll throw away,
> And that shall be the end on't.
>
> Clear the house, the tarnal stuff,
> Shan't be here so handy,
> Wife has given the winds her snuff,
> So now here goes my brandy.
>
> And now, says Jonathan, towards rum
> I'm desperate unforgiving,
> The tyrant never more shall come
> Into the house I live in.
>
> Kindred spirits, too, shall in-
> To utter darkness go forth,
> Whiskey, Toddy, Julep, Gin,
> Brandy, Beer, and so forth.[58]

While the Washingtonian movement was sweeping through the country, a few theatrical managers saw in it the possibil-

[57] *Washingtonian Teetotalers' Minstrel* (1845). See also *Temperance Lyrics* (1844), *Songs of the Washingtonians* (1845), *The Fountain Minstrel* (1846), *Temperance Songster* (1846), *The Mountain Minstrel* (1847).

[58] Marsh, *Temperance Recollections*, p. 161; *Washingtonian Teetotalers' Minstrel.*

ity of increased profits. If temperance appeals were effectively dramatized, they reasoned, popular interest in the
reform would insure generous returns from the venture.
Such was the belief of the manager of the Boston Museum in
1843, when he secured the right to produce *The Drunkard,
or, The Fallen Saved,* a moral drama in five acts adapted
from a series of temperance dialogues. The play was produced under the supervision of W. H. Smith, an actor turned
playwright, who also took the leading rôle. On February
12, 1844, the first performance, given before an enthusiastic
audience, assured the play's success. A phenomenal run of
140 consecutive performances was a sufficient testimonial of
public interest in the plot and its effective presentation.[59]

The Drunkard contains in a disguised form most of the
appeals that had long proved valuable to the reformers.
The opening scenes in the home of a young couple recently
married reveal the mainspring of the action, the husband's
fondness for spirituous liquors. The numerous temptations
in the pathway of youth, the easy transition from temperate
drinking to drunkenness, the terrors of delirium tremens,
the physical and mental suffering of the drunkard's family;
all are carefully developed as the play progresses. The
climax is reached when the young husband, penniless and
friendless, is prevented from committing suicide by a member
of a temperance society, who persuades him to sign the
pledge. Tragedy is averted, the pledge works its magic cure
and domestic bliss reigns once more where misery and poverty so lately held their sway. In the Boston presentation,
it is said, the portrayal of delirium tremens was particularly effective, while the distress of the drunkard's family
brought tears to the eyes of many. Probably, the play's

---

[59] *The Drunkard, or the Fallen Saved* (Boston, 1847); Mary F. Ayer,
Early Days on Boston Common, p. 62. Mrs. Presbrey's Wax Work Exhibition showing in Boston at the time contained a group representing
the drunkard's family.

sentimental theme, rather than its crudely enforced moralizing, accounts for its unusual success.

The apparent popularity of temperance drama encouraged other managers and producers to venture into the field.
Shortly after the *Drunkard* departed from the Boston Museum, *One Cup More, or the Doom of a Drunkard* went on
the boards at the National Theatre in the same city. It,
too, was successful, though not so well written as the former
play.[60] In 1847 the Park Theatre in New York City, where
Dunlap had secured so much of the material for his novel,
housed an English production known as *The Bottle*. It was
a drama in two acts with a plot similar to that of *The
Drunkard*. Its author, Thomas P. Taylor, had received his
inspiration from several drawings by George Cruikshank,
which portrayed conditions in a home wrecked by intemperance. The play's run at the Park seems to have been prolonged by William B. Chapman's clever performance in the
comedy rôle of *Coddles*, a potboy.[61]

In the meantime companies of strolling players had found
the temperance theme popular. In 1843 a certain Dr. Robinson and several Washingtonians in New Hampshire organized a group to present the *Moral Exhibition of the Reformed Drunkard*. They sought the patronage and support of temperance advocates by advertising the fact that
a percentage of the proceeds from the play would be donated
to local Washingtonian societies. In Worcester, Massachusetts, a stronghold of temperance sentiment, they were well
patronized until the board of selectmen stopped their performances. This action, based on a town law against
theatrical exhibitions of any sort, was roundly applauded
by the officers of the American Temperance Union. In an
editorial the *Journal* rebuked those who were trying to
further temperance principles through the agency of the

60 Mary F. Ayer, *op. cit.*, p. 62; *Journal*, July, 1844, p. 107.
61 Thomas P. Taylor, *The Bottle* (New York, 1847).

theatre. The temperance cause, said the editor, "is the cause of God and humanity, and needs not the aid of buffoonery, mountebanks, and theatrical exhibitions, which are, after all, money-making affairs." [62]   In spite of this attitude on the part of the national organization, Dr. Robinson's company continued to receive the support of temperance people in many of the cities which it visited. The argument that the theatre was indecent and unscriptural, that it had never before aided moral reform, that it was only doing so now because of financial returns did not convince all reformers of the danger of propaganda in the form of drama. Whether the American Temperance Union approved or not, some societies welcomed theatrical companies as important allies in the work of reform.[63]

Prior to 1850 there were few organized efforts to discredit temperance principles. This does not imply that the reformers encountered no serious opposition. While indifference was usually their greatest enemy, at times they were forced to bear the brunt of formidable attacks. There were, for example, such works as Calvin Colton's *Protestant Jesuitism* and Bishop Hopkins' *The Primitive Church* which carefully analysed and criticized the principles and methods of temperance societies. In the course of his caustic comments on the propaganda of the movement, Colton said:

The great public, busy about other matters and their private concerns, but finding gratification at intervals of repose in sympathizing with philanthropic projects, are always ready to be wrought upon by an adequate machinery. Voluntary and hasty organization have been the fashion of the day. Whatever is started, a national society must at once be got up, which is imposing in its very name; a list of respectable names must be obtained, as members and patrons, which is also imposing and influential; a secretary and an adequate corps of assistants must

[62] *Journal*, August, 1843, p. 125.
[63] *Ibid.*, July, 1844, p. 107, August, 1845, p. 121, March, 1846, p. 43.

be appointed and provided for from the first fruits of collections; a band of popular lecturers must be commissioned, and sent forth as agents on the wide public; the press with its many-winged messengers, is put in operation; certificates fitted for the purpose are made out, submitted, subscribed, and sworn to; the entire machinery is put in operation; subsidiary societies are multiplied over the length and breadth of the land; the end proposed is manifestly a good one; and how can the community resist the sway of such an influence? Nobody feels it his duty to oppose, for the cause is good; everyone believes, because everybody else does; credit in all statements goes by authority, not by conviction; the prime agents believe, first, because it is their business and next, because, having told the story so long, they have no doubt of its truth; new discoveries are made, new sophistries invented, new facts developed on hypothetical state-ments; tracts and books are written and find a ready market; the daily and weekly journals are burdened with the weight of new matter, and with new visions or representations of old; it is "line upon line, and precept upon precept, here a little and there a little"; the heavens above and the depths beneath, fire, earth, air, wind, and water are ransacked, and fail not to yield their treasures of things new and old. In a word, the public is over-whelmed—literally carried by storm—there is no resisting it. Thinking is out of the question. The fashion and necessity are, to fall in with the current, and float along with it. It is the easiest and cheapest. Who can stop to examine such an accumu-lation—such a world of materials? Who so presumptuous as to dissent from such a weight and amount of authority? [64]

Not all of the protests were so ably voiced, but their import was as easily understood. At a meeting called to form the first temperance society in Providence, Rhode Island, an opposition group secured control of affairs and voted to form a debating society instead. In Northamp-ton County, Pennsylvania, an attempt in 1833 to establish a permanent organization among the temperance people was

[64] Colton, *Protestant Jesuitism*, pp. 53–54.

frustrated by a mob. In southeastern Pennsylvania there was considerable anti-temperance sentiment among the Germans. This was particularly true of Bucks, Chester, York, Adams and Cumberland counties, where agents of the Pennsylvania State Society found it difficult to arouse any enthusiasm.[65] The editor of the *Doylestown Democrat* was inclined to laugh at the earnest efforts of the reformers. Of total abstinence he wrote:

We certainly do not approve of the present system of anti-fogmatics, phlegm-cutters, mint juleps, and the whole tribe of liver murdering preparations that infest our country, but we hold with Anacreon, Horace and Tom Moore, that the juice of the grape is not to be eschewed. We are poor devils of humanity altogether, and if a glass of Champagne or Madeira or Port will drive away the clouds of care, why should we not indulge it?
    Let us have whiskey, punch and mirth and laughter;
    Sermons and soda water the day after.[66]

More serious in tone was the protest that came from another section of the state. On March 14, 1834, a special meeting at Georgetown, Mercer County, condemned total abstinence associations as organizations subversive of government and dangerous to society. The temperance reform, said the resolutions, destroyed family harmony, setting father against son and brother against brother. It was in reality a form of nullification, since it ignored the laws of the state which sanctioned the trade in intoxicants. These views were similar to those expressed by an anti-temperance conclave at Elizabeth City in 1833, which recorded its abhorrence of the whole system of cant and hypocrisy symbolized by the temperance pledge.[67] Current objections to

---

[65] *Pa. Temp. Rec.,* October, 1835, p. 64, November, p. 71, December, pp. 78-79.

[66] Quoted in W. H. Davis, *Doylestown, Old and New,* pp. 85-86.

[67] *New York Evangelist,* Aug. 10, 1833; *History of Mercer County, Pennsylvania* (Chicago, 1888).

the religious aspect of the reform found expression in a pamphlet published at Richmond in 1836 with the title *Reasons for not joining the Temperance Society.*[68] The anonymous author, who described himself as a clergyman, maintained that abstinence had nothing in common with temperance, that the methods of the reformers tended to foster intolerance, that the movement was using Christian churches as mere agencies to accomplish its ends, that the harmony of congregations was thereby being ruined and the real mission of the church subordinated to a temporary interest in moral reform.[69]

Occasionally temperance propaganda involved its authors in litigation which redounded to the credit of the cause. A notable case in point was that of the libel suit arising out of the publication of *Deacon Giles' Distillery.* In February, 1835, there appeared in the *Salem* (Mass.) *Landmark* under the caption "Inquire at Amos Giles' Distillery" an allegorical narrative of unusual occurrences in the distillery of one Deacon Amos Giles.[70] The story had been written as tem-

---

[68] *Reasons for not joining the Temperance Society* (1836). The pamphlet was published the next year in Baltimore.

[69] One wonders how much mute antagonism to temperance was represented by the following letter to the *Temperance Recorder,* July, 1835, p. 51:

Sir:—By what authority you continue to send me the *Temperance Recorder,* I know not. One thing I do know, which is, that if you do not like to have them returned with double postage, you had better wait till I subscribe before you send me another. We have Anti-Masonry, Anti-Rum, Anti-Gin, Anti-Brandy, and Anti-mind-their-own-business people enough in this small town, without aid from the Regency city [Albany]. Enclosed you have your "extra" which, perhaps, you will want for some one you can more easily gull than Me.

[70] *The Dream, or Deacon Giles' Distillery* became a popular piece of temperance fiction as a result of this widespread publicity. The story related how Amos Giles, a prominent deacon in the church and treasurer of a Bible society, had quarrelled with his labourers in the distillery. One evening as he was sitting in his counting room a gang of singular fellows appeared and offered to work for him on his own terms. These new workers were demons in disguise, who proceeded

perance fiction by Rev. George B. Cheever, a Congregational
clergyman in Salem, with too great fidelity to facts known
by residents of the town. Deacon John Stone, proprietor
of the largest local distillery, immediately brought suit for
libel, contending that the clergyman had resorted to fiction
as a thin veil to cover an unwarranted attack on his character and the good repute of his business. The case was
heard before the Common Pleas Court of Essex County,
Peleg Sprague and Rufus Choate representing the defendant.
Their defence was brilliant, but not effective, for the jury
found Cheever guilty on the strength of evidence which
established identical incidents in the career of Deacon John
Stone and the supposititious Deacon Amos Giles. Though
Cheever carried his case to the state Supreme Court, he was
not so much interested in securing a favourable decision as in
advertising the evils of intemperance and the tactics of the
liquor dealers. He succeeded in his real purpose, for the
higher court found against him, and his thirty-day imprisonment was regarded as a martyr's fate by temperance advocates throughout the country. Retribution came seven
years later, when the Washington Temperance Society of
Salem was organized in the building formerly used as Deacon
Stone's distillery.[71]

to do the work of the distillery in highly efficient fashion. On each
barrel and keg, however, they secretly inscribed invisible labels. As
soon as the retailer sold the first draught of liquor out of the keg, the
label become plainly visible in large letters. Some of the inscriptions
read *Consumption Sold Here, Insanity and Murder, For Delirium
Tremens Inquire Deacon Giles' Distillery.* So frightened were retailers and customers that Deacon Giles' business was ruined.

[71] *The True History of Deacon Giles' Distillery* (New York, 1844);
New York Evangelist, Feb. 21, 1835; *Pa. Temp. Rec.,* September, 1835,
p. 51. Another famous lawsuit was that instituted by several Albany
brewers against E. C. Delavan. On February 12, 1835, Delavan published an article in the *Albany Evening Journal* in which he charged
breweries in the city with using polluted water for malting and brewing
purposes. His charges were so well supported by affidavits that the
plaintiffs were not able to collect damages. A full report of the

The most virulent attack upon the temperance propaganda originated in York County, Pennsylvania. Alexander S. Davis, who had retired from a successful business career in Philadelphia, was the outstanding leader in arousing the latent opposition in that section. On March 28, 1842, as a result of an extensive advertising campaign, a "public, independent anti-teetotal abstinence" meeting was held at Hanover. The crowd that attended represented York, Adams and several adjoining counties where temperance workers had always found a hostile sentiment. Addresses were delivered in English and German, denouncing the doctrine of total abstinence as an infringement of personal liberty and a violation of Scriptural injunctions. The methods of the temperance reformers were branded as inimical to political and religious liberty and destructive of republican government. No effort was made by the speakers to justify such a sweeping indictment, for the crowd had assembled to hear unrestrained denunciation. At the conclusion of the invectives resolutions were adopted to express definitely the attitude of the audience. The signers agreed that they would not support any minister or teacher who preached or taught total abstinence; that they would not vote for any person for public office who favoured the temperance cause. The resolutions were to be published in at least three newspapers in the county. Subsequently Davis wrote and distributed a lengthy account of the proceedings.[72] Although such isolated protests indicated a growing hostility to the reform, they represented but a small proportion of the opposition finally aroused by the reformers' attempts to effect the legal destruction of the liquor traffic.

evidence at the trial was printed and distributed by the Albany Temperance Society in 1840. See *A Report of the trial of the cause of John Taylor vs. E. C. Delavan.*

[72] Alexander S. Davis, *A Loud Call to the Freemen of the United States.*

CHAPTER XI

PROPHETS OF PROHIBITION

MUCH of the later propaganda of the temperance movement was concerned with moral suasion and legal coercion,
with petitions and counter-petitions, with licence laws and
amendatory statutes; the demand for restrictive legislation
was constantly gathering force.   It had met with considerable opposition during the decade of the thirties, when few
had been willing to consider it even a remotely possible solution of the liquor question.   The first petitions to state legislatures, for example, had been roundly denounced by leaders
within the temperance ranks, but that had not prevented a
determined minority from pressing the question.   Memorial
followed memorial, each causing dissension among the reform
element and worrying the legislators who sought to appraise
its political significance.   While many of these appeals were
laid on the table, or otherwise lost in the ordinary routine
of legislative procedure, not all were so conveniently disposed of.   In some states an attempt was made to satisfy the
petitioners by the appointment of a special committee to
hear evidence with regard to the operation of existing licence
laws and to report whether modifications seemed advisable.
In a few instances the committees saw fit to incorporate their
ideas in the draft of a law, thus presenting the issue
squarely to the legislature.   Such was the origin of the
"fifteen gallon law" in Massachusetts, a statute which served
as a model for a particular type of legislation in other
states.

A state convention of temperance advocates, held in Boston on February 21, 1838, adopted resolutions against "the practise of licensing men to traffic in intoxicating liquors to be sold as a beverage," and appointed a committee to memorialize the legislature on the subject. The committee, headed by such earnest workers as Dr. Walter Channing, Dr. Ebenezer Alden, Rev. John Pierpont and Deacon Moses Grant, lost no time in framing a petition which asked that all laws authorizing the sale of intoxicating drinks be repealed and their retail sale be made a penal offence. The appeal, with 1500 supporting signatures, reached the legislature at a time when many of its members were favourably inclined toward a policy of restriction. It was immediately referred to a select committee, which reported a bill designed to prohibit the sale of spirituous liquors in small quantities for beverage purposes. The minimum quantity to be sold by licensed dealers was fixed at twenty-eight gallons, except in the case of licensed apothecaries and physicans. With but slight modification the bill was passed by more than a two-thirds vote in both houses. As signed by Governor Edward Everett on April 19, it forbade the sale of spirituous liquors, except for medicinal or mechanical purposes, in less quantity than fifteen gallons, "and that delivered and carried away all at one time." Sales for medicinal and mechanical purposes might be made by licensed apothecaries and physicians, and the wholesale dealer was not limited by its provisions. In its effect, therefore, the law amounted to prohibition of the sale of distilled liquors in taverns and shops for beverage purposes. Though it did not place wine and malt liquors under the ban, it was aimed directly at the grog-shop and tippling-house.[1]

The reasoning responsible for the passage of the "fifteen

[1] *Laws of the State of Massachusetts* (1838), pp. 81–82; *Independent Messenger*, March 2, 1838, April 20, 1838; *Report of the American Temperance Union* (1838), pp. 32–33; Clark, op. cit., pp. 39–40; Marsh, op. cit., pp. 64–65.

gallon law" was clearly set forth in the special committee's report to the legislature. It contained in well documented form a comprehensive and specific indictment of the existing licence system. The ineffectiveness of the licence laws, the committee held, arose from the fact that they recognized the use of spirituous liquors as beneficial and necessary. By their provisions they furnished legislative sanction for the growth of the retail liquor trade. Out of this situation had developed an inconsistency in the legislative policy of the commonwealth. While one set of statutes was designed to protect life, health and reason and to prevent poverty, vice and crime, another set was as carefully framed to protect a business which burdened the state with invalids, lunatics, paupers and criminals. This inconsistency, the committee insisted, was detrimental to the state's prosperity. Investigations during 1836 and 1837 had revealed the fact that more than three-quarters of the pauperism in Massachusetts was caused by intemperance, that the liquor traffic sent its annual quota of victims to the State Lunatic Asylum at Worcester, and that the prisons were filled with men whose crimes were traceable to strong drink. In the face of such incontrovertible evidence it seemed economically unwise to retain a system of so-called regulation, whereby the sale of spirituous liquors was really encouraged.[2] As to the possibility of enforcing the proposed measure the committee entertained some doubts, but it saw no reason for refusing to enact a law because of probable difficulties in enforcement.

Opponents of the new statute began a campaign for its repeal before it had gone into operation. The centre of activity was Boston, for few of the city's representatives had favoured the bill when it was before the legislature. Realizing that the rural communities were responsible for the passage of the act, Boston liquor dealers and their friends issued

[2] *Report of Linus Child to the Legislature of 1838.*

an appeal to voters in the country districts trying to persuade them that under the new system they would lose a good
market for their grain. The friends of temperance issued
a reply in which they emphasized the cost of intemperance
to the tax-payer.[3] As the autumn elections for the legislature drew near, the political situation seemed favourable to
the advocates of repeal. Though the act had been supported by both Whigs and Democrats, the latter party,
making a strong bid for the governorship, believed that it
could capitalize popular dissatisfaction in Boston and vicinity by favouring a return to the old licence system. The
Whigs were badly divided over the question, and the logic
of the situation seemed to indicate that the Van Buren men
could take advantage of their opponents' dissensions.
During the campaign opponents of the law made much of the
fact that it had apparently been framed to benefit the rich.
The fifteen gallon minimum enabled the wealthy citizen to
purchase his stocks of liquor and store them, but it effectually prevented the poor man from securing the smaller
quantities which he could afford. Supporters of the law
countered this attack by charging the Boston aristocracy
with having originated the idea that the law oppressed the
poor. Why, they asked, had the "monied aristocracy"
suddenly become so interested in their less fortunate brethren? This defence of the poor man sounded suspiciously
like an invention of the rum-sellers. The law had not been
passed for the benefit of the wealthy. It had been enacted
without their aid and it would have to be sustained in the
same manner.[4]

---

[3] *A Reply to the Report of the Committee of those opposed to the
License Law; Address by the Hampshire Convention of the Friends
of the License Law.*

[4] *Hampshire Gazette* (Northampton), April 18, Nov. 7, 1838; Peter
Parley, *Five Letters to My Neighbor Smith;* Moses Williams, *The
Cracked Jug, or Five Answers to My Neighbor Parley's Five Letters;*

The November election resulted in the re-election of Governor Everett, who was opposed to an immediate repeal of the law. The liberal Democrats and Whigs, in favour of a return to the old licensing system, were not able to control the legislature. Pressure was soon brought to bear upon the hesitant ones, however, and an investigation of the law was ordered. Harrison Gray Otis, who well represented the old "quality" of Boston, drafted a legal argument against it, which was signed by hundreds of citizens. The public hearings before the select committee were used by both groups in an attempt to influence the legislature. Mayor Samuel A. Eliot of Boston, Benjamin F. Hallett and Franklin Dexter argued the case against restriction, while Peleg Sprague appeared as defender of the law.[5] Dexter summed up the contentions of his colleagues. He argued that the statute in question injured a good moral cause by arousing the antagonism of those who were anxious to effect the reform by moral suasion. It amounted to a prohibition of the retail sale of spirituous liquors and as such it was an unwarranted violation of property rights. Its infringement of personal liberty was serious, but even more so was its conflict with federal statutes which granted the right to import liquor. Furthermore, the law was inexpedient, since it was not based on public sentiment. It could not be enforced. The inevitable reaction, therefore, would be detrimental to the very cause which the law sought to promote.[6]

Essex Register quoted in *Journal,* July, 1838, p. 101; Clark, *op. cit.,* p. 41.

[5] The counsel who appeared against the law were all representative of that wing of the temperance movement which opposed restrictive legislation. Hallett had distinguished himself as a temperance advocate when he was editor of the *Boston Daily Advertiser* from 1827 to 1831. Dexter was a son of Samuel Dexter, first president of the Massachusetts Temperance Society. *Journal,* March, 1839, pp. 34–36.

[6] Franklin Dexter, *Investigation of the Fifteen Gallon Law.* See also *Letters to Harrison Gray Otis,* pp. 2–11; *Journal,* May, 1838, p. 72; Clark, *op. cit.,* p. 41.

For the supporters of restriction Peleg Sprague presented a carefully drawn answer to these arguments. He maintained that the state's action was in conformity with a judicious exercise of its police power. The statute under discussion was of a sort with those restraining the sale of obscene books and pictures, or suppressing gambling, lewdness and drunkenness. It was not in conflict with the constitutional provision granting Congress power to regulate interstate and foreign commerce, for it dealt solely with intra-state commerce. This distinction had been upheld by the United States Supreme Court in the famous cases of *Gibbons v. Ogden* and *Brown v. Maryland*. Furthermore, Sprague argued, Congress itself had prohibited the importation of distilled spirits in any quantity less than fifteen gallons. Massachusetts' legislation was, therefore, in harmony with federal regulation of foreign commerce. As for the contention that the "fifteen gallon law" discriminated between rich and poor, it was manifestly absurd. Anyone, not on the verge of pauperism, could raise five or six dollars to purchase the minimum quantity. The real ground for the apprehension felt by liquor dealers was that the poor man *would not*, rather than that he *could not* purchase so freely as formerly. Finally, Sprague presented evidence to show that in those counties, where commissioners had refused to issue licences under the old law, a significant decrease had occurred in pauperism and crime, which residents of the counties attributed to a decline in intemperance. Such correlations would be noticeable throughout the state under the operation of the new law.[7]

The report of the special committee to the legislature sustained Sprague's arguments and the legislature voted

[7] *Argument of Peleg Sprague Before the Joint Committee of the Legislature.* For confirmation of Sprague's argument in regard to pauperism in no-licence counties see *Salem Register* quoted in *Journal,* May, 1838, p. 86.

against repeal.   The victory of the anti-licence group however, had not settled the question of restrictive legislation.
Supporters of a liberal licence policy continued their agitation, making considerable impression by urging that the law
was a blunder since it could not be enforced.   Public opinion,
they said, approved moral suasion as a method of securing
reforms, but it had not yet been educated to the point of
accepting legislative coercion as a means of correcting manners and morals.   Consequently, any attempt to combat
intemperance by imposing legal restrictions was too far in
advance of public sentiment to be practicable.   Conventions
of tavern-keepers adopted resolutions condemning a law
which seriously interfered with the business of keeping a
public house.   A group of "liberal" Whig members of the
legislature met at the State House on April 8 and appointed
a committee of correspondence to arouse and organize
opinion favourable to repeal.   To counteract such propaganda a campaign of law enforcement was initiated by
supporters of the statute.   Such papers as the *Hampshire
Gazette* and the *Massachusetts Spy* urged all citizens to
abide by the decision of the majority whatever their personal opinions on the subject.   The *Springfield Republican*
rejoiced that the "liberals" were able to make little headway
and that the law would be obeyed.   The mayors of Salem
and Lowell served notice that they would punish severely
all violations of the law.   In Boston committees were organized in each ward to co-operate with the police and the
magistrates.[8]

On May 30, 1839, the Massachusetts Temperance Society,
which was suspected of hostility to prohibitory measures,
adopted a resolution stating that the law of 1838 deserved
the support of every citizen who had the interests of the

[8] See the extracts from Massachusetts papers in *Journal*, May,
1839, p. 75; *Springfield Republican*, June 8, July 6, 1839; *Hingham
Patriot*, April, 1839,

commonwealth at heart.   Hubbard Winslow, who was Lyman Beecher's successor in the Bowdoin Street Church,
Boston, voiced the sentiment of most of the temperance
people, when he insisted that the issue was no longer the
desirability of restrictive measures, but the enforcement of
existing statutes.   He answered the argument that the
"fifteen gallon law" could not be enforced by asserting that
the principle which allows *one* law to be trampled upon will
allow *every* law to be trampled upon.   "If this spirit of in-
subordination," he warned the liquor dealers and their
friends, "is allowed to go on in our country, the time will
come when no law will be sacred." [9]

The refusal of liquor dealers in some sections to close their
grog-shops and tippling-houses aroused extraordinary public
interest in the matter of prosecutions.[10]   In Boston the
arrest of an inn-keeper, who refused to pay his fine or go to
jail, almost resulted in a riot.   Several thousand citizens
assembled with the intention of preventing the imprisonment
of the liquor dealer, but the authorities were able to avoid
a clash with the mob by collecting the fine.[11]   From almost
every town came word of indictments, trials, convictions,
fines and appeals.   Some retailers paid their fines and continued in business, hoping that the second prosecution would
be long deferred.   Others agreed to abandon the sale of
spirituous liquors.   Many appealed their cases, when fines
were imposed by the lower courts.   In a few instances the
police courts sentenced those found guilty of maintaining
common tippling-houses to serve a short term in the house of
correction.[12]

During the late summer and early autumn both the licence
and anti-licence groups campaigned vigorously to control

[9] *Documents and Records of the Massachusetts Temperance Society,*
p. 80; Hubbard Winslow, *The Importance of Sustaining the Law.*
[10] *Conn. Courant,* June 25, 1839.
[11] *Journal,* July, 1839, p. 105.
[12] *Ibid.,* September, 1839, p. 139,

the new legislature.   Opponents of the existing law established a paper called *The Liberal*, while the opposite party
issued a weekly, *Facts for the People*, until after the election.
To offset the charge that the question was a political one,
Whig supporters of the "fifteen gallon law" persuaded
Robert Rantoul, Jr., one of the most prominent Democratic
politicians in the state, to undertake a speaking tour in behalf of law enforcement.[13]   Wherever he spoke, he counselled the friends of temperance to send representatives to
the legislature who would make no concession to the liquor interests.   He also assured his hearers that the licence
question cut across party lines and that Democrats and
Whigs did not represent opposite views on the subject.   On
October 23, a temperance convention in Middlesex County
reiterated these statements, warning voters not to be misled
by party labels, but to investigate the candidate's record.
"The time has arrived," said the committee, "when all the
friends of our republican institutions, and of good order,
are signally called upon to maintain their principles by
vigorous action.   Every means that interest and art can
devise, to defeat the operation of the People's law, has been
put in requisition, and great efforts will be made throughout
the Commonwealth, to elect men to the Massachusetts Senate,
as well as to the House of Representatives, who will repeal
the law which protects us from the evils of dram-shops, and
give the triumph to the spirit of misrule and sordid interest.
Will not the friends of the law be awake to the sense of their
danger and their duty at this important crisis?" [14]

The temperance forces were much embarrassed by the
gubernatorial campaign.   It was rumoured that a vote for
Marcus Morton, the Democratic candidate, was a vote for
repeal, yet Morton had long been known as a temperance
advocate, having served as the first president of the American

13 *Journal,* October, 1839, p. 149.
14 *Journal,* November, 1839, p. 172.

Temperance Society. His position in regard to the "fifteen gallon law," however, had never been clearly stated, whereas Governor Everett was on record in opposition to the repeal of the statute. Democratic workers were urging all "liberals" to support Morton, if they desired a change in the liquor laws. The result of the election was in doubt for some time owing to the closeness of the vote, but it was finally decided that Everett had lost the governship by one vote. In the legislature the friends of law enforcement appeared to have suffered important reverses. Nevertheless, the *Boston Mercantile Journal* felt that the liquor law would not be repealed and doubted whether the new governor would approve any change in policy. The *Journal of the American Temperance Union* maintained that the defeat of Governor Everett had no bearing on the licence question whatever. Was not Morton a temperance man? [15] Such hopes were soon dispelled by the governor, for in his first message to the legislature he demonstrated that he was not the kind of temperance advocate who believed in legal coercion. He characterized the act of 1838 as a "sumptuary regulation" which interfered unnecessarily with "private business" and consequently violated the property rights of persons engaged in a particular form of commercial enterprise. He, therefore, recommended that the legislature repeal the law and revert to the licence system of 1837. The legislature was not slow to act on the governor's recommendation and on February 9, 1840, the "fifteen gallon law" was repealed.[16]

The response of the temperance forces was voiced at a state convention held in Marlboro Chapel, Boston, on February 12, with more than 1400 delegates in attendance.

[15] *Boston Mercantile Journal,* November 25, 1839. Cited in *Journal,* January, 1840, p. 9.

[16] *Journal,* March, 1840, p. 38. This return to the law of 1837 meant that county commissioners could at their discretion refuse to grant any liquor licences.

Samuel Hoar of Concord presided over the sessions and sounded the keynote.[17]   The repeal of the law of 1838, he said, had thrown open the floodgates to drunkenness.   In such a crisis the future policy of the temperance advocates in the state was a matter of grave concern.   He himself favoured explicit pronouncements on the governor's message and the action of the legislature.   A special committee was appointed by the chair to draft appropriate resolutions.   It reported a lengthy document which approved the principle of total abstinence, condemned the old system of liquor licences, criticized the governor and legislature and demanded more stringent legislation.   The resolution referring to political action in the future aroused a storm of protest. It was finally adopted in the following form:

Resolved, that until the laws of this state, concerning the sale of intoxicating liquors, are fully established upon the basis of prohibition and sustained by a correct general sentiment, like the other criminal and penal laws of the Commonwealth, it is, in our opinion, the duty of the temperance men, to vote only for those men as candidates for legislative and executive offices, who are known and inflexible friends of such a course of legislation.

The vote on this question proved that more than sixty were opposed to its adoption, among them Samuel Hoar of Concord and Emory Washburn of Worcester, two of the leading lawyers in the state.   The dissenters insisted that the suggested course could mean only one thing, a third political party.   The majority, however, maintained that the resolution was designed merely to give a preference to temperance men over all others in their own party.[18]   But the difference of opinion was not sufficient to prevent the

[17] Samuel Hoar was the father of Judge E. R. Hoar and Senator George F. Hoar.

[18] Clark, *op. cit.*, pp. 232–234; *Journal*, March, 1840, pp. 38–39; *P. T. D.*, III, 193–4; *Manufacturers and Farmers Journal*, Feb. 24, 1840.

convention from serving notice that the fight against licence laws was not at an end.[19]

In the meantime temperance workers had been politically active beyond the confines of Massachusetts. We have already noticed the efforts of Flournoy in Georgia to secure a repeal of the licence laws, a movement which resulted so disastrously for the reformers.[20] For two decades after this failure Georgia made no change in the system of regulation, the state legislature continuing to confer upon authorities in the incorporated municipalities or the counties the right to grant licences and punish unlicensed dealers.[21] But several states attempted to follow Massachusetts' policy of restricting the retail sale of spirituous liquors.[22] Numerous petitions to the legislature of Mississippi finally resulted in a modification of the existing statutes in 1839, when Henry S. Foote introduced a bill prohibiting the sale of vinous or spirituous liquors in less quantity than one gallon. Inn-keepers and taverners were

[19] During the campaign against the "fifteen gallon law" the dismissal of Rev. John Pierpont from the First Unitarian Church caused considerable excitement in Boston. It was charged that the liquor dealers and their friends had instigated the action because of the clergyman's activity in temperance reform. A storm of protest in Boston and New York newspapers gave the matter much publicity and within a few weeks the congregation voted to reinstate Pierpont and give him a free pulpit. See extracts from the *Boston Mercantile Journal, New York Commercial* and *The New Yorker* in *Journal,* November, 1839, p. 169 December, p. 189; *Portland Transcript,* April 25, 1840.

[20] *Supra,* p. 174.

[21] Scomp, *op. cit.,* pp. 452–458.

[22] The legislature of Tennessee had taken an important step toward prohibitory legislation in 1838 by repealing all laws licensing the sale of spirituous liquors in taverns and stores. Such sale was made a misdemeanor and the courts were authorized to impose fines at their discretion; all fines and forfeitures to be appropriated to the use of the common schools. The act remained in force until 1846, when a system of high licences was substituted. *Acts of the State of Tennessee* (1837–1838), pp. 186–187, (1845–1846), pp. 154–158; *Journal,* March, 1838, p. 40.

forbidden to sell to guests except in quantities above the minimum. The bill was passed by the legislature with little difficulty and received the signature of Governor McNutt in February, 1839.[23] It seems to have been reasonably well enforced during the three years that it was in effect, for the Alabama state temperance convention in 1841 petitioned the legislature for a law similar to the Mississippi "gallon law." [24]

The anti-licence people in South Carolina staged an extensive campaign for repeal of the liquor laws in 1839. Several parish societies sent resolutions to the legislature recommending that the sale of spirituous liquors in any quantity less than twenty gallons be prohibited. Judge John B. O'Neale, president of the state temperance society, and Albert Rhett, a member of the legislature, were selected to argue the cause of restriction before a select legislative committee. Although the proposed measure had the active support of such a prominent politician as Robert Barnwell Rhett and was championed in the columns of the *Charleston Courier* and the *South Carolinian,* the committee reported against modifying the existing law. Judge O'Neale attributed this failure to the attitude of the state temperance society and its official organ, the *South Carolina Temperance Advocate.* Neither the executive committee of the Society, nor the editors of the periodical were enthusiastic over restrictive legislation, and their lukewarm support of O'Neale was partially responsible for the defeat of the anti-licence group before the committee.[25]

---

[23] *Laws of the State of Mississippi* (1839), pp. 26–28; *Journal,* March, 1839, p. 38. The law was repealed on February 22, 1842, and a system of high licence fees was adopted. *Laws of the State of Mississippi* (1842), pp. 110–114.

[24] *Journal,* May, 1839, p. 69; *Mobile Commercial Register,* May 19, 1841.

[25] *Charleston Courier,* September 10, 1839; *Journal,* September, 1839, p. 141, October, p. 156, November, p. 173, February, 1840, pp.

The legislatures of Connecticut, Rhode Island and Illinois, afraid to ignore the temperance petitions and unwilling to enact restrictive legislation, passed the responsibility to the local governments. The situation in Connecticut was particularly interesting because of the well organized opposition of those engaged in the liquor traffic. Grocers, tavern-keepers and other retailers of intoxicants in New Haven announced their intention of fighting for their rights. At an organization meeting in 1838 they charged the temperance societies with maintaining paid informers to detect violations of the licence laws and with financing the prosecution of those against whom information was obtained. They further denounced the reform movement as a conspiracy to procure political power for purposes of oppression. For their own part, they had endured in silence long enough. It was now time to take action against the hypocrisy of their persecutors. They had a fund of three thousand dollars with which to begin a legal assault on the constitutionality of any law restricting their business interests. Every person opposed to intolerance and persecution, every person to whom political and personal liberty was dear, was invited to join them.[26] But in spite of this threat from New Haven the Connecticut legislature in May, 1839, passed a law making it a penal offence for any person to sell wines and spirituous liquors without a licence granted by a majority vote of the town meeting.[27]

The principle of local option was gaining popularity rapidly. Even before Connecticut's action Rhode Island in

35–36. In 1839 Ohio limited sales of spirituous liquors to tavern bars. *Acts of a General Nature of the State of Ohio* (1839).

[26] Leonard Bacon, *Discourse on the Traffic*, pp. 51–54.

[27] *Public Acts of Connecticut* (1839), pp. 55–56; *P. T. D., Report for 1839*, p. 21. This act was repealed in 1842 in order to permit the licensing of taverns to sell in small quantities. In 1845 public investigators were appointed to report violations of the law. *Public Acts of Connecticut* (1842), p. 40, (1846), pp. 46–48.

January, 1839, had conferred upon the freemen in the respective towns the right to decide by ballot whether any liquor licences should be issued. The selectmen and aldermen were bound to abide by the result of the vote.[28] During the same year Illinois limited the jurisdiction of the county courts over licences. An act of March 2, 1839, provided that no licences should be issued in the county, if a majority of the legal voters so petitioned the court. This prohibition was to remain in effect until a majority of the voters petitioned for a re-issuance of licences.[29] In both states local option proved disappointing to the temperance supporters. It was extremely difficult to enforce the law because of the proximity of licence territory to the no-licence towns.[30] Besides, few of the communities pursued either policy long enough to allow an intelligent comparison of effects. One year a town would reject liquor licences and the next it might authorize the authorities to issue as many as seemed desirable. As a result the temperance people came to regard local option as of doubtful value to the cause. The American Temperance Union urged state and local societies to campaign for restrictive laws which would operate uniformly throughout the state.[31]

Still, the most notable victories continued to be won by popular vote under local option laws rather than by state action. During the decade of the forties the legislature of Pennsylvania granted to particular counties the right to ballot on the licence question. By 1847 eighteen counties

[28] *Acts of the State of Rhode Island* (1838–1839), pp. 75–78.

[29] *Laws of Illinois* (1838–1839), pp. 71–72.

[30] Difficulties of enforcing the local option law in Rhode Island led to the passage of an act in 1846 which provided for public informers in each town. *Acts of the State of Rhode Island* (1846), p. 63; Edward Peterson, *The Bible Temperance Review*, pp. 21–25.

[31] For example, Providence in 1840 and 1841 granted no licences, but in 1842 at least sixty-three were permitted to sell ardent spirits in small quantities. *Providence Daily Journal*, April 25, 1842. Also see *Journal*, November, 1839, p. 169; *P. T. D.*, II, 274.

enjoyed this privilege and five had already forbidden the sale of spirituous liquors within their borders.[32] In Rhode Island in 1845 every town but three voted no-licence, while more than three-fourths of the towns in Connecticut did likewise. The following year a popular referendum in Vermont resulted in the prohibition of the sale of ardent spirits by retailers. Local option laws in Wisconsin and Michigan enabled about half of the towns to bar grog-shops and tippling-houses. In Iowa every county except Keokuk voted no-licence in 1847. Although many of these victories were temporary, it was evident, said the reformers, that sentiment in favour of restrictive legislation was rapidly increasing.[33]

The conflict in New York state was of special interest to temperance workers in all parts of the country, not only because of the importance of the state, but also because of its pre-eminent position in the reform movement during the early years. New York had long ranked first in the number of societies, in total membership, in contributions and in the distribution of propaganda. Would the state rank as high in the fight for prohibitory legislation? During the spring of 1845 the constant stream of petitions to the legislature and the work of a strong temperance lobby at Albany finally forced the select committee to report a bill designed to amend the existing excise system. The proposed measure provided that the electors in the several towns and cities were to determine at a special election whether licences to sell

[32] See *Laws of Pennsylvania* (1845), pp. 327–328, (1846), pp. 383–384; (1847), p. 53; *P. T. D., Report for 1847*, p. 5.

[33] *Laws of Vermont* (1846), pp. 18–21; *Laws of the Territory of Wisconsin* (1847), pp. 218–220; *P. T. D., Report for 1847*, pp. 4–6; Silas Farmer, *History of Detroit and Wayne County; Journal*, April, 1848, p. 61. In 1847 the Supreme Court decided the famous Licence Cases in favour of state regulation. The power of the state to suppress as well as license the sale of liquors was upheld in *Thurlow v. Massachusetts, Fletcher v. Rhode Island* and *Pierce v. New Hampshire. 5 Howard 504–633.*

intoxicating liquors should be granted. If the result of the balloting in any town or city was in favour of no-licence, the board of excise was bound by the decision to refuse to grant any permit for the sale of intoxicants. This decision was to stand until one-fourth of the number that voted at the special election should petition, in writing, for another vote on the question.

This bill was approved by the assembly without a recorded vote, but in the senate considerable opposition developed. In order to carry any kind of a local option measure it was necessary to exclude New York County from the provisions of the act. A compromise was finally reached by granting to the excise commissioners in New York County the power to issue licences at increased fees and by increasing the penalties for Sunday sales in New York City. In this form the bill passed the legislature and received Governor Wright's signature on May 14.[34] The date for the special election was fixed as the first Tuesday before the first Monday in May, 1846. This allowed the anti-licence forces one year in which to campaign for their principles. The leaders admitted that they needed every minute of the time. Organization work began immediately. On April 25 at the call of the executive committee of the New York State Temperance Society a convention was held at Albany for the purpose of discussing the features of the proposed excise law. Some were inclined to think that it would amount to little, since New York City was not included within its provisions. A few were opposed to any sort of legislation against the liquor traffic, but the majority were convinced that an energetic campaign should be undertaken in every town and city to secure a no-licence vote. Horace Greeley, Edward

[34] *Journal of the Assembly of the State of New York*, 68th session, 514, 1392; 69th session, 420; *Journal*, May, 1845, p. 74, June, 1845, p. 88. *The New York Tribune* charged that the "Loco-focos" were responsible for the exclusion of New York from the provisions of the bill. May 15, 1845.

C. Delavan and Rev. John Marsh, as the committee on resolutions, recommended that a union of the temperance organizations be effected in each community for the purpose of discussing the excise law and distributing suitable literature in regard to it. Furthermore, each county was urged to hold a convention before the meeting of the state convention in October.[35]

One of the chief concerns of the local committees, as they worked to secure a repudiation of the licence system, was to avoid political entanglements. The *Poughkeepsie Safeguard*, a strong advocate of no-licence, warned the temperance workers of their great problem:

The difficulty will be to consolidate our forces and bring our power to bear with a concentrated energy upon the question. "United, we stand—divided, we fall," should be the motto of the friends of temperance; and let us most carefully and constantly bear in mind that this is not a political question. It is not to be decided by arraying the two great political parties against each other—*nor by forming a third party*. In this controversy the friends of Polk and Dallas, and those of Clay and Frelinghuysen, preserve their political predilections, and remain firm in their respective political views and principles, and as free to vote for their favorite candidates at the political elections as ever, while they now unite without any distinction of party, to put down a common foe to whom they are equally opposed. The temperance question is common ground for men of all political complexions. The enemy they resist is a common enemy; an enemy who riots with equal zest and equal power upon Whig and Loco-foco blood.[36]

Not all of the reformers gave heed to this timely warning. Greeley invariably linked his temperance propaganda with his political arguments. In the *Tribune* he denounced the

[35] *Journal*, July, 1845, p. 100.

[36] Quoted in *Journal*, July, 1845, p. 103. See also same copy of the *Journal*, p. 105.

"Loco-focos" as the party of the liquor interests. They were responsible for the provision in the excise law which prevented New York County from ridding itself of the licence system. They had defended the liquor dealer by their votes in the state legislature. It was evident that the temperance forces could hope for little support from the "Loco-foco" ranks.[37] As the autumn elections approached, Greeley advocated Whig-Temperance tickets to prevent control of the legislature from passing into the hands of the enemies of local option. Furthermore, if such tickets could be elected in certain assembly districts, there was a possibility that the excise law might be amended so as to permit every part of the state to vote on the question of liquor licences.[38] This, of course, was a plea for local option in the metropolis. Although Delavan and Marsh, who were managing the campaign throughout the state, scrupulously avoided all political entanglements, they allowed Greeley to play his own game, for they found that his influence with the Whigs more than offset the power of the enemies he made among the "Loco-focos." Besides, the large circulation of the *Tribune* in northern and western counties was one of the greatest factors in unifying the efforts of widely scattered temperance organizations.

As early as July, 1845, the no-licence workers began their drive for votes. In every county vigilance committees were formed which supervised the publication and distribution of literature. A central vigilance committee, of which Edward C. Delavan was chairman, received reports from county workers and furnished speakers and funds to the sections that most needed them. On August 27 a convention of the western districts was held at Rochester to establish a closer connection between the various town and city committees. This was preliminary to a state convention which met at

[37] *N. Y. Tribune,* July 18, August 30, 1845.
[38] *Ibid.,* Sept. 4, 1845.

the same place in October and made provision for adequate
revenues to finance the campaign. The state central committee was authorized to place temperance pamphlets in
every home just prior to the election. Accordingly, during
March and April, 1846, appeals designed to interest merchants and manufacturers, farmers and mechanics were
distributed in each county through the co-operation of the
local organization. A special circular was prepared for
the most numerous foreign element in the state, the Irish.[39]

This widespread and wisely directed propaganda, supplemented by the personal work of hundreds of enthusiasts,
proved surprisingly effective. The result of the balloting
on April 27 was a victory that went far beyond the expecta-
tions of the most optimistic. Nearly five-sixths of the
towns and incorporated municipalities reported no-licence
majorities. In a number of counties every town voted
against the sale of intoxicants. The reformers had been
confident of carrying the smaller towns in sections where
temperance societies had long been numerous, but they
doubted the popularity of their cause in the urban districts.
It was gratifying to them, therefore, to discover that some of
the most notable victories had been won in such cities as
Albany, Buffalo, Brooklyn, Rochester, Schenectady, Troy
and Utica. When one went behind the returns, it became
evident that the business interests were willing to give the
no-licence principle a trial.[40]

But the rejoicings of the temperance folk were speedily
stilled. No sooner was the result known than the liquor
dealers began to circulate petitions for another election the
following year.[41] When the necessary signatures had been
secured, the legislature set April 27, 1847, as the date for a

---

[39] *Journal,* October, 1845, p. 146, December, 1845, p. 184, April, 1846,
pp. 50–51.
[40] *Ibid.,* June, 1846, pp. 89–90, July, p. 97.
[41] *Ibid.,* July, 1846, p. 97.

second referendum.   In the ensuing campaign the chief issue was the enforcement of the prohibitory features of the excise law.   Supporters of the old licence system insisted that the retail liquor trade could not be suppressed by legislation, since laws of a prohibitory character could not be enforced. They stated their position succinctly in the slogan: More has been sold since no-licence than before.   This line of attack was calculated to win the votes of those temperance advocates who had acquiesced unwillingly in the repeal of the former licence system.   It proved to be excellent strategy, for the failure to suppress the liquor traffic in no-licence communities was heralded abroad as an indication that no sort of prohibitory statute could be enforced.   The "lawlessness" that was encouraged by the refusal to grant liquor licences was a compelling reason for a return to the old order of lawful sale under state control.

In the face of this attack the friends of the existing law were apathetic.   Whether they believed that the results of the experiment spoke for themselves, or that the previous decision at the polls would not be reversed, does not appear. At any rate, they failed to make the same vigorous campaign in 1847 that they had made in 1846.   Some of the leaders felt that this lack of enthusiasm was a direct result of reliance on legislation, and they minced no words in denouncing the theory that a law could banish intemperance.[42]   In view of this indifference and disillusionment it was not surprising that the no-licence advocates suffered a defeat at the polls. More than half of the towns and cities which had prohibited the sale of liquors a year before voted to authorize the grant-

[42] Reuben Tinker, *Address* (Westfield, N. Y., 1847); J. Henry Clark, *The Present Position and Claims Of the Temperance Enterprise*, pp. 9–15; L. Armstrong, *The Temperance Reformation*, pp. 47–48; *N. Y. Tribune*, July 15, 17, 18, 1846. Greeley denounced the *Buffalo Daily Globe* for urging the liquor dealers to support the "Loco-Foco" ticket. *Tribune*, Sept. 29, 1846.

ing of licences for the ensuing year.[43] The dealers in intoxicants had recovered much lost ground. Political leaders were not slow to appreciate the significance of the verdict. Immediately Democrats and Whigs in the legislature vied with each other to secure a revision of the excise law. A bill to repeal the local option provisions and restore the licence system in all towns and cities of the state passed the lower house by a vote of 69 to 38. In the senate there were only two votes against it.[44] The politicians, encouraged by a popular referendum, had put an end to local option, but the temperance leaders served notice that they had only begun to fight.

At the same time that New York voters were registering their dissatisfaction with restrictive measures, the electorate of Maine had returned candidates to the legislature who were in favour of suppressing the retail sale of intoxicants. In no other state were the forces hostile to the liquor interests so well organized or so completely under the spell of a single leader. For almost a decade Neal Dow, a well-known merchant of Portland, had been recognized as the astute director of temperance propaganda. Neither in the tanning business of Josiah Dow and Son, nor in his own speculations in timber lands, did Dow display more ability than in the task of marshalling votes against the liquor dealers. Born in 1804 of Quaker parents, he had grown to manhood in a home where the discipline of the Society of Friends was faithfully observed. Scarcely had he reached his majority when he became an earnest advocate of the teachings of his sect with regard to the use of alcoholic stimulants. At

[43] *Journal,* June, 1847, p. 92.

[44] *N. Y. Assembly Journal,* 70th session, p. 1403. The vote in the lower house stood: For repeal of local option, 39 "Loco-focos" and 30 Whigs; against repeal, 11 "Loco-focos" and 27 Whigs. *Journal,* June, 1847, p. 92.

every opportunity he made his influence felt in the community. As a member of the Deluge Engine Company he was instrumental in persuading the firemen to enforce the principle of total abstinence at all their meetings. With the assistance of William W. Thomas, an associate in his timber land ventures, he succeeded in preventing the drunken excesses so long associated with Fourth of July celebrations in Portland. He was responsible for the adoption of a resolution by the Maine Charitable Mechanics' Association urging master workmen to stop furnishing journeymen and apprentices with ardent spirits.[45]

As his business interests broadened, Dow became more firmly convinced of the evils of the liquor traffic. It seemed to him that the economic aspects of the problem were worthy of careful consideration. As an employer, he was impressed by the relation of intemperance to labour efficiency; as a governor of the alms-house and house of correction, he came in contact with some of the worst victims of the grog-shop. For the first time he realized just how much of the tax-payer's money was spent to repair the havoc wrought by alcohol. His experience was causing him to take a radical position in the reform movement. When the Maine State Temperance Society refused in 1837 to alter its pledge in order to place all intoxicants under the ban, Dow was one of the first to withdraw and help form the Maine Temperance Union, which championed total abstinence. At the time he warned his associates in the new organization that the temperance battle would never be won by moral suasion. Not until the manufacture and sale of spirituous liquors had been made a penal offence would Maine be freed from the curse of intemperance.[46]

Such a pronouncement was startling to many reformers

[45] Dow, *Reminiscences,* pp. 81–110.

[46] Dow, *Reminiscences,* pp. 232–233; Henry S. Clubb, *The Maine Liquor Law,* p. 12.

in the state, but others agreed that it indicated the future course of the reform. A resolution had already been introduced in the legislature asking for the appointment of a special committee to investigate the operation of the licence laws. The author of the resolution was General James Appleton who belonged to that class of men generally known as fanatics. From business he had turned to politics that he might encourage legislation to remedy a number of social ills. In sympathy with every humanitarian movement, he endorsed Birney's views on slavery, advocated generous and systematic relief for the pauper, and championed the cause of popular education. But his real hobby was temperance. Its promotion had been his chief reason for seeking public office. In 1832 he had published in the *Salem Gazette* a series of articles to the effect that intemperance would never be banished from the nation until the trade in intoxicants was made illegal. Five years later, as a member of the Maine legislature, he was in a position to propose a specific law. As chairman of the select committee on liquor licences, he wrote the report to the legislature, recommending repeal of the existing licence system and prohibition of the sale of intoxicants in less quantities than twenty-eight gallons. Such a measure would be sufficient for the present, said the committee, but the ultimate aim was state-wide prohibition of the liquor trade.[47]

Though the legislature tabled the report without discussion, Appleton's effort had not been in vain, for it inspired Neal Dow to undertake a campaign in Portland to modify the method of granting licences. Under the state law the board of aldermen in each municipality was authorized to issue a licence whenever an applicant met the conditions imposed in the statute. Dow insisted that so far as his own city was concerned the authorities granted permits without regard to the qualifications of the dealer

[47] *Ibid.,* pp. 243, 244–247.

and without investigating the character of the shops kept by the licensees. He believed that the public was thoroughly disgusted with such a system and, if given the opportunity, would register its disapproval at the polls. Therefore, he urged the board of aldermen to submit the matter to the voters at a special election, which should be a referendum to determine whether any licences for the retailing of intoxicants should be granted. In 1839 the aldermen, feeling that the people of the city had been aroused by Dow's propaganda, declared that they would abide by the mandate of the citizens. For this first test of voting strength the temperance forces organized a house to house canvass, concentrating particularly on the business men in an effort to convince them that a vote in favour of licence was a vote against their own best interests. The liquor traffic, argued the reformers, took its toll from the employer in the form of incompetent and irresponsible employees, and from the tax-payer in the form of increased assessments for poor relief and penal institutions. The intensive campaign proved to be only an effective preparation for subsequent work, since the electorate instructed the aldermen to issue the usual licences.[48]

Convinced, in spite of this defeat, that he would soon gain a victory, Dow continued to keep the question before the public. During the spring of 1841 the effects of the Washingtonian movement were evident in Portland, and the temperance ranks were augmented by hundreds of enthusiastic converts. Dow was quick to see the possibility of using the Washingtonians in his own campaign. Once more, while intemperance was being widely discussed, he pressed the city authorities to refer the licence matter to the voters, and won his point. In an ensuing election in 1842 the liquor interests fared badly as a result of Dow's success in effecting an alliance with the Washingtonians, who seem to have worked in

[48] A majority of 38 was given in favour of licensing in a total of 1160. T. W. Organ, *Biographical Sketch of General Neal Dow*, p. 2,

harmony with the older organizations. By a vote of 943 to 498 Portland refused to permit the retail sale of intoxicants within the city limits.[49] It was an unmistakable triumph for the astute leadership of Dow. The rejoicing of the victors, however, was soon changed to indignation and disgust, when it was discovered that the overthrow of the licence system did not mean the passing of the grog-shop. Those who had sold under fraudulent licences while the old system was in force were not unwilling to sell without a licence. Rumour had it that disreputable establishments, where liquor was retailed illegally, had multiplied rapidly after the refusal of the aldermen to grant permits. It was almost impossible, however, to secure evidence that would justify prosecution. When convictions were obtained by the authorities, the municipal courts imposed either suspended sentences or trifling fines. A few months of this flagrant violation of the law convinced the prohibitionists that it would be impossible to drive the liquor traffic out of Portland so long as it was tolerated in other parts of the state.

Out of this conviction developed the movement to secure relief from the legislature. During 1843, as if by common consent, there were circulated in every county petitions demanding the enactment of a law which would make the "traffic in intoxicants an infamous crime." In February of the following year Neal Dow appeared before a legislative committee to support the petitions with arguments drawn from the experience of Portland. In conformity with his suggestions the committee introduced a prohibitory bill, which passed the lower house but failed to secure a majority in the senate. For almost a year the prohibitionists lobbied with more zeal than discretion and failed to force the legislature to take action. Finally, they appealed to the people over the heads of the obstinate legislators. It was soon evi-

[49] Dow, *op. cit.*, pp. 271–280; *Portland Tribune*, Oct. 26, 1842, November 16, 1842.

dent that spontaneous enthusiasm for a prohibitory statute was sadly lacking.   The people would have to be aroused to the perils of the existing system.   Once more Dow took the lead in the attempt to create an opinion which would lead to legislative action.   Teams of workers were organized to visit every school district in the state, that the voters might receive first hand information on the necessity for prohibitory measures.   Musicians accompanied many of the speakers and offered varied programs which attracted large audiences to the meetings.   Enthusiasm ran high in the rural districts, where almost every school building housed at least one rally during the campaign.   Dow himself was indefatigable.   No matter how inclement the weather, he was always ready to meet his speaking engagements, which were legion during the summer and autumn of 1845.   Neither storms nor snow-drifted roads caused him to deviate from an exacting schedule, and.more than one companion who accompanied him on his trips was unable to keep up with the pace set by the leader.   Many an audience was inspired by his forceful reasoning and his oratorical denunciation of the "traffic and traffickers."   Everywhere his theme was the same—a compelling appeal to the voters that they support only those candidates for the legislature, who were pledged to give the state a prohibitory law.[50]

As the campaign progressed, Dow grew confident of victory.   Just prior to the election he wrote to a friend:

I have within two months travelled over four thousand miles, and have come in contact with many thousand citizens, and can testify that I have never before witnessed so deep-rooted and widespread enthusiasm among the people.   They now understand that talking temperance and working for temperance will do little good unless they vote for temperance also; and this they are resolved to do.   The result of our agitation will be the expulsion from all the states of the traffic in intoxicating liquors

[50] Clubb, *op., cit.,* pp. 17–18; Dow, *Reminiscences,* pp. 291–293.

to be used as a drink, but we hope that the state of Maine will have the honor of leading in this glorious reform.[51]

This faith was well founded, for the work of persuading voters to support temperance candidates had been skilfully done under experienced leaders. Dow's associates were no novices in the art of creating public opinion. John T. Walton, prominent in the councils of the Whig party, was ever at hand to give advice and encouragement. Luther Severance, editor of the *Kennebec Journal*, kept the liquor question before the people of Augusta, while Austin Willey's editorials in the Portland *Inquirer* advocated prohibitory legislation. The distinguished anti-slavery editor, George H. Shirley, was a consistent supporter of Dow's views.

Indeed, the one group on which the prohibitionists could always rely was the anti-slavery element in the state. The determined enemies of human bondage wanted to be considered foes of the traffic which enslaved men to the vice, intemperance. They never tired of pointing to the similarity between the two movements. Dow testified to the understanding and co-operation between these reforms when he wrote:

The prohibitory movement received invaluable assistance from the distinctively anti-slavery element in the state, that from 1842 to the organization of the Republican party in 1854 maintained a political organization in Maine known first as the Liberty party, and afterwards as the Free Soil. . . . Most of the leaders in each reform were interested and active in both, exerting their influence to make the efforts for one contribute to the development of the other, as far as it could be done consistently and with prudence. To this end the state and county gatherings of both agitations were generally held upon succeeding days, that those attending the one might more conveniently participate in the other.[52]

[51] Organ, *op cit.,* pp. 2–3.
[52] Dow, *Reminiscences,* pp. 306–307; *Portland Transcript,* Feb. 27, 1841.

In Maine, as elsewhere, a too close association with abolitionists was not apt to be an unmitigated blessing for the
temperance cause, but the matter seems to have been handled
"with prudence," for many of the anti-slavery leaders
brought sorely needed strength to the prohibitory movement.
Such prominent members of the Liberty Party as James Appleton and Samuel Fessenden were conspicuous foes of the
liquor traffic. Charles A. Stackpole, George H. Shirley,
Ezekiel Holmes, Samuel R. Leavitt and S. M. Pond, all followers of Birney or Garrison, were in the front ranks of the
prohibitionists. The avowed Free-Soilers among the clergy,
David Thurston, D. B. Randall, O. B. Cheney and C. C.
Cone, were numbered among Dow's most valuable lieutenants
in the campaigns after 1848. It required consummate skill
to hold the support of this group without losing the good
will of those who refused to be classed with the radical anti-
slavery agitators.[53]

Political snares, also, were carefully avoided by the prohibitionists. They refused to allow themselves to be in-
trigued into admitting alliance with any party. Dow constantly urged his supporters to cut across party lines and
vote for candidates whose opinions on the liquor problem
were acceptable. In more than one district prohibition
Whigs and Democrats united their votes to elect their man.
As a result, the demands of the reformers were ably championed in both major parties, though the Whig politicians
were generally more interested in the cause than the Democratic leaders. When the relative strength of the licence
and anti-licence forces was appraised in the session of 1846,
it was evident that the friends of prohibition could muster
a majority in both houses of the legislature. At once a bill
was introduced. After public hearings before a joint com-

[53] Appleton and Fessenden had both been Liberty candidates for
governor. Dow, *Reminiscences,* pp. 306–307.

mittee the final draft became law on August 7, 1846. The licence system had been overthrown. By the terms of the statute the sale of intoxicating liquors for beverage purposes was prohibited, except in the case of wholesalers and importers who sold in quantities greater than twenty-eight gallons. The selectmen in each town were authorized to license persons to retail for mechanical and medicinal purposes. While the law was not satisfactory to the more radical reformers, since their goal was absolute prohibition rather than highly restrictive regulation, it contained what the legislators thought their constituents desired at the time.[54]

The possibilities of evading the new statute were obvious. Its enforcement depended largely upon the manner in which the town selectmen used their licensing power. Since no state enforcement machinery was created, the sentiment of the local group determined the extent to which the law was obeyed. In communities unsympathetic with the purposes of the new regulations it was a simple matter to permit the grog-shop and tippling-house to thrive under regular licences. Local authorities in the larger towns became notorious for their refusal to punish retailers who made illegal sales. Resorts of low character found refuge behind the pretext that they were selling liquor for mechanical and medicinal purposes. It required endless litigation to prove that they were violating the law. The prohibitionists got little satisfaction when they appealed to the state government, for John W. Dana, the Democratic governor, was opposed to restrictive legislation. Pressure brought to bear upon the legislature, however, was more productive of results. In 1849 after considerable lobbying a bill supplementary to the act of 1846 was passed, which authorized the

[54] *Public Laws of the State of Maine* (1842–1851), pp. 189–195; Dow, *Reminiscences*, pp. 313–315.

appointment of special enforcement officers in each town to "ferret out and suppress the grog-shops." Governor Dana vetoed the measure, explaining his action in a lengthy attack on the principle of prohibition. The experience of the state under the existing law proved to him that so long as public opinion countenanced the use of intoxicants the most elaborate enforcement machinery ever devised could not suppress the liquor traffic.

The governor's message gave expression to the secret fear of the supporters of the law—that the public was becoming convinced of the impossibility of enforcing restrictive measures. It seemed to Dow that the best antidote to the spread of this conviction would be a striking campaign to suppress illegal selling in one of the cities of the state.[55] He, therefore, determined to strike for the control of the municipal government in Portland that he might make it a signal example of the successful enforcement of all state laws. The announcement of his candidacy for the Whig nomination for mayor in 1850 split his party wide open. The regulars, who apparently had control of the situation, immediately declared a factional war. Two Fillmore appointees in the city, the postmaster and collector of the port, led the attack. Their chief argument against Dow was on the score of party regularity. He was only a nominal Whig. On several occasions he had bolted the regular nominees of his party. He had even run as an independent candidate for alderman. Could the Whigs afford to support an independent in a municipal election? Would they not lose the support of every loyal member of the party by making such a nomination? Why should the reward of public office go to a man who had never turned his hand to build up Whig strength in Portland?

[55] During 1848 and 1849 activity on the part of temperance societies was considerably quickened by the apparent indifference to the law. *Portland Transcript,* May 20, Oct. 7, 1848, Feb. 17, March 3, 1849.

This attempt to read Dow out of the party was unsuccessful. His record as a business man stood him in good stead, and he received the enthusiastic endorsement of those Whigs who had followed him in many a temperance campaign. In the nominating convention the Dow men controlled affairs by an uncomfortably narrow margin, but were able to select an entire city ticket satisfactory to their leader. The event was now in the hands of the disappointed faction. Would they support the candidate? During the campaign Dow tried hard to unite his party, but he could get no statement from the opposing group. When the votes were counted, the trick of the "regular" Whigs was apparent. Rather than vote for a Democrat, they had written in the name of Joseph C. Noyes. Noyes was not a party to the scheme, for he had supported Dow. The result, however, was no election, since no candidate had received a clear majority. In the subsequent "run-off" Dow was attacked as an "abolitionist" and a "fanatic," but enough Democrats voted for him to give him the victory. The city administration was placed in the hands of men friendly to prohibition.[56]

In his inaugural address, April 24, 1851, the new mayor outlined his program. He intended to close every grog-shop in Portland. He would enforce the state law without fear or favour. Since he felt that the law was not well drawn, he would urge the legislature to enact a truly prohibitory statute. At his request the board of aldermen sent a petition to the Portland delegation in the legislature asking them to support such a measure. The representatives replied by asking Dow to come to Augusta and direct the lobby for the kind of law that he wanted. The mayor accepted the invitation and took a committee of aldermen with him to the capital to support his efforts. Events moved rapidly after

[56] Dow, *op. cit.*, pp. 321–326; Rev. A. A. Miner, "Neal Dow and his Life Work," *The New England Magazine*, June, 1894, pp. 397–412; *Portland Transcript*, Feb. 24, 1849, April 26, 1851.

he reached Augusta—so rapidly, in fact, that the people of the state did not keep up with developments.[57]

A special committee from the legislature, whose membership was designated by Dow, was instructed to prepare a prohibitory measure. Within two weeks it reported a bill, which conformed in every detail to the suggestions of the reformers from Portland. In order that the measure might not be side-tracked, Dow kept in close touch with its progress in both houses. An attempt to postpone deliberation in the lower house was defeated by a vote of 89 to 16. Such a decisive victory enabled the prohibitionists to force an early closing of the debate. Their plans were carried out with such precision that the fate of the bill was never in doubt. It passed the house by a vote of 81 to 40, a majority of the Democrats and Whigs and all the Free-Soilers supporting it.[58] In the senate a short filibuster was staged under the direction of Senator Cary of the Aroostook district, who dismissed the idea of prohibition as colossal nonsense and centred his attention on the author of the measure. His caricature of Dow was sufficiently broad to amuse even its subject.

This new manifestation of the spirit of fanaticism [said the Senator] originates in the city of Portland under the auspices of that prince of fanatics, the present Mayor of that city. . . . It embodies the ultra notions of the wring-necks of that city, of whom the Mayor is chief. Has the legislature of Maine, and a Democratic legislature, too, become so lost to dignity and to self-respect, as to sit here the registrar of the inquisitorial edicts of the temperance fanatics of Portland, headed by the popinjay Mayor, a Whig abolitionist of the most ultra stripe? I met the Mayor the other day on the stairway. He is a pretty little

[57] Dow, *Reminiscences*, pp. 331–333; *Portland Transcript*, May 3, 1851.

[58] In the house the vote stood: For the bill 42 Democrats, 31 Whigs and 8 Free-Soilers; against the bill 25 Democrats and 15 Whigs. In the senate 14 Democrats, 3 Whigs and 1 Free-Soiler supported the measure, while 10 Democrats opposed. *Ibid.*, pp. 334–338.

dapper man, goes well dressed, wears a nice blue jacket and fancy vest, and his hat cocked on one side of his head. He succeeded in getting his bill reported by the committee, word for word and letter for letter, as it was prepared for them. . . . A few years ago the jackdaw Mayor of Portland, this man with the fancy vest, who got up the precious document the legislature is called upon to register, was at the head of the nigger movement in that city. He was formerly a Federalist, but Federalism alone was not low enough for his instincts, and he joined the abolition movement; but even abolitionism was not strong enough for his diseased palate, and he has added temperanceism to his former stock of humbugs. Is this Federal-abolition-wring-neck to be allowed to dictate to a Democratic legislature what enactments it shall pass? [59]

The question which Senator Cary raised was speedily answered in the affirmative, for the Democratic senate approved Dow's measure by a majority of eight votes. There was no doubt of the governor's attitude. John W. Dana had been succeeded by John Hubbard, a country doctor whose prejudices were all against the liquor interests. He had repeatedly served notice that he would sign any prohibitory statute sent to him by the legislature. On June 2, 1851, he announced his approval of a law which forbade the manufacture and sale of intoxicating liquors within the confines of Maine; authorized justices of the peace and municipal judges to grant search and seizure warrants on the complaint of three voters; and encouraged enforcement by granting all fines to the prosecuting officers. Dow's prophecy for his state had been fulfilled.[60]

The passage of the Maine Law was hailed by the prohibitionists as an unmistakable sign that the temperance movement had been transformed into a campaign for prohibitory legislation. Two generations of combat with intemperance,

[59] Dow, *Reminiscences*, pp. 338–339.

[60] *Public Laws of the State of Maine* (1842–1851), pp. 416–424. One dealer was to be licensed in each town to sell liquors for mechanical and medicinal purposes. *Kennebec Journal*, June 5, 1851.

they said, had carried the reform far beyond the first feeble protests against the use of ardent spirits. Dow's victory, remote as it seemed from the pioneer efforts of Rush and Beecher, was, nevertheless, a direct result of the forces which those early temperance advocates had set in motion. It bore witness to the fact that the reformers had finally been forced to accept prohibition as the true solution of the liquor problem. They had tried moral suasion for half a century and had found it wanting. Legal coercion was, therefore, their last resort. Principles and methods were being changed; new leaders had supplanted old. But the continuity of the movement had not and would not be broken. The purpose of the reform remained the same. Dow, like Beecher and Rush, had only one objective—to drive intemperance from the land.

CHAPTER XII

A SUMMARY VIEW

ONE cannot study the growth of temperance sentiment in the United States and escape the conclusion that the Eighteenth Amendment was long on its way. Its ratification was not the result of temporary conditions taken at their flood, but the final expression of a fundamental change which had been more than a century in the making. This formative movement, now revealing itself in the guise of prohibition, reaches back beyond any efforts to amend the Constitution; it took its rise from early attempts to curb the intemperate use of intoxicants. It was not a simple movement. Many factors, at times apparently working at cross purposes, determined its varying course and ultimate goal. Its ranks were swelled by recruits from every walk of life, representing an infinite variety of ideas and ideals. The wide range of its propaganda was a fair indication of the multitude of motives which inspired those who laboured for its success.

It is obviously futile to regard any or all of these motives as a complete explanation of the present state of affairs, for some new forces entered the prohibitory movement after Neal Dow won his first victory in Maine. No true appreciation of these later developments is possible, however, without an understanding of the early reform. Fortunately the reformers themselves, though normally too busy with the minutiæ of ways and means to philosophize about their cause, probed occasionally beneath surface indications in search of fundamentals. Whether their search revealed anything of great value may be questioned, but that their findings are worth consideration is certain. In the first place, they were convinced that their cause was truly American, that it squared with American ideas and institutions, that it was growth of the soil. Was it not an important element in the national awakening which followed the War of 1812? Did it not indicate a quickened consciousness on the part of the American people that domestic problems, quite as serious as any foreign complications, had been neglected? A nation, expanding politically, industrially and territorially, needed to take thought of the materials with which it was building. It could afford to support generously a movement against disease and poverty, against filth and misery, against drunken husbands who beat their wives and sent their children into the street to beg, against liquor dealers who grew rich while their customers filled the alms-houses and debtors' prisons.

Temperance reformers who saw their cause in this light were prone to emphasize its affiliation with other American efforts to establish a more perfect social order. The people of the United States, it seemed, were testing out new theories regarding the individual's relation to the group. Extreme individualism, so characteristic of the young and growing nation, was being modified by a keener realization of society's responsibility for those unfortunates who had lost out in life's struggle. A generation so sincerely interested in the fate of the pauper, the lunatic and the criminal could not long remain unconcerned about the far-reaching consequences of intemperance. Furthermore the liquor problem was involved in more than the question of caring for human derelicts; it was linked up with any general scheme of social reorganization. No community, whether large or small, could order its affairs "for the greatest good of the greatest number," unless its inhabitants had learned the lesson of individual self-control. Many temperance enthusiasts, therefore, felt that their idea was basic. Stressing the principle of self-denial, abstinence not only freed men from slavish subjection to appetite, but it prepared them through the purifying influence of this asceticism for greater co-operation with their fellows.

There was also in the temperance philosophy a strong conviction that the reform was typically American in its defence of the home.   One finds this both expressed and implied in the writings of Lydia H. Sigourney, Lucius M. Sargent and Timothy Shay Arthur.   At the heart of the matter was a passionate concern for the sanctity of marriage and the integrity of the family circle, a determination that no home should be wrecked and no child denied a fair chance in life because of a drunken parent.   How shocking a travesty on the ideal family group was a household in which an intemperate husband forced the wife to become the sole breadwinner!   Were children who spent the impressionable years of youth in such an environment receiving the full advantages of "the land of equal opportunity"?   Surely, a nation which championed the principles of liberty and equality was under compulsion to guarantee to its children an even start in life, free from all unnecessary handicaps.   This, insisted the reformers, should be part of every American youth's priceless heritage.

Some contemporary writers seem to have believed that the most significant fact about the temperance movement in the United States was its bearing upon the great experiment being made in democratic control.   A government based on the consent of the governed, they reasoned, could not rise any higher than the people from whom it took its source. Consequently, if democracy was to succeed, and the whole world was watching the experiment, the American voter would have to be safeguarded on every side, even from the folly of his own vices.   It was ridiculous to talk of the "will of the sovereign people," when intoxicated citizens were taken to the polls, and legislators were not ashamed to parade their inebriety while discussing important public measures. Intemperance might be tolerated in a divine-right monarchy, but in a republic it endangered the very existence of the state. No popular government could long endure, unless the electorate was persuaded or forced to follow the straight and narrow path of sobriety.

Both opponents and supporters of the campaign against the use of intoxicants felt that the greatest single force in the movement was the power of evangelical Protestantism. Here, again, there seemed to be something distinctively American about the situation. Evangelical sects in Europe were not noted for their insistence on conformity to the principle of total abstinence. Calvinism, for example, presented no dogmatic teachings on the subject. John Calvin, himself, classed the question of the proper use of alcoholic beverages among "matters indifferent." Scotch Presbyterianism could scarcely be considered hostile to the interests of the liquor dealer, and it is doubtful whether Dutch and Swiss Reformed churches were any more severe than German Lutheran in their attitude toward the social glass. But the case was different in the United States. It was a matter of grave concern to the New England Puritan that his neighbour's manners and morals should be acceptable unto God. Though the explanation of the fact may escape us, it is true that American evangelical Protestants, whether Calvinists or not, were far more inquisitorial and censorious than their European brethren.

This was early appreciated by temperance propagandists and they made the most of it. Through Congregationalism, through the far-flung Methodist and Baptist societies, and to a less degree through Presbyterianism the reform was given a religious significance which placed it on the plane of things spiritual. Intemperance was of the devil; it marked a person as belonging with the unregenerate. His path took him among atheists and agnostics, among infidels and scoffers! The spirit of God could not dwell in him until he had

abandoned his sin and been converted. Since this unregenerate state resulted directly from the use of alcoholic beverages, it was obvious that such use constituted an obstacle
of no mean proportions in the path of the church militant.
Any movement designed to remove the obstacle would be of
incalculable benefit to the cause of religion. Consequently,
in the thinking of many a religious zealot the temperance reform and prohibitory movement became integral parts of the
church's earthly mission. Hear Reverend George B. Cheever, staunch defender of orthodox Calvinism, explain what
he considers fundamental:

This moral enterprise is removing one of the most dreadful
obstacles ever yet opposed to the spread of the gospel. Self-
denying and holy men have almost fruitlessly devoted their
lives to this blessed object, because along with every supply of
that word which conveys the gift of eternal life, there has been
sent to the perishing nations the gift of intoxication, the sure
producer of death temporal and eternal. Preach to the hea-
then that spiritual gospel which commands the denying ungod-
liness and every earthly lust, and at the same time place in their
hands and put to their lips the provocation to every sort of
crime that can be named! Appeal to the reason and the conscience, and at the same time give them to drink what debases
reason, and stupefies the conscience, and makes the whole being
earthly, sensual, devilish! Let the temperance reformation go
hand in hand with the Bible, and the Sabbath school, and the
tract in its distribution among the wretched, and truth will
have power, and the world's regeneration will be speedily accomplished.[1]

Of course, not all of the reformers thus idealized the movement. For an ever increasing number the chief concern was
not the suffering and cruelty which drink caused, or the souls
which it sent to perdition, but the economic waste which it
involved. Judge Cranch's estimate of 1831 that more than

[1] *American Quarterly Observer*, March, 1833.

ninety-four million dollars were lost to the American people each year through the liquor traffic was hailed by the practical temperance advocate as an unanswerable argument. It expressed in terms of dollars and cents the major offences of intoxicants. Drink lowered the worker's efficiency, reduced production, decreased consumption, increased taxation and endangered business prosperity. Here was a matter of supreme importance. The burden of the liquor traffic on the tax-payer, said some, would be more effective in arousing the nation to action than any philanthropic desire to save the intemperate from disease and poverty. Not long would the man of property pay an annual tax for the support of alms-houses and poor relief, work-houses and jails, hospitals and asylums, made necessary in large part by the consequences of intemperance. He would relieve himself of this financial burden by putting an end to the business which was responsible for it.

A further reason to believe that this event would not be long delayed seemed apparent in the changing industrial system. As workers were slowly but steadily concentrated under one management in larger enterprises, the relation of intemperance to labour efficiency became a problem of more than passing interest to the factory-owner. Arguments, which lacked force when addressed to farmers employing a few labourers, were more influential with manufacturers who regarded unnecessary labour-turnover from the viewpoint of diminished profits. The industrial enterpriser was beginning to see in the liquor business a potential menace, a menace not at all lessened by the constant infiltration of foreigners into the United States. By the middle of the nineteenth century the prohibitory movement enrolled in its ranks some of the rising "captains of industry," who were not unaware of the economic implications of the trade in intoxicants.

Even if the foregoing theories are accepted as explanatory of the movement for total abstinence, there still remains a

question concerning prohibition. Why did prohibitory laws
become the approved method of solving the problems connected with intemperance? A partial answer is to be found
in the experience rather than the philosophy of the reformers. During the first four decades of the nineteenth century
temperance advocates generally refused to consider restrictive legislation as a proper means of effecting their object.
With a high faith in the ultimate success of their cause and
an optimistic belief in man's perfectibility, they relied entirely on precept and example to persuade their fellow-men
of the right. Through the instrumentality of voluntary associations, bound by an ordinary pledge of good faith, they
carried their propaganda into thousands of American homes.
Each achievement meant a challenge to greater effort.
From moderation in the use of alcoholic beverages they
moved forward to abstinence from ardent spirits, and then
to "total abstinence from all that can intoxicate."

Their cause was growing in popularity all the while, but it
was not progressing rapidly enough for the more impatient
ones. By 1840 many were convinced that the lure of profits
to be gained from the liquor traffic was nullifying their efforts. As population increased, the problem grew ever
larger. Intemperance seemed to keep a step ahead of the
most vigorous pursuit. Years of experience in reasoning
with individuals and groups were wearing down faith in the
efficacy of persuasion alone. After all, the task seemed a
bit too large for the reformers' unaided efforts. Like so
many other American citizens, face to face with a proposition too big for individual initiative, they turned to the
Government. Legal coercion would prevail, they reasoned,
where argument and persuasion had failed. The work of the
voluntary associations would be crowned with success, if supported by the "strong arm of the law."

This turning to legislation indicated no fatuous faith on
the part of the reformers in the possibility of effecting an

immediate revolution in social customs. Some of them realized the difficulties of their new course, difficulties of enforcement as well as of enactment of satisfactory statutes. But they were determined that legal coercion should receive the same full and fair trial which had been accorded moral suasion. In the Maine Law of 1851 they won their first important victory. It indicated that the major portion of the temperance forces would follow their leaders into the prohibitory movement, and it forecast some of the tactics and methods of future campaigns. The story of those campaigns, it seems well to leave to a subsequent volume, wherein may be chronicled the enlightening successes and failures of the later reformers.

BIBLIOGRAPHY

I. PRIMARY SOURCES

1. PUBLIC RECORDS

Acts of the General Assembly of the Province of New Jersey, Samuel Allinson, editor. Burlington, 1776.

Archives of Maryland. 41 vols. Baltimore, 1883–1922.

A Collection of the Statutes of England now in force in the State of North Carolina, Francois Martin, editor, Philadelphia, 1792.

Colonial Laws of New York from the Year 1664 to the Revolution. 5 vols. Albany, 1894–1896.

Colonial Records of North Carolina. 26 vols. Raleigh, 1886–.

Colonial Records of the State of Georgia. 24 vols. Atlanta, 1904–1915.

Documents and Records relating to the Province of New Hampshire. 31 vols. Concord, 1867–1907.

Documents relative to the Colonial History of the State of New York. 15 vols. Albany, 1856–1887.

Duke of Yorke's Book of Laws. Harrisburg, 1879.

Public Laws of South Carolina, J. F. Grimke, editor. Newbern, N. C., 1790.

Public Records of the Colony of Connecticut. 15 vols. Hartford, 1850–1890.

Pennsylvania Archives. Third series. Philadelphia, 1852–1899.

Records of the Colony of New Plymouth. 12 vols. Boston, 1855–1861.

Records of the Colony of Rhode Island and Providence Plantations. 10 vols. Providence, 1856–1865.

Records of the Governor and Company of Massachusetts Bay. 5 vols. Boston, 1853–1854.

*Statutes at Large, being a collection of all the laws of Virginia,
1619–1792.* 13 vols. Philadelphia and New York, 1823.
(Hening.)

2. TEMPERANCE RECORDS AND REPORTS

*Anniversary Report of the Pennsylvania State Temperance
Society.* Philadelphia, 1833.

Annual Report of the Maryland State Temperance Society.
Baltimore, 1842.

*Annual Report of the Massachusetts Society for the Suppression
of Intemperance.* Boston, 1818–1820.

Annual Report of the New York State Temperance Society.
Albany, 1833.

Constitution and Laws of the Temperance Beneficial Association. New York, 1838.

Constitution of the Providence County Temperance Society.
Providence, 1838.

Documents and Records of the Massachusetts Temperance Society. Boston, 1855.

First Annual Report of the Congressional Temperance Society.
Washington, D. C., 1834.

*Journal of the Proceedings of the Grand Division of the Sons
of Temperance of New York.* New York, 1845–1846.

*Journal of the Proceedings of the Grand Division of the Sons of
Temperance of Pennsylvania.* Philadelphia, 1848–1849.

Permanent Temperance Documents. 4 vols. New York, 1852.

*Proceedings of the Convention for the Promotion of the Cause
of Temperance.* Washington, D. C., 1833.

*Report of the Committee of the Massachusetts Society for the
Suppression of Intemperance.* Boston, 1831.

3. CONTEMPORARY HISTORIES AND DESCRIPTIONS

Abdy, Edward S., *Journal of a residence and tour in the United
States of America from April, 1833 to October, 1834.* 3
vols. London, 1834.

Acrelius, Israel, *Description of the former and present condition of the Swedish Churches in what was called New Sweden.* 1759. *Historical Society of Pennsylvania, Memoirs, XI.*

Alexander, J. E., *Transatlantic Sketches.* 2 vols. London, 1833.

Alsop, George, *A Character of Maryland,* N. D. Mereness, editor. Cleveland, 1902.

Blanchard, Claude, The Journal of, Thomas Balch, editor. Albany, 1876.

Bradford, William, *History of Plymouth Plantation, 1606–1646,* William T. Davis, editor. New York, 1908.

Brissot de Warville, J. P., *New Travels in the United States of America.* Translated from the French. New York, 1792.

Burnaby, Andrew, *Travels through the Middle Settlements in North America, in the years 1759 and 1760.* London, 1775.

Candler, Isaac, *A Summary View of America.* London, 1824.

Chastellux, Francois-Jean de, *Travels in North America in 1780, 1781, 1782.* New York, 1828.

Coke, R. T., *A Subaltern's Furlough.* 2 vols. New York, 1833.

Danckaerts, Jasper, Journal of, B. B. James, and J. F. Jameson, editors. New York, 1913.

Duncan, John M., *Travels through part of the United States and Canada in 1818 and 1819.* 2 vols. New York, 1823.

Dunton, John, *Letters from New England.* Prince Society, Boston, 1867.

Fearon, Henry B., *A Narrative of a Journey . . . through the Eastern and Western States of America.* 2nd ed. London, 1818.

Finch, I., *Travels in the United States of America and Canada.* London, 1833.

Hall, Basil, *Travels in North America in the years 1827 and 1828.* 3 vols. Edinburgh, 1829.

Hall, Francis, *Travels in Canada and the United States in 1816 and 1817.* Boston, 1818.

Hamilton, Thomas, *Men and Manners in America.* 2 vols. Philadelphia, 1833.

Alexander Hamilton's Itinerarium, Albert B. Hart, editor. St. Louis, 1907.

Harriott, John, *Struggles Through Life.* 2 vols. London, 1808.

Hodgson, Adam, *Letters from North America.* 2 vols. London, 1824.

Holmes, Isaac, *An Account of the United States,* London, 1824.

Itinerant Observations in America (London, 1745). *Historical Society of Georgia, Collections,* IV.

Jameson, J. Franklin, editor, *Narratives of New Netherland.* New York, 1909.

Janson, Charles William, *The Stranger in America.* London, 1808.

Jones, Hugh, *The Present State of Virginia* (1724). New York, 1865.

Josselyn, John, *An Account of Two Voyages to New England Made During the Years 1638, 1663.* Boston, 1895.

Kalm, Peter, *Travels into North America.* 2 vols. Warrington, 1770.

William Logan's Journal (1745). *Pennsylvania Magazine,* XXXVI.

Lechford, Thomas, *Plain Dealing.* Boston, 1867.

Mather, Cotton, *History of the War with the Indians in New England,* Samuel G. Drake, editor. Boston, 1862.

Melish, John, *Travels in the United States of America in the years 1806, 1807 and 1809, 1810 and 1811.* Philadelphia, 1812.

Mereness, Newton D., editor, *Travels in the American Colonies.* New York, 1916.

Michaud, F. A., *Travels to the West of the Alleghany Mountains.* 2 vols. London, 1805.

Neilson, Peter, *Recollections of a six years' residence in the United States.* Glasgow, 1830.

Ramsay, David, *The History of South Carolina.* 2 vols. Charleston, 1809.

Robb, Kate M., editor, *A Tour through Indiana in 1840.* New York, 1920.

Royall, Anne, *Sketches of History, Life and Manners in the United States.* New Haven, 1826.

Stuart, James, *Three Years in America.* 2 vols. Edinburgh, 1833.

Tudor, Henry, *Narrative of a Tour in North America.* 2 vols. London, 1834.

Winthrop, John, *The History of New England,* James Savage, editor. Boston, 1825.

4. TEMPERANCE PERIODICALS

(Dates indicate files consulted)

Almanac of the American Temperance Union. New York, 1840–1845.

American Quarterly Temperance Magazine. Albany, 1833–1834.

American Temperance Preacher (monthly). New Haven, 1848.

The Cold Water Army (weekly). Boston, 1841–1842.

Columbia Washingtonian (weekly). Hudson, N. Y., 1842–1843.

The Crystal Fount (monthly). Baltimore, 1847.

The Enquirer (quarterly). Albany, 1843–1844.

The Fountain (annual). Boston, 1847–1848.

The Fountain (annual). Philadelphia, 1847.

Journal of the American Temperance Union (monthly). Philadelphia and New York, 1837–1850.

Journal of Humanity (weekly). Andover, Mass., 1829–1832.

National Temperance Offering (annual). New York, 1850–1851.

New York Organ (weekly). New York, 1844–1846.

Pennsylvania Temperance Recorder (monthly). Philadelphia, 1835–1837.

Temperance Almanac (annual). Albany, 1840–1843.

Temperance Herald (weekly). Baltimore, 1834–1836.

Temperance Offering (annual). New York, 1848–1850.

The Temperance Offering (monthly). Salem, Mass., 1845.

Temperance Offering and Youth's Cascade (monthly) Boston, 1846.

Temperance Recorder (weekly). Albany, 1832–1836.

Youth's Temperance Advocate (monthly). New York, 1839–1850.

5. TEMPERANCE TRACTS AND PUBLICATIONS

Abbot, Abiel, *An Address delivered before the Massachusetts Society for the Suppression of Intemperance.* Cambridge, Mass., 1815.

Adams, John Q., *Address to the Norfolk County Temperance Society.* Boston, 1842.

Address by the Hampshire Convention of the Friends of the License Law. Northampton, 1838.

An Address to the Churches and Congregations of the Western District of Fairfield County. Hartford, 1813.

Appleton, Jesse, *An Address delivered before the Massachusetts Society for the Suppression of Intemperance.* Boston, 1816.

Arthur, Timothy S., *A Christmas Box for the Sons and Daughters of Temperance.* Philadelphia, 1847.

Six Nights with the Washingtonians. Philadelphia, 1842.

Ten Nights in a Bar-Room. Philadelphia, 1855.

Bacon, Leonard, *A Discourse on the Traffic in Spirituous Liquors.* New Haven, 1838.

Bannatyne, J., *Intemperance Among Literary Men.* Portland, Maine, 1842.

Barbour, I. Richmond, *A Statistical Table showing the influence of intemperance on the churches.* Boston, 1831.

Barnes, Albert, *The Causes of Intemperance in Cities and Large Towns.* Morristown, N. J., 1828.

Bates, Joshua, *Two Sermons on Intemperance.* Dedham, Mass., 1814.

Beecher, Lyman, *Six Sermons on the nature, occasions, signs, evils and remedy of intemperance.* Boston, 1827.

Beman, Nathan S. S., *The Crisis and the Triumph.* Troy, N. Y., 1846.

Benezet, Anthony, *The Mighty Destroyer Displayed.* Philadelphia, 1774.

Remarks on the Nature and Bad Effects of Spirituous Liquors. Philadelphia, 1778.

Bonner, T. D., editor, *The Mountain Minstrel.* Concord, N. H., 1847.

Bound, John James, *The Means of Curing and Preventing Intemperance.* New York, 1820.

Brantly, William T., *Total abstinence from all intoxicants—the only safeguard.* Philadelphia, 1833.

Cary, S. F., *The Liquor Manufacture and Traffic.* New York, 1849.

Channing, Walter, *Thoughts on the Origin, Nature, Principles and Prospects of the Temperance Reform.* Boston, 1834.

Channing, William Ellery, *An Address on Intemperance.* Boston, 1837.

Cheever, G. B., *The Dream, or Deacon Giles' Distillery.* Boston, 1838.

The True History of Deacon Giles' Distillery. New York, 1844.

Circular to Immigrants. New York, 1833.

Clark, J. H., *The Present Position and Claims of the Temperance Enterprise.* New York, 1847.

Cleaveland, E. L., *A Discourse on the Existing State of Morals in the City of New Haven.* New Haven, 1850.

Considerations on the customary use of Spirituous Liquors. By a Philanthropist. Burlington, N. J., 1811.

Correspondence on the Principles of Right Reasoning Applicable to Temperance. Geneva, N. Y., 1836.

Cranch, W., *An Address delivered at the annual meeting of the Washington City Society.* Alexandria, Va., 1831.

Cross, Marcus E., *The Mirror of Intemperance.* Philadelphia, 1849.

Davis, Gustavus F., *A Sermon.* Hartford, 1831.

Davis, James M., *The Two Immortal Queens.* Woonsocket, R. I., 1846.

Delavan, E. C., *Adulterations of Liquors.* New York, 1850.

Dickinson, Austin, *Appeal to the American Youth on Temperance.* New York, 1848.

Dimmick, Luther F., *Intemperance.* Newburyport, Mass., 1824.

The Drunkard, or the Fallen Saved. Boston, 1847.

Duffield, George, Jr., *Samson Shorn, and his lock renewed.*
  Philadelphia, 1855.

Dunlap, William, *Thirty Years Ago, or Memoirs of a Water
  Drinker.* New York, 1837.

Edwards, Justin, *Letter to the friends of Temperance in Massachusetts.* Boston, 1836.

  The Well-Conducted Farm. Andover, Mass., 1825.

  Temperance Manual. New York, 1847.

Finn, Matthew D., *Moral and Temperance Table Book.* New
  York, 1843.

Frost, Henry R., *Address.* Charleston, S. C. 1832.

Gallaudet, Edward, *Progress of Intemperance.* Boston, 1831.

Greeley, Horace, *Alcoholic Liquors, Their essential nature and
  necessary effects on the Human Constitution.* New York,
  1849.

Hall, Edward B., *The Temperance Reform.* Boston, 1840.

Hall, John, *The Harvey Boys.* Philadelphia, 1834.

Harbaugh, Henry, *A Word in Season, or, A Plea for legislative
  aid in putting down the evils of Intemperance.* Chambersburg, Pa., 1846.

Hertell, Thomas, *An Expose of the Causes of Intemperate
  Drinking.* New York, 1819.

Hitchcock, Edward, *An Argument for Early Temperance.* Boston, 1837.

  *An Essay on Alcoholic and Narcotic Substances, as articles of
  common use.* Amherst, Mass., 1830.

Hoover, Charles, *Intemperance in Relation to Family Interests
  and Happiness.* New York, 1849.

Hunt, Thomas P., *The Cold Water Army.* Boston, 1840.

  It will never injure me. Philadelphia, 1846.

  The wedding days of former times. Philadelphia, 1845.

Jeffries, Henry, *The Religious Objection to Teetotalism.* New
  York, 1840.

Jewett, Charles, *The Temperance Cause, Past, Present and Future.* Hartford, Conn., 1865.

  The Temperance Toy. Boston, 1840.

  Youth's Temperance Lecturer. Boston, 1840.

Keener, Christian, *The House Old Nick Built.* Baltimore, 1834.

Kercheval, John, *An Address proposing a new temperance organization*. St. Louis, 1848.

Kitchel, H. D., *Appeal to the People for the Suppression of the Liquor Traffic*. New York, 1848.

Kittredge, Jonathan, *An Address upon the Effects of Ardent Spirits*. Boston, 1829.

Letters to the Hon. Harrison Gray Otis by a citizen of Massachusetts. Boston, 1839.

Letters to the Mechanics of Boston. Boston, 1831.

Lincoln, Abraham, *An Address delivered before the Springfield Washingtonian Temperance Society, Feb. 22, 1842*. Springfield, Ill. 1882.

Mann, Cyrus, *The Clinton Family*, Boston, 1833.

Mann, Horace, *Effects of Intemperance on the Rich and Educated*. Syracuse, 1852.

Marsh, John, *The Boy's Temperance Book*. New York, 1848.
    An Exposition of the Excise Law of the State of New York. New York, 1846.
    The Hand of God in the Reformation of Drunkards. New York, 1842.
    Hannah Hawkins, the Reformed Drunkard's Daughter. New York, 1849.
    Putnam and the Wolf. Hartford, Conn., 1829.

Marshall, Thomas F., *The Speeches of Thomas F. Marshall on Alcohol and Intemperance and Fashionable Wine-Drinking*. New York, 1842.
    Substance of an Address on Temperance delivered before City Hose Company #33. New York, 1842.

Mather, Cotton, *The Bostonian Ebenezer*. Old South Leaflets, I, 67.
    Sober Considerations on a Growing Flood of Iniquity. Boston, 1708.

Mather, Increase, *Woe to Drunkards*. Boston, 1673.

Mussey, Reuben D., *An Address on Ardent Spirits*. Hanover, N. H., 1828.

Nott, Eliphalet, *Lectures on Bible Temperance*. Albany, 1847.

Palfrey, John G., *Discourses on Intemperance*. Boston, 1827.

Parker, Joel, *An Address before the Association in Keene.* Keene, N. H., 1830.

Parley, Peter, pseud., *Five Letters to My Neighbor Smith touching the Fifteen Gallon Jug.* Boston, 1838.

Peterson, Edward, *The Bible Temperance Review.* Providence, 1848.

Pickering, David, *The Effects of Intemperance.* Providence, 1827.

Plain Facts Addressed to the Inhabitants of Boston. Boston, 1834.

Porter, Ebenezer, *The Fatal Effects of Ardent Spirits.* Hartford, 1811.

Potter, Robert, *Boston Temperance Songster.* Boston, 1846.

Prime, Nathaniel S., *A Sermon delivered at the opening of the Presbytery of Long Island.* Brooklyn, 1812.

An Address to the Cambridge Branch of the Moral Society of the County of Washington. Albany, 1815.

Reply to Bishop Hopkins' Attack on the Temperance Society, By An Episcopalian. Philadelphia, 1836.

A Reply to the Report of a Committee of those opposed to the License Law. Boston, 1838.

A Report of the trial of the case of John Taylor vs. Edward C. Delavan. Albany, 1840.

Rhett, Albert, *The Temperance Reform Vindicated.* Charleston, S. C., 1843.

Sir Richard Rum. At a Court Held at Punch-Hall in the Colony of Bacchus. Boston, 1724.

Rush, Benjamin, *Directions for preserving the health of soldiers. Military Surgeon,* March, 1908.

Inquiry into the Effects of Ardent Spirits on the Human Body and Mind. Boston, 1811.

Sargent, Lucius M., *A Letter on the State of the Temperance Reform to the Rev. Caleb Stetson.* Boston, 1836.

The Temperance Tales. 6 vols. Boston, 1884.

Sewall, Thomas, *Effects of Intemperance on the Intellectuai, Moral and Physical Powers.* Albany, 1841.

Shelton, William, *An Address before Citizens of Buffalo.* Buffalo, 1835.

Sigourney, Lydia H., *The Intemperate*. Boston, 1833.

Songs of the Washingtonians. New York, 1845.

Sparhawk, Ebenezer, *A Sermon delivered at Templeton, Mass., January, 1776*. MS. in possession of Dean H. E. Hawkes, Columbia College.

Speech of a Creek Indian Against Immoderate Use of Spirituous Liquors. London, 1754.

Spring, Samuel, *The Only Safe Expedient*. Hartford, 1832.

Sprague, Peleg, *The Argument of Peleg Sprague, Esq., before the committee of the legislature*. Boston, 1839.

Stewart, Alvan, *An Essay on the Evils of Intemperance*. Utica, N. Y., 1833.

   Prize Address on licenses to retail ardent spirits. Baltimore, 1835.

Stow, Baron, *Address before the Portsmouth Temperance Society*. Portsmouth, N. H., 1830.

Stuart, Moses, *Scriptural View of the Wine Question*. New York, 1848.

Sweetser, William, *A Dissertation on Intemperance*. Boston, 1829.

Taylor, Thomas P., *The Bottle—A Drama in two acts*. New York, 1847.

Temperance Fables for the American People. New York, 1850.

Temperance in the City of New York. New York, 1844.

Temperance Lyrics. Boston, 1844.

Temperance Manual of the American Temperance Society. Boston, 1836.

Ticknor, Caleb, *Prize Address to the Honorable Corporation of the City of New York*. New York, 1834.

Ware, Henry, *The Criminality of Intemperance*. Boston, 1823.

Tucker, Mark, *A Plea for Entire Abstinence*. Boston, 1830.

Wayland, Francis, *An Address before the Temperance Association*. Providence, 1831.

Washingtonian Teetotalers' Minstrel. New York, 1845.

Weems, Mason L., *The Drunkard's Looking Glass*. Philadelphia, 1818.

Wetmore, George B., *An Appeal to the Protestant Christians*. New York, 1851.

White, P. S., and Ely, Ezra S., *Vindication of the Order of the Sons of Temperance.* New York, 1848.

White, P. S., and Pleasants, H. R., *The War of Four Thousand Years.* Philadelphia, 1846.

Williams, Moses, *The Cracked Jug, or Five Answers to my neighbor Parley's five letters.* Boston, 1838.

Winslow, Hubbard, *The Importance of Sustaining the Law.* Boston, 1839.

Withington, Leonard, *A Review of the late Temperance Movement in Massachusetts.* Boston, 1840.

6. NEWSPAPERS AND PERIODICALS

(Dates indicate files consulted)

Alabama: *Mobile Commercial Register and Patriot.* 1841–1842.

Connecticut: *Connecticut Courant.* (Hartford) 1800–1825.
Connecticut Evangelical Magazine. (Hartford) 1814–1815.
Connecticut Journal. (Hartford) 1822–1829.
Religious Intelligencer. (New Haven) 1817–1818.

Delaware: *Delaware Gazette.* (Wilmington) 1841–1843.

District of Columbia: *National Intelligencer,* 1840–1841.

Georgia: *Georgia Journal.* (Milledgeville) 1830–1832.
The Georgian. (Savannah) 1833–1834.

Illinois: *Alton Commercial Gazette,* 1839–1840.
The Galenian. (Galena) 1834–1835.
Illinois Advocate and State Register. (Springfield) 1834.

Indiana: *Indiana State Sentinel.* (Indianapolis) 1845.

Kentucky: *Frankfort Argus,* 1831–1833.
Maysville Eagle, 1842.

Maine: *Kennebec Journal.* (Augusta) 1849–1851.
Portland Transcript, 1840–1851.
Portland Tribune, 1842–1846.

Maryland: *Baltimore Patriot,* 1840–1842.

Massachusetts: *Boston Christian Herald,* 1831–1832.
Boston Daily Journal, 1846.

Boston Daily Mail, 1841.

Boston Recorder, 1829–1831.

Essex Register. (Salem) 1812–1821.

Hampshire Gazette. (Northampton) 1838.

Massachusetts Spy. (Worcester) 1829–1836.

Panoplist and Missionary Herald. (Boston) 1806–1819.

Springfield Republican, 1838–1839.

Mississippi: *The Ariel.* (Natchez) 1829–1830.

Columbus Democrat, 1839–1840.

Statesman and Gazette. (Natchez) 1829.

New York: *Albany Argus,* 1837–1838.

Christian Advocate. (New York) 1826.

Commercial Advertiser. (New York) 1841.

New York Evangelist, 1828–1834.

New York Observer, 1830–1836.

New York Herald, 1850–1851.

The Sun. (New York) 1836–1838.

New York Tribune, 1841–1851.

North Carolina: *North Carolina Standard.* (Raleigh) 1835–1838.

Star and North Carolina Gazette. (Raleigh) 1830–1831.

Western Carolinian. (Salisbury) 1834–1835.

Ohio: *Anti-Slavery Bugle.* (Salem) 1845–1846.

Cincinnati Daily Enquirer, 1848–1849.

Cleveland Daily Plain Dealer, 1848–1850.

Cleveland Herald, 1841–1842.

Ohio State Journal. (Columbus) 1841–1843.

Pennsylvania: *National Gazette.* (Philadelphia) 1840–1842.

Rhode Island: *Manufacturers and Farmers Journal.* (Providence) 1840–1841.

Providence Daily Journal, 1841–1844.

South Carolina: *Charleston Courier,* 1839–1841.

Southern Chronicle. (Columbia) 1841–1843.

Tennessee: *The Standard.* (Knoxville) 1845–1847.

Vermont: *The State Banner.* (Bennington) 1841–1843.

Virginia: *Richmond Enquirer,* 1839–1844.

Richmond Whig, 1842–1845.

7. DIARIES, JOURNALS AND OTHER PERSONALIA

Ames Diary, Dedham Historical Register, II, Dedham, Mass., 1891.

Asbury, Francis: *Journal of Francis Asbury.* 3 vols. New York, 1901.

Beecher, Lyman: *Autobiography, correspondence, etc., of Lyman Beecher, D.D.,* Charles Beecher, editor. New York, 1865.

Belknap, Jeremy: *Belknap Papers. Massachusetts Historical Society, Collections,* Fifth Series, I–II, Sixth Series, IV.

Bentley, William: *Dairy of William Bentley, D.D.* 3 vols. Salem, Mass., 1914.

Bicker, Henry: *Orderly Book of the 2nd Pennsylvania Continental Line. Pennsylvania Magazine,* XXXVI.

Boucher, Jonathan: *Letters of Jonathan Boucher. Maryland Historical Magazine,* VII.

Byrd, William: *Writings of Col. William Byrd,* J. S. Bassett, editor. New York, 1901.

Cartwright, Peter: *Autobiography of Peter Cartwright,* W. P. Strickland, editor. New York, 1857.

Chalkley, Thomas: *The Journal of Thomas Chalkley.* Philadelphia, 1866.

Coke, Thomas: *Extracts of the Journals of the late Rev. Thomas Coke.* Dublin, 1816.

Dow, Neal: *The Reminiscences of Neal Dow.* Portland, Me., 1898.

Finley, James B.: *Autobiography of Rev. James B. Finley,* W. P. Strickland, editor. Cincinnati, 1855.

Fithian, Philip: *Journal and Letters, 1767–1774,* John R. Williams, editor. Princeton, N. J., 1900.

Fisher, George: *Narrative of George Fisher. William and Mary College Quarterly,* XVII.

Gough, John B.: *Autobiography and Personal Recollections of John B. Gough.* Springfield, Mass., 1870.
Platform Echoes. London, 1885.
Sunlight and Shadow. Hartford, Conn., 1881.

Grant, Anne Macvicar: *Memoirs of an American Lady*, James G. Wilson, editor. 2 vols. New York, 1901.

Gridley, Luke: *Luke Gridley's Diary of 1757*. Hartford, Conn., 1907.

Hempstead, Joshua: *Diary of Joshua Hempstead*. *New London County Historical Society, Collections*, I.

Hone, Philip: *Diary of Philip Hone*, Bayard Tuckerman, editor. 3 vols. New York, 1889.

Hopkins, Samuel: *Works of Samuel Hopkins*. 3 vols. Boston, 1854.

Howells, W. C.: *Recollections of Life in Ohio*. Cincinnati, 1895.

Knight, Sarah Kemble: *The Private Journal of Madame Knight*, W. R. Deane, editor. Boston, 1858.

Marsh, John: *Temperance Recollections*. New York, 1866.

Mather, Cotton: *Diary of Cotton Mather*. *Mass. Hist. Soc., Collections*, Seventh Series, VII–VIII.

Mather, Increase: *Diary by Increase Mather*, S. A. Greene, editor. Cambridge, Mass., 1900.

Reynolds, John: *My Own Times*. Chicago, 1879.

Rush, Benjamin: *A Memorial containing travels through life of Dr. Benjamin Rush written by himself*, L. A. Biddle, editor. Lanoraie, 1905.

Sewall, Samuel: *Diary of Samuel Sewall*. *Mass. Hist. Soc. Collections*, Fifth Series, V–VII.

Seward, William H.: *Autobiography of William H. Seward*, Frederick Seward, editor. New York, 1877.

Sigourney, Lydia H.: *Letters of Life*. New York, 1868.

Thacher, James: *A Military Journal*. Boston, 1823.

Watson, Elkanah: *Men and Times of the Revolution; or Memoirs of Elkanah Watson*, W. C. Watson, editor. New York, 1856.

Woolman, John: *The Journal and Essays of John Woolman*, Amelia M. Gummere, editor. New York, 1922.

8. MISCELLANEOUS

Benezet, Anthony, *Pennsylvania Spelling Book*. Philadelphia, 1779.

Broadsides, Ballads, etc., in Massachusetts, 1639–1800, W. C. Ford, editor. *Mass. Hist. Soc., Collections,* LXXV.

Colton, Calvin, *Protestant Jesuitism.* New York, 1836.

Coxe, Tench, *A View of the United States of America.* Philadelphia, 1794.

Commerce of Rhode Island, 1726–1800. Mass. Hist. Soc., Collections, Seventh Series, IX–X.

Davis, Alexander S., *A Loud Call to the Citizens of this Nation.* Hanover, Pa., 1842.

Delavan, E. C., editor, *Temperance Essays.* New York, 1884.

Dexter, Franklin, *Investigation of the Fifteen Gallon Law.* Boston, 1839.

Doctrines and Discipline of the Methodist Episcopal Church in America. New York, 1808.

Early Records of the Town of Providence. Providence, 1893.

Essex County Court Files. Historical Collections of Essex Institute, XLIV.

First Annual Report of the Managers of the Society for the Prevention of Pauperism in New York. New York, 1818.

First Ten Annual Reports of the American Board of Commissioners for Foreign Missions. Boston, 1822.

Hopkins, John H., *The Primitive Church.* Burlington, 1836.

Huntington Town Records, C. R. Street, editor. 3 vols. Huntington, L. I., 1887.

Journals of the General Conference of the Methodist Episcopal Church, 1796–1856. New York, 1856.

Minutes of the Methodist Conference Annually Held in America. New York, 1813.

Oyster Bay Town Records. New York, 1916.

Parker, Thomas J., *Teetotalism Unmasked.* New York, 1851.

Pease, J. C. and Niles, J. M., *A Gazetteer of Connecticut and Rhode Island.* Hartford, 1819.

Reasons for not joining the Temperance Society. By a Clergyman. Baltimore, 1836.

Records and Files of the Quarterly Courts of Essex County, Mass. 8 vols. Salem, 1911–1921.

Records of the Court of New Castle, 1676–1681. Lancaster, Pa., 1904.

Report of the Committee on petitions in relation to the license laws. Printed by order of the Legislature. New Haven, 1838.

Report of Linus Child to the Legislature of 1838. Boston, 1867.

Rush, Benjamin, *Essays—Literary, Moral and Philosophical.* Philadelphia, 1798.

Seybert, Adam, *Statistical Annals.* Philadelphia, 1818.

Sigourney, Lydia H., *Boy's Reading Book in Prose and Poetry.* New York, 1839.

II. SECONDARY MATERIALS

1. GENERAL WORKS ON TEMPERANCE

Armstrong, Lebbeus, *History of the Temperance Reformation.* New York, 1868.

Buckingham, J. S., *History and Progress of the Temperance Reform in Great Britain.* London, 1854.

Cherrington, Ernest H., *The Evolution of Prohibition in the United States.* Westerville, O., 1920.

Couling, Samuel, *History of the Temperance Movement in Great Britain and Ireland.* London, 1862.

Clark, George F., *History of the Temperance Reform in Massachusetts, 1813–1883.* Boston, 1888.

Dorchester, Daniel, *The Liquor Problem in All Ages.* New York, 1884.

Dunlop, John, *The Philosophy of Drinking Usage in Great Britain.* London, 1839.

Dunn, J. B., editor, *Centennial Temperance Volume.* New York, 1877.

Scomp, Henry A., *King Alcohol in the Realm of King Cotton.* Oxford, Ga., 1888.

Wheeler, Henry, *Methodism and the Temperance Reformation.* Cincinnati, 1882.

Winskill, P. T., *The Temperance Movement and its Workers.* 4 vols. London, 1892.

Woolley, John G., and Johnson, W. E., *Temperance Progress in the Century.* Philadelphia, 1903.

2. BIOGRAPHIES AND MEMOIRS

T. S. Arthur, His Life and Works. By One Who Knows Him. Philadelphia, 1873.

Baird, H. M., *Life of the Rev. Robert Baird.* New York, 1866.

Bartlett, William S., *The Frontier Missionary: A Memoir of Rev. Jacob Bailey.* Boston, 1853.

Bungay, George W., *Pen Portraits of Illustrious Abstainers.* New York, 1881.

Coad, Oral S., *William Dunlap.* New York, 1917.

Cutler, W. P. and J. P., *Life of Rev. Manasseh Cutler.* 2 vols. Cincinnati, 1888.

William Lloyd Garrison, The Story of His Life told by his Children. 4 vols. New York, 1885–1889.

Hall, Arethusa, *Life and Character of the Rev. Sylvester Judd.* Boston, 1854.

Hallowell, Anna D., *James and Lucretia Mott.* Boston, 1884.

Hallock, W. A., *A Sketch of the Life and Labors of Justin Edwards.* New York, 1855.

Harper, Ida H., *The Life and Work of Susan B. Anthony.* 3 vols. Indianapolis, 1899–1908.

Hawkins, W. G., *Life of John H. W. Hawkins.* Boston, 1859.

The Life of the late Right Reverend John Henry Hopkins. By One of his Sons. New York, 1873.

Howe, M. A. de Wolfe, *Memoirs of the Life and Services of the Rt. Rev. Alonzo Potter.* Philadelphia, 1871.

Jeter, J. B., *A Memoir of Abner Clopton.* Richmond, 1837.

Maguire, John F., *Father Mathew.* New York, 1864.

Illustrated Memoir of Father Mathew. Philadelphia, 1847.

Martyn, Carlos, *John B. Gough, The Apostle of Cold Water.* New York, 1893.

Organ, T. W., *Biographical Sketch of General Neal Dow.* New York, 1880.

Parker, E. P., *Appreciation of Calvin Chapin.* Providence, 1908.

Pettit, Thomas M., *Memoir of Roberts Vaux.* Philadelphia, 1840.

Pilcher, James E., *Life and Labors of Elijah H. Pilcher of Michigan.* New York, 1892.

Prentice, George, *Wilbur Fisk.* Boston and New York, 1890.

Ramsay, David, *An Eulogium upon Benjamin Rush.* Philadelphia, 1813.

Richards, W. C., *A Memoir of George N. Briggs.* Boston, 1866.

Sheppard, John H., *Reminiscences of Lucius Manlius Sargent.* Boston, 1871.

Staughton, William, *An Eulogium in Memory of the late Dr. Benjamin Rush.* Philadelphia, 1813.

Thayer, W. M., *Life and Recollections of Charles Jewett.* Boston, 1880.

Tracy, E. C., *Memoir of Jeremiah Evarts.* Boston, 1845.

Van Santvoord, Cornelius, *Memoirs of Eliphalet Nott.* New York, 1876.

Vaux, Roberts, *Memoirs of the Life of Anthony Benezet.* Philadelphia, 1817.

3. STATE AND LOCAL HISTORIES

Adams, Charles Francis, *Three Episodes of Massachusetts History.* Boston and New York, 1893.

Arnold, Samuel G., *History of the State of Rhode Island and Providence Plantations.* Providence, 1894.

Babson, John J., *History of the Town of Gloucester, Mass.,* Gloucester, 1860.

Bacon, Nathaniell, *Annalls of Ipswiche,* W. H. Richardson, editor. Ipswich, 1884.

Baird, C. W., *History of Rye, N. Y.* New York, 1871.

Baldwin, Edgar M., *The Making of a Township.* Fairmount. Ind., 1917.

Barry, J. S., *Historical Sketch of the Town of Hanover, Mass.* Boston, 1853.

Bates, S. A., *Records of the Town of Braintree.* Randolph, Mass., 1886.

Blackman, Emily C., *History of Susquehanna County, Pa.* Philadelphia, 1873.

Bliss, W. R., *Colonial Times on Buzzard's Bay.* Boston, 1889.

Boyd, John, *Annals of Winchester, Conn.* Hartford, 1873.

Bruce, P. A., *Economic History of Virginia in the Seventeenth Century.* 2 vols. New York, 1896.

Institutional History of Virginia in the Seventeenth Century. New York, 1910.

Cabot, Mary R., *Annals of Brattleboro, Vt.* Brattleboro, 1921.

Chalkley, Lyman, *Chronicles of Scotch-Irish Settlement in Virginia.* 2 vols. Rosslyn, Va., 1912.

Chase, G. W., *History of Haverhill, Mass.* Haverhill, 1861.

Clark, S. J., *History of McDonough County, Ill.* Springfield, Ill., 1878.

Cochran, Joseph, *History of Mifflin County, Pa.* Harrisburg, 1879.

Coffin, Charles C., *History of Boscawen and Webster.* Concord, N. H., 1878.

Dahlinger, C. W., *Pittsburgh, A Sketch of Its Early Social Life.* New York, 1916.

Davis, W. W. H., *Doylestown, Old and New.* Doylestown, Pa., 1905.

Eastman, J. R., *History of Andover, N. H.* Concord, N. H., 1910.

Emery, Edwin, *History of Sanford, Me.* Fall River, Mass., 1901.

Fairbanks, E. T., *The Town of Saint Johnsbury, Vt.* St. Johnsbury, 1914.

Fairchild, James H., *Oberlin, The Colony and the College.* Oberlin, 1883.

Farmer, Silas, *History of Detroit and Wayne County.* Detroit, 1890.

Felt, Joseph, *Annals of Salem.* 2 vals. Salem, 1845–1849.

History of Ipswich, Essex and Hamilton. Cambridge, 1834.

Fox, D. R., *The Decline of Aristocracy in the Politics of New York.* New York, 1919.

Hall Henry, *History of Auburn, N. Y.* Auburn, 1869.

Harman, John N. Sr., *Annals of Tazewell County, Va.* Richmond, 1922.

Hazard, Samuel, *Annals of Pennsylvania from the Discovery of the Delaware.* Philadelphia, 1850.

Head, James W., *History of Loudoun County, Va.* Park View Press, 1909.

Hollister, H., *History of Lackawanna Valley.* Philadelphia, 1885.

Howe, Henry, *Historical Collections of Ohio.* Columbus, 1891.

Hudson, Alfred, *History of Sudbury, Mass.* Sudbury, 1889.

Hurlbut, Henry H., *Chicago Antiquities.* Chicago, 1880.

Jenkins, Howard M., *Historical Collections of Gwynedd.* Philadelphia, 1897.

Judd, Sylvester, *History of Hadley.* Springfield, Mass., 1905.

Kimball, Gertrude S., *Providence in Colonial Times.* Boston, 1912.

Kuhns, Oscar, *German and Swiss Settlements of Colonial Pennsylvania.* New York, 1901.

Lapham, W. B., *History of Bethel, Me.* Augusta, Me., 1891.

Larned, Ellen D., *History of Windham County, Conn.* 2 vols. Worcester, Mass., 1880.

Maxwell, Hu, *History of Tucker County, W. Va.* Kingwood, W. Va., 1884.

Mead, Spencer P., *Ye Historie of Ye Towne of Greenwich.* New York, 1911.

Merrill, Georgia D., editor, *History of Carroll County, N. H.* Boston, 1889.

Morrison, Leonard A., *History of Windham, N. H.* Boston, 1883.

Morton, Oren F., *History of Rockbridge County, Va.* Staunton, 1920.

Munsell, Joel R., *Annals of Albany.* 10 vols. Albany, 1850–1860.

Murray, Louise W., *Old Tioga Point and Early Athens, Pa.* Athens, Pa., 1908.

Neill, Edward D., *Threads of Maryland Colonial History.* Philadelphia, 1867.

Nourse, H. S., *The Early Records of Lancaster, Mass.* Lancaster, 1884.

Orcutt, Samuel, *History of New Milford and Bridgewater, Conn.* Hartford, 1882.

History of Torrington, Conn. Albany, 1878.

Phelps, Charles S., *Rural Life in Litchfield County.* Norfolk, Conn., 1917.

Randall, E. O., and Ryan, D. J., *History of Ohio.* 5 vols. New York, 1912.

Roberts, Millard, *History of Remsen, N. Y.* Remsen, 1914.

Sanford, C. E., *Early History of Hopkinton.* Boston, 1903.

Sheperd, W. R., *History of Proprietary Government in Pennsylvania.* New York, 1896.

Stiles, H. R., editor, *The History of Ancient Wethersfield, Conn.* 2 vols. New York, 1904.

Stone, W. L., *Reminiscences of Saratoga.* New York, 1880.

Thompson, Francis, *History of Greenfield, Mass.* Greenfield, 1904.

Turner, J. K., and Bridges, J. L. *History of Edgecombe County, N. C.* Raleigh, 1920.

Usher, J. M., *History of the Town of Medford.* Boston, 1886.

Waters, Thomas F., *Ipswich in the Massachusetts Bay Colony.* 2 vols. Ipswich, 1917.

Watson, J. F., *Annals of Philadelphia and Pennsylvania in the Olden Times.* Philadelphia, 1887.

Wayland, John W., *History of Rockingham County, Va.* Dayton, Va., 1912.

Weeden, W. B., *Economic and Social History of New England, 1620–1789.* 2 vols. Boston and New York, 1890.

Wells, F. P., *History of Newbury, Vt.* St. Johnsbury, Vt., 1902.

White, Alain C., *History of the Town of Litchfield, Conn.* Litchfield, 1920.

Wilson, Erasmus, editor, *History of Pittsburgh.* Chicago, 1898.

Wise, Jennings C., *Eastern Shore of Virginia.* Richmond, 1911.

Woods, Edgar, *Albemarle County in Virginia.* Charlottesville, 1901.

Young, Andrew W., *History of Chautauqua County, N. Y.* Buffalo, 1875.

History of Warsaw, N. Y. Buffalo, 1869.

4. MISCELLANEOUS

Ayer, Mary F., *Early Days on Boston Common.* Boston, 1910.

Bliss, W. R., *Side-Glimpses from the Colonial Meeting House.* Boston, 1894.

Brown, Alexander, *The Genesis of the United States.* Boston, 1890.

Clubb, Henry S., *The Maine Liquor Law.* New York, 1856.

Documentary History of the Maine Law. New York, 1855.

Earle, Alice M., *Customs and Fashions in Old New England.* New York, 1902.

The Sabbath in Puritan New England. New York, 1893.

Field, Edward, *The Colonial Tavern.* Providence, 1897.

Fisher, Sydney G., *Men, Women and Manners in Colonial Times.* Philadelphia, 1898.

Griffiths, T. S., *A History of Baptists in New Jersey.* Hightstown, N. J., 1904.

Hanscom, Elizabeth D., *The Heart of the Puritan.* New York, 1917.

Hitchcock, Edward, *Reminiscences of Amherst College.* Northampton, 1863.

Houck, G. F., *The Church in Northern Ohio and in the Diocese of Cleveland.* New York, 1887.

Kittredge, George L., *The Old Farmer and His Almanac.* Boston, 1904.

Lord, John K., *History of Dartmouth College, 1815–1909.* Cambridge, 1913.

Mathews, Lois K., *The Expansion of New England.* Boston, 1909.

Mesick, Jane Louise, *The English Traveler in America, 1785–1835.* New York, 1922.

Neill, E. D., *History of the Virginia Company of London.* Albany, 1869.

Purcell, Richard J., *Connecticut in Transition. 1775–1818.* Washington, 1918.

Riley, Woodridge, *American Thought from Puritanism to Pragmatism.* New York, 1915.

Shea, John G., *A History of the Catholic Church within the Limits of the United States.* New York, 1892.

Smith, Helen E., *Colonial Days and Ways.* New York, 1900.

Stanard, Mary N., *Colonial Virginia, Its People and Customs.* Philadelphia, 1917.

Stinness, J. H., *Rhode Island Legislation Against Strong Drink.* Providence, 1919.

Strobel, P. A., *The Salzburgers and Their Descendants.* Baltimore, 1855.

Sweet, W. W., *Circuit-Rider Days in Indiana.* Indianapolis, 1916.

Thomann, G., *Colonial Liquor Laws.* New York, 1887.

Tucker, George, *Progress of the United States in Population and Wealth.* New York, 1843.

Tyler, L. G., *The Cradle of the Republic.* Richmond, 1900.

Webb, Sidney and Beatrice, *The History of Liquor Licensing in England.* London, 1903.

INDEX

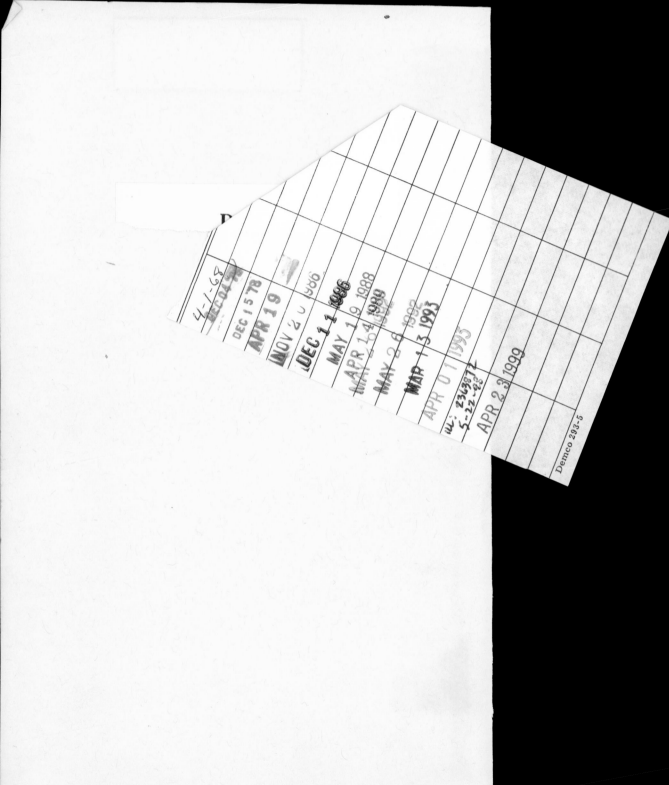